THE SCREENWRITER'S WORKOUT

by
WILL HICKS

Stretch Your Creativity
Strengthen Your Craft
Sell Your Screenplay

© 2019 Will Hicks
All Rights Reserved
ISBN: 978-1793197313

A Dedication, a Thanks and an Apology

Dedication

To Mom
for teaching me to dream

To Dad
for teaching me how
to make dreams reality

and

To You
for daring to dream

Thanks

I'd like to thank the following people for their contributions to this journey:

To Tim, one of the finest screenwriting mentors I've ever known

To Christa, für die offenen Einsichten

To Klaus, for those eye-opening summers

To Candace, for the inspiration long ago

To Rashel and Dan, for our adventures in filmmaking (POIK!)

To Jess, for believing

To Frederic, for taking a chance

To my students, for teaching me

To Tommy -- miss you, man

To Kirk, Hannah, Lovinder and all the screenwriting gang, for so many good times

To George, for making a certain movie

and

To my family, for being my reason.

Apology

I'd like to respectfully apologize to my seventh-grade English teacher for the conversational writing style used to write this book. She didn't take kindly to people abusing her beautiful language, so Mrs. Williams, I'm sorry for all the sentence fragments, comma splices, the gotta's, kinda's and sorta's, the superfluous apostrophes I just used, the split infinitive in the first sentence of this paragraph, the ellipses, and, gulp, even the occasional emoticon you'll encounter. Maybe everyone should get an apology for that last one. ;)

Also, I use 'they' as my gender-neutral pronoun of choice. Except when I don't.

If the casual writing style and occasional abuse of grammar can't be overlooked, feel free to edit as you go – it's good practice for proofreading your scripts.

THE SCREENWRITER'S WORKOUT
TRAINING GUIDE

Introduction

Welcome to The Screenwriter's Workout! In this section we'll explore how to use the workout to strengthen your craft and stretch your creativity. Think of it as a weight training for your mind, with exercises designed specifically for screenwriters. In particular, <u>this workout is designed to work the neural pathways that generate story</u>. As you hone and strengthen these pathways, they become almost second nature, similar to the principle of muscle memory. And, like muscle memory, once a skill becomes second nature you no longer have to think about it. Instead, you can devote your time and creative thought to executing a great screenplay – your great screenplay.

Athletes spend hundreds, thousands of hours in the gym before competing professionally, why can't screenwriters do the same? Sure, we can read books on screenwriting, attend seminars, take classes, listen to podcasts, study screenplays, but most of these activities are passive, more informational in nature – a good thing to be sure, but we learn by doing. That's where this book comes in. Think of it as a gym, our gym, a place for you to stretch, strengthen and hone your skills. The activities and exercises are like different pieces of gym equipment, each designed to work aspects of the screenwriting craft. How you approach your workout is up to you, but don't just read -- <u>write in this book</u>. Scribble in its margins. Correct its errors. To be a writer, you have to write. And, here's the place to do it.

The Exercises

Your workout is divided into three main sections:

1. The Warmup

This is a long section intended to be completed sequentially. The warmup contains the lessons and theories you'll use later in your workout, so it's to be completed first.

2. The Workout

This section contains exercises shorter than the ones in the warmup as we target and hone specific skills. These exercises can be completed in any order, depending on the particular skills you wish to work.

3. The Cooldown

This section offers additional theories and approaches to screenwriting. It's mostly reading. It's also there to give you something to bear down on as you write in the latter portions of this book.

Exercises are divided into two main categories: craft and creativity.
Please note: there is an additional THEORY category for the Cooldown.

Craft

This is a broad category, encompassing numerous skills specific to screenwriting. While there can be considerable crossover with creativity, craft exercises focus more on the nuts and bolts of writing screenplays.

Creativity

These exercises are broader in nature and can apply outside of screenwriting. They're designed to stretch your imagination and foster outside the box thinking.

The main difference between the two lies in their application. Creativity focuses more on developing creative approaches to your craft.

Each exercise group begins with a header that looks like this:

Sets

Similar to weight training, a set is usually one specific exercise. Each set works a precise skillset for a certain number of repetitions, otherwise known as…

Reps

Reps are the number of times you do a particular exercise within a set. For our purposes, a single rep usually denotes something you do – whether it's writing the name of a character or writing a scene. Some activities will be worth more reps to account for increased complexity, but when taken as a whole with the simpler ones, the work tends to balance out.

So, in the sample header above, you'd be doing <u>three sets of craft for a total of 18 reps</u>. Sets often contain different types of exercises to work the same skill using a variety of approaches as we thoroughly hone those story chops from multiple angles.

Each exercise group ends with a chart to track your workout progress. The chart lists the exercises in a particular exercise group, the type of skill worked, the type of activity and the number of reps in each set.

EXERCISE	SKILL GROUP		TOTAL REPS	
	SET #	TYPE	ACTION	AVAILABLE	COMPLETED
Name of Exercise	1	Craft	Analysis	6	
Another Exercise	2	Craft	Application	8	
And Another	3	Craft	Analysis	4	
And... You Get the Idea	Bonus	Craft	Application	20	
			TOTAL REPS		

Some exercise groups contain a <u>bonus set</u> of additional exercises. Bonus sets usually involve applying an exercise to a screenplay you've written. Because you may or may not have a screenplay to apply the exercise to, bonus sets are optional.

Action refers to what you'll be doing in a particular set and is subdivided into two broad categories – <u>analysis</u> and <u>application</u>. Analysis is just that – you'll analyze scripts and films. Application can involve a number of activities, but it usually involves applying an exercise to create something new.

After the progress chart, each exercise group contains a <u>summation</u> of the total number of reps available, including the bonus, to mark the end of the section and to make it easier to track the total number of reps you've completed.

So, in this section you have a maximum total of 38 reps of Craft, including the bonus set.

The next page contains a list of exercises, sets and reps, followed by a blank chart to help you plan your workout by weekly or daily goals for reps or sets, start/completion dates, or as simply a place to track or log your progress.

The Exercises

MODULE			TOTALS		
NAME	PAGE	TYPE	SETS	REPS	BONUS
ACT 1: THE WARMUP					
A Most Difficult Crossword Puzzle	1	Craft	6	22	
Hollywood Character Design	13	Craft	13	55	13
The 8-Turn Structure	83	Craft	2	18	9
Ancient Greek Hero Design	101	Craft	2	2	
Archetypical Characters	107	Craft	2	16	
Myth Structure	119	Craft	2	30	
Dualing Structures (hmm... interesting spelling)	167	Craft	2	45	
ACT 2: THE WORKOUT					
Sticks and Tomes	185	Craft	2	6	
Building Better Loglines	199	Craft	4	6	2
Character Introductions	211	Craft	2	16	2
Oh, the Troubles I've Scene	219	Craft	4	11	
Scenic Efficiency and Functionality	237	Craft	2	4	2
Build-a-Tale 1	249	Craft	1	6	1
Personal Dictionary	257	Creativity	3	12	
Indirect Characterization	263	Craft	4	24	5
Setting for Two	275	Creativity	1	8	1
Mixed Relations and Revealing Character	279	Craft	2	19	
Something Like an Outline	301	Craft	2	20	
Any Way You Say It	313	Craft	3	57	2
The Twisting Cliché	323	Creativity	2	10	25
Build-a-Tale 2	329	Creativity	1	10	
Driving Through Kansas	335	Creativity	2	7	1
The Obstacle of Course	341	Creativity	1	7	
The Curious Question of Conflict	349	Craft	4	12	
Delivery Drivers	371	Craft	1	9	4
Making Connections	379	Creativity	3	30	
Build-a-Tale 3	383	Craft	2	11	
Positively Negative	389	Creativity	1	27	1+
Dancing with Devils	391	Creativity	1	4	2
Guessed Speakers	399	Creativity	2	16	
ACT 3: THE COOLDOWN					
Interactive Screenwriting	405	Theory	1	1	
Totals			78	521	70

MY SCREENWRITING WORKOUT

Okay, let's get this workout started! Only 591 reps to go!

THE SCREENWRITER'S WORKOUT

ACT 1

THE WARMUP

The World's Most Difficult Crossword Puzzle

With a title like that, this doesn't need much of an introduction.

SET 1: Puzzling   **CRAFT**   **Total Reps: 1**
Complete the crossword puzzle below.

Down
1. Shock and _____

Across
2. What is it good for? Absolutely nothing. Say it again!

Hmm... perhaps difficult is a relative term. Let's try this again.

Introducing the New and Improved **World's Most Difficult Crossword Puzzle**!

SET 2: Less Puzzling   **CRAFT**   **Total Reps: 1**
Complete the crossword puzzle below.

Down
1. Awe

Across
2. War

Wait a second. No clues. No 70s music references. With the answers provided, you don't even have to think. You just copy them to the puzzle. That's not more difficult. Perhaps we should try a different approach.

Imagine a much larger version of each of these crossword puzzles.
> Version 1: you get clues you must figure out to solve the puzzle.
> Version 2: you're given the answers so all you have to do is copy them.

Which puzzle would be more interesting, more fun to complete?

Hopefully, you picked Version 1. How boring would that second version be? Just transcribing already formed answers. Seems more like work than fun.

And, that's the problem.

Because these aren't crossword puzzles. They're screenplays.
Or, at least different approaches to writing screenplays.

To explore how a screenplay is a crossword puzzle, let's bring back our puzzles and break them down into their screenwriting equivalents.

Here's the first one:

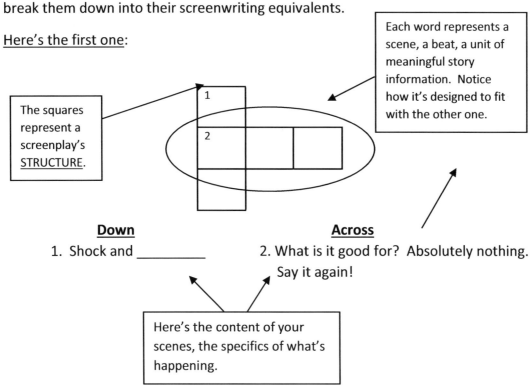

Down
1. Shock and _____

Across
2. What is it good for? Absolutely nothing. Say it again!

Now that we've identified some equivalents between screenplays and crosswords, let's dive a bit deeper into each component.

Notice how the structure of the puzzle helps you fill it in? It works in conjunction with the content, our clues, to help you figure out what each clue actually means. In this way, the clues are subtext, requiring you to fill in the meaning. We'll explore this aspect in a moment -- let's stick with structure for now.

2

The relationship between content and structure in your screenplay works something like this:

SET 3: Content and Structure   CRAFT   **Total Reps: 1**

Complete the crossword puzzle below.

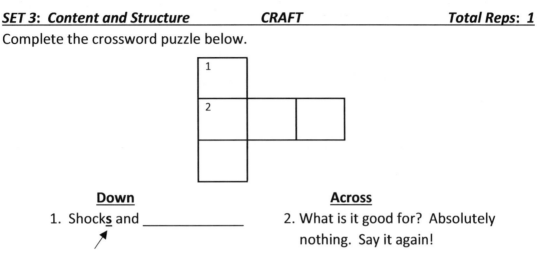

        Down　　　　　　　　　　　　　　　　**Across**

1. Shock<u>s</u> and _____　　2. What is it good for? Absolutely nothing. Say it again!

The clue suggests the correct answer should be 'awes', but that doesn't fit the structure. Or, put another way – the structure doesn't support the content.

In your screenplay, when content and structure don't mesh, when they don't fit together, you're asking the audience to solve this last puzzle. And, when they can't because of the ill-fitting design, frustration ensues. Or, they become fixated on trying to figure out that one aspect and begin missing other pieces of the puzzle because they're still focused on that one section. This is especially problematic for cinematic narrative, because, unlike our puzzle, in which you can pause to ponder a particularly difficult clue, information in a movie hurdles at a blistering 24 frames per second.

Bottom line: structure and content must work together for an audience to complete the picture.

Of course, our second puzzle solves that issue rather nicely by simply giving you the answers.

        Down　　　　　　　　　　　　　　　　**Across**

1. Awe　　　　　　　　　　　　　　　2. War

Done and done. Hey, who needs structure?

The clues for this puzzle, as you can see, aren't really clues at all. For screenplays, this is the equivalent of <u>on the nose</u> content. Whether it's on the nose dialogue, on the nose action or simply scenes without any sort of nuance or subtlety, the results are remarkably similar -- spoon-feeding content removes the fun, the sense of discovery, the joy of using other clues to confirm our suspicions, test our predictions.

Yes, it's clearer. Much clearer. And, if your goal is to tell a story – well, there you go. But, look at what it does to the experience of the story. With nothing to interpret, nothing to wonder about or interact with, the audience is left to do… you guessed it -- nothing, except maybe munch on popcorn. Hope the refills are free.

Are there times when you need to be crystal-clear in your storytelling? Absolutely. Imagine coming across the following in a crossword puzzle:

SET 4: *Clue Less*   ***CRAFT***   **Total Reps: *1***

Fill in the correct word.

1									

    1. Rainy day state

That clears it up. Yes?

Well, not quite, depending on your answer. While that's not a big deal in this context, imagine if you couldn't proceed until you found the correct answer from that rather vague clue. How would that feel?

Frustration comes to mind.

Mild irritation.

If it goes on long enough, apathy even.

Frustration. Irritation. Apathy. Not exactly selling points for a movie. But, this is what an audience feels when presented with something they can't figure out. And, if that something is vital to understanding the story, the level of irritation can be way more than mild.

I suppose we could resort to the on the nose approach. Just give it to 'em. After all, we did start this page by saying sometimes we should be clear. But, as we discovered earlier – where's the fun in that?

What we're exploring here is the flipside of subtext -- when the clues, the hints, aren't enough to create the connection we intended. Often this leads filmmakers to shy away from the technique. But, let's lean into it. Because there's a far more cinematic way to solve this clarity problem. And, ironically, you already have the answer.

Speaking of answers, have you found that ten-letter word for rainy day state yet?

The cinematic answer you already have lies in the second clue of the first puzzle. Here it is again:

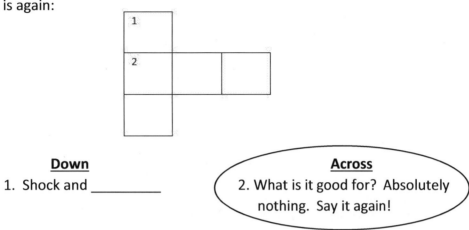

Down
1. Shock and _____

Across
2. What is it good for? Absolutely nothing. Say it again!

Notice how the clue relies on your knowledge – in this case, I was counting on you knowing lyrics to the song "War", Edwin Starr's smash protest anthem from 1970.

If you know the song, that clue is super easy. Probably too easy to be entertaining. Unfortunately, I have no way of knowing if you know the song or not, so I did two things to account for this:

1. I picked a lengthy lyric.
2. I used the first clue to (hopefully) help you fill in the second.

This is how subtext works, and by extension, cinematic narrative as a whole. The content of one scene has to inform the content in other scenes in addition to successfully doing its own thing. In the puzzle this is represented by the W in awe feeding in to the answer for the other clue.

When you are trying to convey something subtextually, you're relying on the audience collaborating with you to co-construct the narrative. It's a minimalistic approach, which is one of its strengths, allowing you to tell more complex stories, or at least tell your story in a more nuanced way, because you're allowing the audience to add their contributions to the content you present, the whole 'sum is more than its parts' sort of thing. Because we're only hinting rather than spelling things out, we save time, which you can use to develop a more complex story. However, that time savings can be misleading. Just in my simple example, I felt the need to provide another clue (shock and awe), which in cinematic terms would eat time, and I resorted to three statements in the second clue that could have been covered by simply saying WAR, which also eats up time. Let's examine that second clue a bit more closely.

Because I wasn't certain anyone would get the reference, I expanded the clue, hoping that this would help ensure people would get it. However, if I discovered that the clue was too easy, the connection too obvious, I could trim it. And, I could cut it incrementally until I found the sweet spot – not so vague that no one gets it and not so obvious that getting it is boring.

In terms of the puzzle, this approach is similar to the rewrite process for screenplays. For our clue, the process looks something like this:

If this is too obvious...

    2. What is it good for? Absolutely nothing. Say it again!

Then I could do this:

    2. What is it good for? Absolutely nothing. ~~Say it again~~!

If it's still too obvious, this:

    2. What is it good for? ~~Absolutely nothing. Say it again~~!

Another solution would be to keep the less obvious parts of the clue, which to me are 'Absolutely nothing' and 'Say it again.'

Or, I could have chosen a different song. Rather than "War", Edwin Starr's protest anthem, I could have picked something more recent. A song more people may know. That may seem counter-intuitive, but think about it – the more well-known the song, the more obscure the clue can be.

When you solved the first puzzle, would you have gotten it with just the first part of the clue? If I had to hazard a guess, I'd say yes – especially with our other answer providing the first letter. But, without any way of knowing, I played it safe. Unfortunately, playing it safe in movies tends to underwhelm. Finding a balance becomes the key. In screenplays this is the balance between text and subtext.

As you tackle subtext in your screenplay, the task is to find the clues (text) that create the longest connection that the greatest number of people understand (subtext.) In other words, the hint has to spark a connection between text and subtext that's not too easy, but not so obscure that no one can make a connection. The more the audience must bring to the table to make this connection, the better. Makes sense if you think about it – there's more of 'them' in the movie. Connections that challenge, but don't overwhelm, are highly entertaining -- almost as though the filmmakers had you in mind when they created the movie.

This also illustrates the rewrite process as you trim down content to its leanest, most suggestive state. To achieve this you need to get eyes on your screenplay to get feedback on whether you need to use stronger, more obvious subtext or be less obvious in your approach. The trick is to find the right balance, that elusive sweet spot, if you will. And, the process to do that cinematically takes us back to our rainy day state…

SET 5: *Clueless*   CRAFT   **Total Reps: *1***

Fill in the correct word.

1									

    1. Rainy day state

The same thing. Again?
If you're sick of this puzzle, welcome to how an audience takes redundancy. :)

Before we explore how to handle this puzzle cinematically, let's examine one of the context clues audiences use to dissect your story.

What if, instead of calling this exercise '*Clueless*', it was called*: Clueless in Seattle*. Would that help fill in the puzzle? The title in this case represents genre. Remember, Hollywood is in the business of making genre films. The main reason for this is marketing; however, for us, genre carries a host of story implications, one of which is helping an audience decipher your movie. Genre creates a set of expectations that you can then use to guide your content. How it works is by narrowing the set of possibilities within the film, which helps the audience put together clues by eliminating choices that don't adhere to the genre. When genre and content work together, you can achieve powerful results. When they don't? You might get this:

Clueless in Seattle

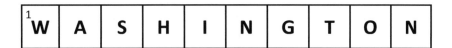

    1. Rainy day state

Makes sense. It's a state. It's rainy. Seattle. Makes perfect sense actually, and if that was your answer, congratulations, you are correct! And yet, it's not the right answer. Well, not intended answer. It's not your fault; it's mine. Given the context clues I provided, Washington should be correct. That's where the clues point. The genre (exercise title) hints at it. The subtext (our clue) alludes to it – especially with the word 'state' in there. Even the structure supports this answer. This leads to an important consideration when dealing with subtext:

You must account for the different interpretations resulting from your combination of story elements.

To do this, ask yourself what logical outcomes could result from this combination of story elements? Then, list them. Once you have your list, you then eliminate the options until all that's left is the one you intended. To do this cinematically, consider the puzzle below:

SET 6: Clued In **CRAFT** **Total Reps: 14**

Figure out our rainy day state by completing the puzzle. Or, if you've already got it, test your prediction to see if you're right.

Across

2. Rainy day state
4. Units of story for drummers
6. Try by dipping these
8. He phoned home
10. Former lover, reversed
12. Where your career is headed
14. My favorite kind of pet

Down

1. This is one, but less in Seattle
3. Hollywood's business
5. One down, in screenwriting terms
7. Starr's clue was a _____ anthem
9. In other words, abbreviated
11. Pick this to say it on the _____
13. What you should be writing

Before we move on, let's talk about the types of clues you were given – especially **14 Across**. My favorite kind of pet? Really? How are you supposed to know that? This clue illustrates situations where the subtext is too obscure, the reference too personal. Remember, subtext is meant to help the audience create connections, and what may be obvious to us as writers, may not be to your audience. At least the structure of that clue helped narrow the possibilities. The correct answer is cat.

I know, I know, don't hate. But then, some other three-letter possibilities include: dog, rat, eel (hey, it's possible!), pig, and a bunch of other three-letter critters. Notice, if you chose DOG for **14 Across**, it would have thrown off the clue for **13 Down**, which in turn, may have thrown off **2 Across**, which is what we're trying to ascertain. This illustrates an important facet of indirect nature of cinematic storytelling – all the clues have to work together.

The types of clues you were given represent two basic types of subtextual content.

If you examine the ACROSS clues, these are external to the text, relying on knowledge the audience, or reader in this case, brings to the material. External subtextual content tends to be broader, a bit more basic, to ensure the largest number of viewers will be able to make a connection.

The DOWN clues are mostly internal to the text. With the exception of clues 5 and 7, the rest are references to what you've (hopefully) been reading. These are clues everyone should get because, unlike the others, they are not dependent on prior knowledge – you, the filmmaker, have taught them to us. In ways, this represents a setup/payoff pair. The first encounter with this specific content introduces the idea so the second can pay it off. This also illustrates another aspect of cinematic storytelling: movies become increasingly self-referential as they progress. Once again, this makes sense if you think about it. Early in the film you haven't had time to teach the audience the setups, so subtext must rely on what the audience brings to the table. Later in the film, once you've had time to teach us a few things, you can refer back to what you've taught, and chances are, most of your audience will get the reference because everyone in the theater has experienced it. This technique is especially useful for story critical details the audience must understand to follow the narrative. Let's examine one of these referential clues a bit more closely:

7 Down, Starr's clue was a _____ anthem.
If that one gave you trouble, it's likely because it wasn't set up very well. There are two setups for this particular clue, both in Set 4. This part's good. If the answer was a story critical detail, we'll want to hit it more than once, in case it was missed the first time. Unfortunately, each setup was buried among other details and thus could be easily missed or overlooked. Or, because it seems like such a throwaway fact in a discussion of screenwriting it may have been dismissed as unimportant. This part's not so good. To keep that from happening in your movie, you must draw attention to your setups either through repetition or by making them memorable (or both.) Making them memorable is faster and more efficient, but can be more challenging creatively. What makes something memorable? Suppose many things, but the big one is... it's different. Think about the days in your life that stand out. I should think

the one commonality they hold is that they differ from the everyday, the routine. It's the same with the content of your screenplay – it needs to stand out, be different, yet also be relevant. In other words, it should have meaning. And, meaning is why we've been talking so much about subtext. After all, subtext is what something really means – whether it's a line of dialogue or your movie as a whole.

Okay, now that I've stalled so you wouldn't have the answers to the blank puzzle on the adjacent page, here's the solution:

Across

2. Rainy day state
4. Units of story for drummers
6. Try by dipping these
8. He phoned home
10. Former lover, reversed
12. Where your career is headed
14. My favorite kind of pet

Down

1. This is one, but less in Seattle
3. Hollywood's business
5. One down, in screenwriting terms
7. Starr's clue was a _____ anthem
9. In other words, abbreviated
11. Pick this to say it on the _____
13. What you should be writing

Which, of course, leaves us with our word of the day:

| L | U | G | U | B | R | I | O | U | S |

Meaning sad or gloomy looking, like the state a person might appear to be in on a rainy day. Because lugubrious isn't a particularly common word, notice all the supporting clues to help decipher it. Even then, if the term is unfamiliar, we still may not get it. This leads us to another aspect of cinematic narrative:

The more complex an idea is, the more support it needs to be communicated cinematically.

The key part of that last sentence is: cinematically.

In general, movies don't handle complexity very well. The medium itself, with its reliance on visual storytelling, has a difficult time communicating complex, abstract ideas. It's just not built to do it. It's like using a screwdriver to hammer a nail. Yes, it can be done, but it wasn't really designed for that purpose. The level of audience interpretation involved in visual storytelling makes it extremely difficult to convey complexity with any degree of accuracy.

Notice how complex communicating just a simple idea is in film. What would it be like communicating something far more abstract or esoteric? Usually films that attempt this have to utilize less cinematic means of communicating, covering the script in dialogue, or voice over, or other such ways of conveying information. Are these part of our palette? Of course. And, such attempts can be entertaining. I love good dialogue and intelligent filmmaking. Just be aware that tackling such topics often comes at the expense what film does do well – show, don't tell, as the saying goes. This process of showing not telling is what makes a film a film. And, it's what makes a screenplay the world's most difficult crossword puzzle.

WORKOUT PROGRESS – CRAFT

Compile your workout totals for this unit.

EXERCISE	SKILL GROUP			TOTAL REPS	
	SET #	TYPE	ACTION	AVAILABLE	COMPLETED
Puzzling	1	Craft	Application	1	
Less Puzzling	2	Craft	Application	1	
Content and Structure	3	Craft	Analysis	1	
Clue Less	4	Craft	Application	1	
Clueless	5	Craft	Application	1	
Clued In	6	Craft	Application	14	
			TOTAL REPS		

CRAFT — Total Reps + Bonus — 19

WHAT A BUNCH OF CHARACTERS!
THE HOLLYWOOD APPROACH TO CHARACTER DESIGN

Don't let the title fool you – yes, we're examining how Hollywood films approach character design, but that doesn't mean you can't use this exact same tool set to create fiercely independent characters. Uniqueness comes not from the tool, but from your application of it. With that in mind, here are some of the patterns found in Hollywood characters.

General Tendencies of Hollywood Characters

- ✓ Underdogs
- ✓ Best at what they do/Worst at what they do/ Sometimes BOTH
- ✓ Larger than life (situations, personalities or characteristics)
- ✓ Hero is OBSESSED with a problem (which is also a problem)
- ✓ Active and driven
- ✓ Hero faces choices under pressure (which reveals character)
- ✓ Hero elicits emotion
- ✓ Identifiable and universal
- ✓ The hero's strength is his/her flaw

Let's examine each of these design features in greater detail to explore WHY these tendencies are used in Hollywood characters and character design in general.

Underdogs
Probably the most prevalent of these characteristics and with good reason. Positioning your main character as an underdog ups the drama – after all, no one expects them to win, amps the conflict through obstacles that are far more challenging for an underdog to overcome. It's also satisfying – who doesn't want to see an underdog triumph?

Underdog characters also offer opportunities for stronger character arcs (they have more room to grow), and place the characters in empathetic positions, creating almost instant relatability.

Being an underdog doesn't necessarily mean you're downtrodden or powerless. Indeed Hollywood films often have heroes who are just the opposite. So, how do you turn someone powerful into an underdog? Consider the following:

Let's say you're a billionaire, playboy philanthropist who's the genius behind one of the biggest arms manufacturers in the world. Not exactly our traditional underdog. So, the writers of *Iron Man* had to place the main character, Tony Stark, in positions where he would be an underdog. If you've ever been kidnapped, outnumbered, stuck in a cave, with your heart hooked up to a car battery, you were probably an underdog in that situation. After Tony becomes Iron Man, the film thrusts him into another underdog position – facing someone in a more powerful supersuit. Let's call these types of characters Hollywood Underdogs – essentially powerful characters who the plot sticks in underdog positions, either by confronting antagonists that are even more powerful, by stripping away the advantages the character has or by placing these characters in situations where their abilities can't help them.

Placing your characters in positions where they're the underdogs accomplishes so much in terms of story, relatability and audience satisfaction, it's no wonder we see it so often.

ADVANTAGES	DISADVANTAGES
Highly relatable	May seem cliché
Ups the conflict	
Helps create unpredictability	
Satisfying to audiences	
Strengthens character arcs	

SET 1: Underdogs   **CRAFT**   **Total Reps: 8**

List THREE movie characters who are traditional underdogs.

1. _____   _____
   (character)   (movie)

2. _____   _____
   (character)   (movie)

3. _____   _____
   (character)   (movie)

Now, list TWO movie characters who might be considered Hollywood underdogs.

1. _____   _____
          (character)   (movie)

2. _____   _____
          (character)   (movie)

Using one of these two characters, briefly describe in the space below what the movie does to place this character into underdog positions.

Situations	How the situation makes the character an underdog

Best/Worst/Both

This one's a bit trickier than our previous characteristic, but the idea here is no less profound. Hollywood characters tend to be either great at what they do, terrible at what they do, or sometimes they're both the best and the worst simultaneously. This last one is the key, because it's inherently ironic that characters' strengths are also their weaknesses (more on this in a bit.)

This one also amplifies the conflict and drama, while simultaneously making these aspects of story more accessible to your audience. Put another way, the greater the height, the greater the fall. Likewise, the deeper the hole, the more challenging it is to overcome.

Because being the best or worst is so extreme, it helps the audience see and understand the dilemmas the characters face and their character arcs. Character changes are easier for an audience to spot simply because of the heightened contrast between extremes.

Something to think about: comedies tend to utilize the 'worst at what they do' dynamic more than other genres. Why do you think this is?

Jot some thoughts in the space below:

ADVANTAGES	DISADVANTAGES
Adds dramatic irony	Runs the risk of being cliché
Helps audience understand arcs	May lead to simplistic characters
Amplifies conflict and drama	

SET 2: Best/Worst/Both   CRAFT   Total Reps: 6

List TWO movie characters who are the BEST AT WHAT THEY DO.
First one's filled out as an example.

1. _____Maverick_____   _____*Top Gun*_____
   (character)   (movie)

   Character is best at: ___being a fighter pilot_____

2. _____   _____
   (character)   (movie)

   Character is best at: _____

3. _____   _____
   (character)   (movie)

   Character is best at: _____

List TWO movie characters who are the WORST AT WHAT THEY DO.
We'll use the same example.

1. _____Maverick_____   _____*Top Gun*_____
   (character)   (movie)

Character is worst at: ___being a teammate/wingman_____

2. _____   _____
   (character)   (movie)

Character is worst at: _____

3. _____   _____
   (character)   (movie)

Character is worst at: _____

List TWO movie characters who are BOTH the BEST AND WORST AT WHAT THEY DO.
If you like, try this with any of the characters you listed previously.

1. _____Maverick_____
   (character)

Best at: _____being a fighter pilot_____

Worst at: _____being a fighter pilot (because he's a bad teammate/wingman)__

> **How?** The film presents the character as an extremely talented pilot, BUT his desire to be the best prevents him from being a good teammate. This is a manifestation of the character's FLAW (more on this in a bit….)

Now it's your turn.

Remember: if you like, try this on a character you've chosen previously.

2. _____
         (character)

Best at: _____

Worst at: _____

> **How?**

3. _____
         (character)

Best at: _____

Worst at: _____

> **How?**

Larger than Life

Hollywood characters tend to have aspects that are larger than life. Whether it's an ordinary person caught in extraordinary circumstances or an extraordinary person in ordinary circumstances, Hollywood is in the business of portraying extreme versions of what we find in everyday life. Makes sense – after all, you get everyday life for free. Even in realistic genres, you'll find characters with oversized personalities, situations that are out of the ordinary, and characteristics that are extreme versions of their real-life counterparts.

Why is this so prevalent? In part, it's due to time constraints of the medium. With approximately two hours to convey story, characters, plot, rules of the world, backstory, etc. , the medium itself dictates using extremes as shortcuts to capture the audience's attention and pique curiosity. Put another way, larger than life extremes are unusual; therefore, they stand out and draw attention to themselves simply through the design.

ADVANTAGES	DISADVANTAGES
Quickly piques curiosity	Runs the risk of being unrealistic
Stands out	Can lead to cliché
Lets audience to explore the unusual	

SET 3 – Larger Than Life   **CRAFT**   **Total Reps: 3**

Using any of the characters/movies you listed previously, <u>describe</u> the larger than life aspects. If you want more of a challenge, think of a realistic movie depicting everyday life and see if you can find its larger than life characteristics.

1.

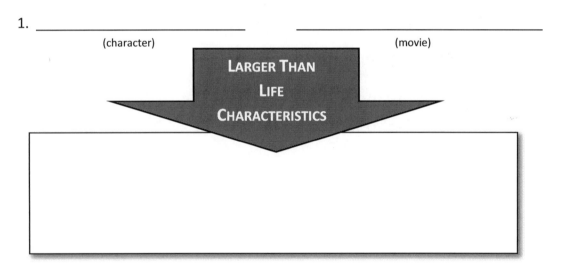

Just for fun, examine the list you just created. Depending on your choices, you may see the larger than life aspects tilted toward either the character or the plot of the movie.

The combination of realistic and larger than life details can soften those extreme aspects of the movie that may strain relatability.

Okay, one more time! Practice makes perfect...

2. _____   _____
         (character)   (movie)

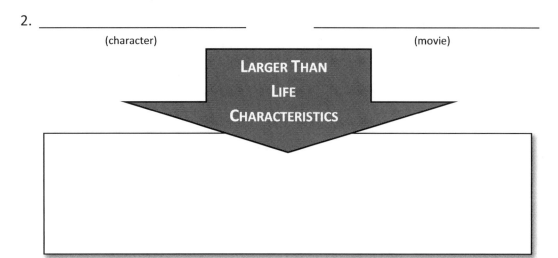

If you encounter characters AND story situations that are larger than life, examine the film a bit closer to see if there are any aspects of it that are rooted in reality. Chances are you may discover some everyday aspects in the film to help keep the audience grounded and engaged.

For example – in *The Incredibles*, Mr. Incredible is an extraordinary character (an animated superhero!) in an extraordinary world (that's outlawed superheroes), so the film adds some realistic aspects to keep the audience grounded and to help them relate to the more unusual aspects. Thus, we have Mr. Incredible struggling in a dead end job and dealing with family issues. This blend helps make the character relatable, while still enabling the filmmakers to explore a fantastical world full of larger than life characters.

Obsessed Heroes
Hollywood heroes tend to be obsessed, goal-driven creatures. This obsession tends to cause all sorts of problems for the character, leading to internal conflict and irony. Obsession also feeds into other aspects of character design, like the character's flaw.

By creating characters who are obsessed with the issues they face, you are able to explore the extremes of their personalities. After all, an obsessed character will go to any length to solve their problems, enabling you to have built-in motivation for extreme behaviors that reveal character. Just how far a character is willing to go tells you a lot about who they are.

Obsession also reveals and defines a character's flaw. Hollywood movies tend to use POSITIVE FLAWS. Simply put, a positive flaw is a normally desirable attribute taken to an extreme, which causes all sorts of problems for the character, thus creating the flaw. Think of it as simply too much of a good thing.

Something to think about: Why do you think this type of flaw would be prevalent in Hollywood films? Jot some thoughts in the space provided:

If you're thinking in terms of creating movies and characters with broad appeal, then you wouldn't want to risk creating a main character with a truly detestable flaw. Doesn't mean you can't go there, but to minimize the risk of alienating the audience from the main character, Hollywood films tend to take positive attributes (things we like or admire) and turn those into character flaws through the use of obsession. So, while it may be desirable to strive for success, having a character obsessed with success can lead them to do anything, sacrifice anything to get it, thus forming the flaw and leading to conflict.

Of all the tendencies on this list, obsession is perhaps the most useful. Through the design alone, you're able to take the story and characters to extraordinary extremes while maintaining relatability. Given the degree of obsession, it's perfectly understandable for characters to react in extreme ways to satisfy their obsessions. This maintains the audience's bond with the character while simultaneously allowing you to push the envelope in other aspects of the story.

So, in *Pirates of the Caribbean – Curse of the Black Pearl*, Captain Jack Sparrow is obsessed with capturing his ship, the Black Pearl. This obsession alienates him from friend and foe and provides narrative drive for the character. The character's obsession is relatable – chances are if you had something taken, you'd want it back. This also feeds into the larger than life aspects of the character. While you might want to recapture something that's been stolen, you may not necessarily go to the extremes Jack does to get it. Obsession also makes the character active and driven (our next design tendency) and helps delineate the character. Remember, the character's insistence that he be referred to as CAPTAIN Jack Sparrow. Hard to be a captain when you don't have a ship.

In short, if you had to pick ONE aspect of character design around which to build a character, it's hard to go wrong with obsession.

ADVANTAGES	DISADVANTAGES
Relatable	May seem unrealistic
Creates internal *and* external conflict	
Reveals character	
Keeps character active and driven	
Provides built-in character motivation	
Feeds into character arc	
Creates positive character flaw	

SET 4: Obsession   CRAFT   Total Reps: 4

Using any of the characters you listed previously, <u>describe</u> their obsessions (if any). If the characters you chose weren't obsessed, think of some who are.

1. _____
   (character)

Obsessed with: _____

Which causes: _____
(list some problems caused by this obsession)

Why?

Ask yourself why the character is obsessed. Is there something in the character's past that would cause this obsession? An old wound? A psychological scar? If you locate the source of the obsession, you may have just found the character's FLAW. Describe **why** the character is obsessed here:

Now, think of another obsessed movie character to explore below:

2. _____
   　　　　　　　(character)

Obsessed with: _____

Which causes: _____
　　　　　　　　　(list some problems caused by this obsession)

Why? Describe **why** the character is obsessed here:

If the obsession was born from a plot event in the film (or revealed in its backstory), did this event create a **flaw** in the character that manifests itself though this unhealthy obsession? If so, briefly describe the flaw here:

_____

Now, examine the plot of the movie. Is it somehow designed to reveal and explore this character flaw? If so, describe the plot events that explore the character's flaw here:

Flaw: _____

Plot Events Briefly note some of the plot events that reveal and explore the character's flaw, either through the problems caused by obsession or some other aspect of the flaw.

If you discovered a relationship between story events and the character's flaw, the movie you picked is likely a flaw-based story in which a character must learn to overcome a flaw to solve the plot of the film. This is classic Hollywood storytelling –

exploring internal conflict through external plot events designed to bring a character's flaw to the surface (thus exposing it to both the character and the audience), then using plot to force the character to deal with the flaw, by learning the lesson of the movie (which creates the character's arc.) Sometimes a character will *not* learn the lesson, thus not address the flaw, leading to the character's demise. The former is a typical happy ending. The latter, a downer ending.

BONUS SET: Applied Obsession   CRAFT   Bonus Reps: 4

Okay, if appropriate, try this tool with one of your own characters/screenplays.

1. _____
   (your character)

Obsessed with: _____

Which causes: _____
                (list some problems caused by this obsession)

> **Why?** Describe **why** the character is obsessed here:

Does your WHY create a **flaw** in the character that manifests itself though this unhealthy obsession? If so, briefly describe the flaw here:

_____

Now, examine the plot of your movie. Is it designed to reveal and explore this character flaw? If so, describe the plot events that explore it here:

> **Plot Events** Briefly note some plot events that reveal and explore the character's flaw, either through the problems caused by obsession or some other aspect of the flaw.

While we'll discuss character flaws in the second half of this exercise, obsession is closely related to the flaw, or is often the manifestation of the flaw.

Active and Driven

This one's self-explanatory – Hollywood characters tend to be very active, driven individuals -- obsession has a way of doing that to a person. But, even if the character is not necessarily obsessed, characters who are actively pursuing their goals keep the story moving forward.

While this aspect is straightforward, it's application often isn't. Typically, this drive and propensity for action aren't directed where they should be. How it works is like this: characters actively pursue solving the plot of the movie without addressing their flaws. Makes sense. Often a flaw is a source of pain or sorrow for characters, so the last thing they want to do is face it. So instead, they devote their energies toward solving the plot to avoid dealing with flaws. This has a subtle psychological effect on the audience of demonstrating just how hurtful the flaw is to a character. The harder they try to avoid the flaw, the more painful it must be. Notice how this approach blends character and plot design into a singularity – story.

Active and driven characters help externalize the plot and reveal character through the choices characters make, helping the audience to understand both a character's personality as well as the internal conflict the character faces.

ADVANTAGES	DISADVANTAGES
Drives story forward	None
Externalizes internal dilemmas	
Contextualizes character flaw	

> Training Tip: Have your characters try to solve the plot of your movie in all the wrong ways. This helps demonstrate a character's WANT and NEED to the audience.

How it works is simple: when characters try to solve the plot of the movie without changing or facing their flaws (want), what they really should do is address their flaws and change (need). This dichotomy creates internal conflict for the character that's externalized so audiences can understand it.

SET 5: *Active and Driven*   **CRAFT**   **Total Reps: 2**

Using any of the characters you've chosen so far (including yours if appropriate), think of a movie character who actively tries to solve the plot of the film without addressing the flaw, then do the activity below.

PLEASE NOTE: for this one, you'll need to pick a character with a well-defined flaw.

1. _____
               (character)

Goal: _____
        (what's this character trying to do? Typically this defines the character's <u>WANT</u>)

Plot Problem: _____
        (what's the issue the character faces because of the plot? May be the same as the goal)

What: _____
        (what does the character do (actions) to achieve the goal or solve the plot problem?)

How: _____
        (how SHOULD the character solve the plot problem? Typically defines the <u>NEED</u>)

Below is a timeline for the movie you chose for this exercise. Watch the movie again (if necessary) and note the approximate times the following events occur:

    1. Mark when the plot problem is presented to the character with a '?'
    2. Mark when the character decides to take action to solve the plot with a '!'
    3. <u>Underline</u> the sections of the timeline where the character is actively trying to solve plot question WITHOUT addressing the flaw
    4. Is there an 'aha!' moment where the character realizes the flaw is the real issue they must address? If so, mark when this happens with a '+'
    5. Finally, overline (is that even a word?) the sections of the film where the character is now somehow addressing the flaw to solve the plot

Your Timeline: (approximate times are listed above the timeline)

	30	60	90	
ACT 1		ACT 2		ACT 3

The next page shows what this timeline might look like for a Hollywood feature.

Hollywood Narrative Approximate Timeline

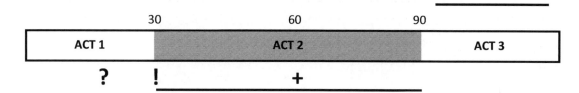

How'd your film compare? Was it similar?
Depending on how you defined these particular story beats, you may have discovered something that looks like this:

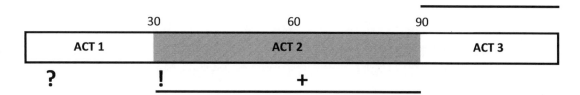

Or this:

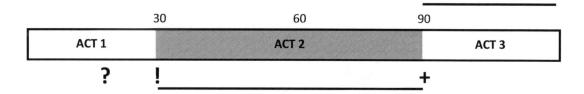

Or even this:

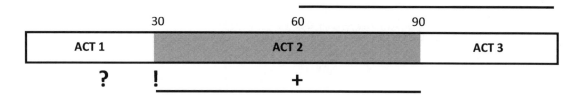

Obviously, your results may vary, but what we're exploring is the relationship between character design and narrative structure. We'll delve into structure in far greater depth in a bit, so for now, let's keep our focus on character and our next design tendency.

> **?** = character encounters main plot question **!** = character begins to solve main plot question
> **+** = character realizes must address flaw to solve plot _____ = character actively trying to solve plot
> _____ = change in strategy in which character uses addressing flaw to solve plot

Choices Under Pressure

This one may go without saying, but the plot must force your characters to face tough choices under duress. If actions speak louder than words, then choices speak louder than actions – and, depending on how you look at it, choices ARE actions, or at least inform the actions to come.

Watching characters struggle with difficult moral dilemmas is extremely satisfying for an audience, allowing us to ask ourselves – what would I do if I were in this character's shoes? Would I choose the same course of action? We then have to watch the movie to see how character choices play out and either confirm these were the right or wrong ways to solve a problem.

If characters make the right choices, the movie typically has a happy ending, and this creates an <u>affirmational learning experience</u>. In other words, right choices demonstrate what to do to solve a problem.

If characters make the wrong choices, the movie typically has a down ending, and this creates an <u>eliminatory learning experience</u>. Put another way, we learned what NOT to do. The film becomes a cautionary tale of sorts.

Audiences tend to prefer the former to the latter, which makes sense. Who wants to leave the movie feeling miserable? Not to mention, discovering what not to do is easy, so the lesson of the movie isn't as valuable. Discovering what to do is far more difficult, thus typically more satisfying.

Although terms like learning and lesson seem more appropriate to the classroom than the movie theater, these facets actually allude to the theme of the movie that you'll explore through its characters, and in a tangential way, the very origin of story itself. Story was THE original teaching tool. Imagine young people sitting around the fire listening to tales told by hunters returning from the hunt. As the tales unfold, listeners are learning what to do, what not to do, what to aspire to, what to avoid. This passing of knowledge and culture from one generation to the next was an early function of story, one which stays with us to this day.

> **Training Tip:** Character choice is the outer manifestation of a character's personality.

Character choice should be the prime mover of plot once your plot gets underway, lending the story an organic feel. So, instead of the audience sensing some writer is driving the plot forward, it now seems like the characters are advancing the story. Creating this feel also helps with plot holes or logical inconsistencies within the narrative; after all, characters, like people, often make illogical decisions, and if these decisions affect the plot, the audience can more easily overlook logic issues.

The 'pressure' part of Choices under Pressure refers to the motivations forcing the choice. In a well-crafted film everything is motivated, and choices are no exception. Pressure can also force the need to make a choice quickly, which helps a film's pace.

Because choices come from character, they carry consequences. A character who makes a bad choice may feel guilt, creating an additional burden to overcome. The right choice can lead to a sense of triumph. Both help the audience 'plug in' to a character, giving us a glimpse inside the character's mind.

ADVANTAGES	DISADVANTAGES
Creates intrigue	You tell me! I can't seem to find one.
Helps audience bond to character	
Helps story feel real	
Adds stakes	
Reveals character	
Creates consequences	
Externalizes inner thoughts	

SET 6: *Choices Under Pressure*   **CRAFT**   ***Total Reps*: 3**

Pick a movie or one of your scripts, and examine a choice a character makes. Then, complete the following:

Choice: _____
(briefly describe the choice a character makes)

Opposing Choice: _____
(what's the opposite to this choice? Describe that here.)

How would making this opposite choice affect the plot? Describe below:

If a character choice doesn't affect the plot, it's a non-event and should be revisited.

Elicits Emotion

Main characters should engender some sort of visceral reaction, one way or another. Obviously, most films prefer to elicit positive emotions for their heroes. This keeps the audience bonded to the character. However, sometimes that kind of response is inappropriate for certain character. We're not meant to like them. These heroes are trickier to pull off. Think of your script as going on a two-hour road trip. Would you rather spend it with someone you love or someone you detest? It's the same with movies. That said, the one thing you don't want is ambivalence – characters we neither like nor hate. I suppose we could add a third choice to our road trip. We could take it with someone we love, someone we hate or someone who's boring. Don't know about you, but I'd still rather have someone I love in the passenger seat. Of course, there are those characters we love to hate, which is also fine. As long as a character gets some sort of emotional response, you're typically in good shape.

At the heart of this aspect of character design is the idea of getting the audience to root for or against characters. When the audience pulls for our hero to win, they're now invested in the outcome of the story – the stronger the pull, the more satisfying the triumph. Likewise, when the audience roots against a character, it's satisfying to see them go down. This polarity helps to create confirmation bias in the audience, which helps you as a storyteller. How it works is simple: when audiences like characters, they tend to ignore their negatives and see only what they want to see that confirms their positive feelings. On the opposite end, when audiences despise characters, they tend to see only those aspects that confirm their negative emotional responses. These polarities help create audience members who are actively adding to the content you're providing, helping you create more complex stories simply because the audience is adding their own layers of complexity.

Ever wonder why people watch movies over and over? On the surface, it doesn't exactly make sense. After all, it's the ultimate spoiler. I'd say we rewatch a film because of how it makes us feel. This feeling comes from characters who elicit emotion.

ADVANTAGES	DISADVANTAGES
Creates polarities	None.
Memorable	
Helps audience engage the film	

SET 7: Elicits Emotion　　　　　　　**CRAFT**　　　　　　　**Total Reps: 2**

Pick a film/character that created an emotional response in you, then consider the following

1. _____   _____
   　　　　　(character)　　　　　　　　　　　　　　　　(movie)

How did the character or movie make you feel? _____

Now, ask yourself why. What was it about the film or the character that elicited that emotional response? Why did you feel the way you did? Jot some thoughts in the space below:

[   ]

Chances are, embedded somewhere in that last response is something that's particular to you, and if the answer was broad enough, a lot of other you's who feel the same way. That's how <u>you</u> contributed to this particular movie. And, that's the power of this technique.

Identifiable and Universal
While this is a separate category on the list, in ways all the tendencies we're exploring are designed to feed into creating characters the audience can identify with or relate to.

Identifiable means you can see some aspect of yourself in a character. Universal means a lot of people can see themselves in a character. Neither of these imply you have to recreate actual, real-life people on the screen. We can identify with superheroes, robots, alien beings, and all sorts of characters drastically different from ourselves. Identifiable and universal simply mean the movie or the characters have at least some aspect to them that we can see in ourselves. Back to Mr. Incredible from an earlier example. I can't identify with being a superhero, but I can identify with the family aspects of the story. Others may identify with being stuck in a dead-end job they detest or having a jerk for a boss or being underpaid and overqualified. Sticking with Mr. Incredible, while I've never found myself in his specific situation (being a superhero in a world that's outlawed superheroes), if we take this character's specific goal – to return to the glory days as a well-respected superhero, and broaden it, we find his goal's universal aspects – to be admired, to be respected, to be himself. From a design standpoint, creating universally identifiable characters means finding values that are universal to human existence, then creating plot-specific characters who explore their particular iterations of these values.

Depending on your particular story, creating identifiable and universal attributes can be as simple as:

- Placing ordinary characters into extraordinary situations an audience can understand (and therefore relate to).
- Placing extraordinary characters in ordinary situations an audience can understand.
- Some blend of these two.

Please note: ordinary doesn't mean boring or plain, but rather, think of ordinary as something that you could realistically encounter in everyday life.

This combination of identifiable yet unusual allows the audience to be grounded by some aspect of the story or characters while simultaneously getting to experience something new. Who says you can't have your cake and eat it, too?

SET 8: *Identifiable/Universal*   ***CRAFT***   ***Total Reps: 4***

Let's look for examples of each of these tool sets.

List an ordinary (identifiable) character caught in extraordinary circumstances:

1. _____ _____
          (character)   (movie)

List an extraordinary character caught in ordinary circumstances:

2. _____ _____
          (character)   (movie)

List a blended character (both extraordinary AND identifiable) then examine both the character and the situations in the film this character is put into.

Then, list some aspects from each that are universal/identifiable and some unusual aspects that are more specific to the character or film, and thus possibly less identifiable

3. _____
                 (character)   (movie)

Ordinary Traits	Ordinary Circumstances
Unusual Traits	Unusual Circumstances

If you were able to identify characteristics in all four quadrants, then you likely found a film (and character) with a mix of traits unusual enough to pique interest yet ordinary enough to be identifiable. Keeping the audience grounded while simultaneously letting them experience something new is a powerful storytelling combination, which is why it's one of the hallmarks of Hollywood character design.

ADVANTAGES	DISADVANTAGES
Grounds and engages audience	None.
Helps audience relate to story	Absolutely none.
Helps create polarities	Seriously. Zero, zilch, zip, nothing.
Makes unique elements accessible	

***BONUS SET**: Applied Analysis* **CRAFT** **Bonus Reps: 4**

Using one (or more) of your scripts and any of your characters...

List an ordinary character caught in extraordinary circumstances:

1. _____   _____
   (character)   (script)

List an extraordinary character caught in ordinary circumstances:

2. _____   _____
   (character)   (script)

List a blended character (extraordinary AND identifiable) and their circumstances:

3. _____   _____
   (character)   (script)

Ordinary Traits	Ordinary Circumstances
Unusual Traits	Unusual Circumstances

Hopefully, you found a healthy blend of identifiable/universal characters and situations to help the audience relate to your script, combined with enough unique content to keep them engaged. If not? Then you know what to do – rewrite!

The Strength-Flaw Combo
Related to heroes being the best and worst at what they do, Hollywood characters tend to possess strengths that are also their flaws. The vice is also versa – a character's flaw can also be a strength.

We've been discussing flaw quite a bit, so perhaps we should define it in more concrete terms.

> **Flaw:** any trait that puts a character at odds with society or the antagonist.

A flaw isn't necessarily something 'wrong' or a defect, but rather, this is the character trait that often sets the force of antagonism against the character. So, in the movie *Amadeus*, Mozart being a musical prodigy causes Salieri (the antagonist) to want to destroy him out of jealousy. Notice that being gifted at something, in this case music, would normally be considered a positive attribute; however, it also draws the wrath of the antagonist. This is an example of a **Strength-Flaw**.

Strength-flaws create a similar sense of irony to the 'best/worst at what they do' design paradigm from earlier. It's inherently ironic that the thing that a helps a character excel is also the exact same thing that gets them into trouble. Going back to Iron Man from our discussion on underdogs, Tony Stark is portrayed in the movie as being the best weapons designer in the world. This forms a strength – brilliant weapons designer. This very strength is why he gets kidnapped at the beginning of the movie, so that he could design weapons for some terrorists (and also because his weapons had harmed these folks in the past.) So, while being brilliant is certainly a strength, by causing problems for our hero, it's also a flaw.

Many of the same advantages to being the 'best/worst at what they do' also apply to strength-flaws. Because you're taking a normally positive attribute and turning it into a flaw, you get the benefits of the positive (audience can admire it, thus admire the character) while simultaneously using that same trait to generate both internal and external conflict. Imagine discovering that the thing you're so good at, is suddenly not so good. Matter of fact, it's actually causing you problems. However, you're reluctant to change this aspect because it's helped you excel. This creates an additional obstacle to the character changing, which increases the conflict.

Whether you decide to go with a strength-flaw for a character, or just a straight-up flaw, this is a critical design component because a character's arc comes from the flaw. Of all the character design tendencies we've explored, flaw is perhaps the most important because it has the greatest influence on the narrative. Without a flaw, you lose much of your internal conflict. The flaw creates the 'need' part of want and need, so that goes POOF as well. The character doesn't need to change, after all there's no flaw to fix, so your character no longer has a tangible arc. Flaws also help humanize your character – real people aren't perfect, so your characters shouldn't be either. This has the added benefit of becoming another point of relatability for the audience.

Flaws are often thematic in nature, helping to convey the theme of your movie to an audience. In overcoming the flaw, typically a character must learn the lesson of the movie. And, as the audience watches the hero learn, they learn, too.

While many of the tendencies of Hollywood character design focus solely on building dynamic characters, the flaw (or strength-flaw) represents a point where plot and character can become one. As a result, flaws should be chosen with great care.

ADVANTAGES	DISADVANTAGES
Forms basis for internal conflict	Hmm…
Helps audience bond to character	
Helps character feel real	
Creates character arc	
Informs subplots	
Can convey theme	
Gives character room to grow	
Can add irony (strength-flaw)	
Creates the 'need' in want and need	

A quick recap:

- Strength-flaws are often simply too much of a good thing.
- Flaws often manifest as obsession.
- Try relating the flaw or strength-flaw to your theme.

You can build an entire movie around something as simple as a character flaw. Consider the case of Marlin from *Finding Nemo*…

Character: Marlin
Strength: He's a great dad – he'll never let anything happen to Nemo
Flaw: He's a great dad – he'll never let anything happen to Nemo.

Story: Marlin is overprotective of Nemo. So, Nemo decides to rebel, leading to his capture. Now Marlin must journey across the sea to save his only son.

Notice what made Marlin so overprotective was shown in the movie's hook in a specialized story beat called the **Birth of the Flaw**.

In the opening, we see Marlin and his spouse tending to hundreds of eggs – their family to be. However, when another fish attacks them, killing everyone but Marlin and sparing only one egg, this scars Marlin to the point where he's afraid to leave his home. The movie sends Marlin about as far away from home as possible to find Nemo, forcing Marlin to overcome the fear created from the Birth of the Flaw.

Lesson of the Movie (Theme): ironically, in some ways the movie could be called *Letting Go of Nemo*. Sure, it's not as catchy, but it's the lesson of the movie. Notice at the end of the film, Marlin is finally reunited with Nemo, but Dory is captured, Now Marlin faces a choice (under pressure) – let Nemo go save Dory or not. Marlin chooses to let Nemo go, thus demonstrating he's changed (character arc), which serves as proof that he's learned the lesson of the movie. Marlin is no longer his old, overprotective self as a result of the journey to find Nemo as illustrated in the film's final scene.

> **Training Tip:** Once you've shown the audience how a character has changed, create a moment/scene that tests this change so we can see if it's lasting.

Using a flaw or strength-flaw as a starting point for your story serves to anchor the script around the main character. The plot then serves as the means you use to explore this flawed character. Plot events then highlight the flaw, bring it to the surface so the character (and audience) understand it's a problem that must be dealt with to solve the plot. Story events are targeted directly at this aspect of the character to maximize the conflict and to force the need to change. They can also reinforce the flaw, creating even more difficulty for a character. Back to Marlin: his greatest fears are confirmed when Nemo is captured due to leaving the safety of home. This entrenches Marlin's fear even more, giving him an even greater challenge to overcome.

The Birth of the Flaw also has the added benefit of increasing relatability. By showing the audience how your character became the flawed person they are today, you generate empathy. After all, this character seemed like an everyday person until the event that gave birth to their flaw. So, by extension, you get the audience subconsciously asking – if that event happened to me, how would I react or how would it have affected me? In addition, because we saw this event occur, we understand WHY a character behaves in a certain way. This gives us a glimpse inside the character, helping to bond us to this person even more because we understand the motivations behind the actions.

SET 9: *Flaws and Strength-Flaws*   CRAFT   Total Reps: 4

Pick a movie character and complete the following:

1. _____
   (character)

Strength: _____
(there may be a few to choose from)

Flaw: _____
(if you're unsure, look at the character's arc and that may help)

Story

List the main story beats related to the flaw (if any). Be sure to check if there's a birth of the flaw!

Lesson of the Movie:
_____

Once we see the character change, is there a beat afterward to test it? _____
If so, briefly describe it here:

Then, go back to earlier in the film. Was there a corresponding beat to this test? A scene or a moment where this same trait is on display? If so, describe that here:

If you encountered a similar moment earlier in the film that explores some aspect of the character's flaw, what you were watching was a technique designed to show the audience what's wrong with a character – one that's easily defined and measured. These repeated scenes serve as litmus tests of a sort, allowing the audience to understand and track changes in the character. If you encounter this technique in a film, be on the lookout for additional moments that test and demonstrate this aspect of the character.

SET 10: Putting it All Together   CRAFT   Total Reps: 2

So far we've been examining each tendency individually. Now let's see if we can find a movie character that exhibits ALL of the tendencies.

Exercise:
Pick a character who exemplifies *all* of the tendencies of Hollywood characters. Check off the tendencies that apply to the character you picked, then briefly describe how the character fits each tendency. I'll pick one to get us started.

1. _____FORREST GUMP_____
   (character)

   ✓ Underdog
      From taking on a hurricane to running from bullies in a truck, the character is placed in numerous situations in which he's the underdog.

   ✓ Best/Worst/Both at what they do
      Let's see. Forrest is the best running back, best ping pong player, best shrimp boat captain, best soldier, best… you get the idea. And worst? This one's more intriguing: I'd say he's both the best and worst lover for Jenny. He's thoughtful, kind, loving. But, how fulfilled could Jenny be with him?

   ✓ Larger than life
      If you've seen the movie, this one doesn't take much explaining – everything in this film is larger than life. But, if you need an example: how many times did he go to the White House? Oh, and how many Dr. Peppers did he drink? While we're at it – how many times did he run across the United States?

   ✓ Obsessed
      He didn't name all the shrimp boats 'Jenny' because he wasn't obsessed…

Note: this wasn't an obsession born from a flaw per se -- it's simply used to provide a continual throughline for the character and the story.

- ✓ Active and driven
  When Bubba is caught under fire in Vietnam, Forrest doesn't hesitate – "I gotta save Bubba!" And, off he rushes into the jungle.

- ✓ Choices under pressure
  "I gotta save Bubba!"

- ✓ Hero elicits emotion
  Whether its Mama dying, Jenny dying, or the moment when Forrest meets his son and expresses worry that his son may have his intellectual ability. The film was a tour de force of emotion.

- ✓ Identifiable and universal
  While I may not be a millionaire shrimp boat captain, I can certainly relate with unrequited love, being picked on, and loving your mom.

- ✓ Strength is flaw
  I'd say there are a couple. Forrest begins the movie with leg braces (flaw) which becomes a strength when he becomes a great runner. A better Strength-flaw might be the character's naiveté, which keeps him oblivious to the tumultuous times that harm the other major characters (Lieutenant Dan, Bubba and Jenny)

Side Note:
Ironically, Forrest Gump doesn't really change or arc as a result of the film, but rather he causes change in others. This is a special form of protagonist known as a Catalytic Hero. Simply put, a catalytic hero remains pretty much the same throughout the film while nearly everything else in the movie exhibits some form of change. Another example of a catalytic hero would be Jack from *Titanic*. While yes, technically he goes from alive to dead (spoiler!), his personality remains consistent throughout the movie. In this particular film, Rose is the hero because she's the character who does change. Likewise, Ferris Bueller from *Ferris Bueller's Day Off* is another catalytic hero bringing change to the movie's actual hero, Cameron.

There's my example. Now it's your turn!

Pick a character that exemplifies all of the tendencies of Hollywood characters. Check off the tendencies that apply to the character you picked, then briefly describe how the character fits each tendency.

1. _____
   (character)

- Underdog

- Best/Worst/Both at what they do

- Larger than life

- Obsessed

- Active and driven

- Choices under pressure

- Hero elicits emotion

- Identifiable and universal

- Flaw or Strength-flaw

So, how'd your character do? Chances are, the more mainstream the movie, the more of these tendencies you'll find.

Now, let's try the same exercise with one of YOUR characters. Same deal as before: list your character, then check off the tendencies that apply then briefly describe.

2. _____
            (character)

- ○ <u>Underdog</u>

- ○ <u>Best/Worst/Both at what they do</u>

- ○ <u>Larger than life</u>

- ○ <u>Obsessed</u>

- ○ <u>Active and driven</u>

- ○ <u>Choices under pressure</u>

- ○ <u>Hero elicits emotion</u>

- ○ <u>Identifiable and universal</u>

- ○ <u>Flaw or Strength-flaw</u>

Remember, these tendencies don't measure the quality of a character, but rather, they're aspects of character designed to HELP you tell your story cinematically.

Now that we've explored some tendencies of Hollywood characters let's examine how to create them.

Hollywood Character Design

Our Hollywood Character Design tool is a remarkably simple, yet robust way of creating characters designed to fit your particular narrative. Think of it as a way of turning character into story and vice versa. While the tool consists of only four parts, these are the parts where character and story meet. In other words, they're the requisite aspects of character necessary for the story to function.

Hollywood Character Design Toolset
The four basic elements of Hollywood Character Design are:

1. Defining Characteristic
   This is a character's main trait or defining attribute. It can be psychological or some other aspect that defines the character, such as an occupation. Think of it as what would be on a character's business card. So for example: a teacher, a firefighter, a terrorist, a self-serving jerk. Whatever it is, this represents the character in a nutshell, so keep the description simple: a single word or two.

2. Humanity
   This aspect is designed to make a character empathetic and relatable. Think of it as some part of ourselves we may recognize in your character. Most often, this is a positive trait – one we admire. But, it can also be negative: pettiness, greed, self-serving jerkiness – all of these are qualities audiences may recognize within themselves, even if we don't care to admit it. Whatever you choose, humanity makes us want to follow the character.

3. Paradox
   Given the character's defining characteristic, this is the thing we'd be surprised to discover about the character. So, for instance, a rugged firefighter who does floral arranging on the weekends. This juxtaposition of characteristics does much for you in terms of storytelling, creating both irony as well as the illusion that this is a three-dimensional character. Let's face it: two hours isn't enough time to convey a story and portray characters as complex as actual human beings, so we use the paradox to hint at additional layers to the character. Because the paradox is a surprise, it suggests there may be more surprising aspects to this character we've yet to experience. Think of it as opening a door to the character, whether or not the story takes

us through that door is up to you, but the very fact that it's open and we get a glimpse at what lies beyond is usually enough to give the audience the illusion that there's more to the character than meets the eye.

A paradox can also create internal conflict for a character, if the juxtaposition of traits between paradox and defining characteristic are set up in opposition to each other.

Paradoxes should be chosen with great care because of all the functions they serve. By adding irony, potential conflict and three-dimensionality to the character the paradox accomplishes a lot with a little. Choose wisely.

4. <u>Flaw</u>
Here it is again! Must be important. And, indeed it is. Flaw gives the character some aspect of themselves they must overcome to solve the problem of the movie. We explored flaw in our last section, so there's no need to delve into depth here, but just as a reminder: a flaw in cinematic terms is the aspect of a character that puts them at odds with the world around them. Also remember: for maximum effectiveness, a character's strength can be their flaw.

That's really all there is to Hollywood Character Design, just these four parameters.

But, wait!

Won't this lead to overly simplistic characters?

After all, you can't reduce entire human beings down into four basic food groups.

The key to this tool is understanding that these four points aren't the sum of who a character is, but rather, these are the points where character meets story. These elements comprise the essential, initial layer of a character that allows the story to function, which in turn allows the audience to explore the more nuanced complexities of your characters. While yes, if these are the only aspects of a character you present to an audience, you run the risk of simplistic characters, but even then, you might be surprised at the amount of complexity you can get out of this tool.

But, you don't have to take my word for it...

SET 11: *Character Design*   **CRAFT**   ***Total Reps: 2***

For this exercise, let's analyze using the Hollywood Character Design Tool. But, before we do this, perhaps an example of this tool in action might be helpful. Consider the case of a certain archeology professor who's afraid of snakes…

Instructions:

For our example, if you haven't seen *Raiders of the Lost Ark*, or for purists: *Indiana Jones and the Raiders of the Lost Ark* (sigh), you may wish to watch it. Then, analyze the character of Indiana Jones using our Hollywood Character Design tool.

To the right is a list of traits for you to assign as the character's:

      Defining Characteristic, Humanity, Paradox and Flaw.

1. _____*Indiana Jones*_____   _____*Raiders of the Lost Ark*_____
               (character)   (movie)

Defining Characteristic: _____
                              (the trait that defines a character)

Humanity: _____
           (this makes the character relatable or likeable)

Paradox: _____
        (something we're surprised to learn about this character)

Flaw: _____
      (puts the character at odds with the world, can be a strength)

Choose from the following:

Archeologist	Adventurer
Professor	Afraid of Snakes
Passionate about Antiquities	Passionate about Marion
Determination	Nerf Herder? ;)

Did I miss one? Add it below!

So, what did you pick? Hopefully, you found it a bit challenging to decide which characteristic goes where. That's okay, there's a degree of subjectivity to this. And, a bit of a secret as well…

To see how your combination of traits compares to some other possible combinations, turn the page.

Here's one possibility:

1. _____Indiana Jones_____   _____*Raiders of the Lost Ark*_____
                   (character)   (movie)

Defining Characteristic: _____Archeologist/Adventurer_____
                                        (the one trait that defines a character)

Humanity: _____Passionate about antiquities/Marion_____
                           (something that makes the character relatable or likeable)

Paradox: _____Professor_____
                           (something we'd be surprised to learn about this character)

Flaw: _____Afraid of snakes_____
               (this trait puts the character at odds with the world, can be a strength, too)

All right, so I cheated a bit with that first one. Who knew adventurer-archeologist was a thing?

How did your combination fare? Look similar? Or, did you assign different traits to our four design paradigms?

Even if our versions don't quite match, that's fine. We'll get to that in a bit. But, there's a problem with the combination above. Did you catch it?

Perhaps, like any good archeologist, we should dig a bit deeper.

When we first meet Indiana Jones, he's deep in the jungles of South America. Scruffy, cool under pressure, every bit the adventurer. So, it makes sense to label the defining characteristic as an adventurer archeologist because when we initially meet movie characters they're typically engaged in a character-defining action. We'll delve into introducing characters later, but back to Indy – there he is among the spiders, poison darts and giant boulders – clearly the stuff of adventurers, not necessarily professors. So, it makes sense, given this introduction to the character, that the last thing we'd expect from this guy in the fedora is that he's a professor – even if it is only part time.

Okay, so far so good. Or, so it seems…

Being afraid of snakes seems like a decent enough flaw. In good, flaw-like fashion, Indy must face snakes to get the prize, the Ark of the Covenant. So, once again, this seems logical. Not to mention, the third movie in the franchise opens on a flashback to when Indy developed his fear of snakes. Seems like a variant on our Birth of the Flaw opening.

And, the character's humanity? Take your pick. You could say it's Indy's dogged determination. Perhaps it's his wit and charm. Or, that he hates Nazis. I chose his passion, typically an endearing trait for most individuals. Indy displays a passion for antiquities, a passion to preserve archeological relics, and of course, a passion for Marion. Passion seems like the strongest choice.

But, something's still not quite right.

Let's go back to that definition of a flaw. The flaw is supposed to set the character at odds with the world, often bringing the antagonist into the character's life. And, being afraid of snakes, while helping to create an antagonist in certain scenes, isn't the main antagonist. And, what about the whole strength-flaw thing? Surely, a movie this well-crafted would take full advantage of the strength of the design.

Hmm...

Perhaps we should try this again.

2. _____Indiana Jones_____   _____Raiders of the Lost Ark_____
             (character)   (movie)

Defining Characteristic: _____Professor   ~~Archeologist/Adventurer~~_____
                              (the one trait that defines a character)

Humanity: _____Passionate about antiquities/Marion_____
               (something that makes the character relatable or likeable)

Paradox: _____Afraid of snakes   ~~Professor~~_____
               (something we'd be surprised to learn about this character)

Flaw: _____Archeologist/Adventurer   ~~Afraid of snakes~~_____
         (this trait puts the character at odds with the world, can be a strength, too)

Ah, this seems better. Being afraid of snakes feels like a solid paradox. Given the demonstrated bravery of our unflappable adventurer, the last thing we might expect is that he'd be afraid of something as simple as snakes. There's that irony paradoxes provide. And, considering the Biblical nature of the first film, snakes hold a certain symbolism as well.

Making 'Professor' the defining characteristic also seems to work. Although, the reveal that Indy's a professor is handled more like a paradox, the important part isn't how or where this information is conveyed, but rather, that this part of the design is present in the character. No need to nitpick its placement in the narrative.

As for humanity -- passion for antiquities and/or passion for Marion seem relatable, particularly the latter. While a fascination with ancient artifacts carries an appeal for some select members of the audience, passion for a lover (or former lover) has a more universal aspect that is greatly humanizing. Juggling careers and relationships seems highly relatable as well. It's worth noting that even though the character has a very specific passion (archeological relics), audiences can relate this passion to one of their own. In other words, a specific audience member may be passionate about…um… let's say, guinea pigs. So, even though Indy's not sporting an **I♡Guinea Pigs!** t-shirt, guinea pig lovers (or anyone with a passion for pretty much anything) can identify or at least possibly relate to characters pursuing their passions.

Hmm… I think we may be onto something here.

Perhaps the key to choosing these characteristics relies on a mix of broad human motivations, such as passion, love, hate, fear, etc…, with applications specific to a character -- fear of snakes, passion for archeological relics, and so forth.

You know, Indy's passion for archeological relics seems almost… dare I say it, an obsession? And, didn't we discover just a few pages ago that obsession can be a character's strength-flaw? Which brings us to…

The flaw. Being the best archeologist in the world (you didn't think Belloq was better than Indy, did you?) attracts the attention of the antagonist (Belloq again), and brings FBI agents knocking on Indy's door, wanting him to get the Ark of the Covenant before the Nazis do. Considering Indy wants to study the ark once he gets it, and considering the government ordered it locked away for future sequels, the agents could be considered antagonists as well. Least they have top men working on it…

So, if flaws attract antagonists, then Indy's obsession with archeology seems a likely candidate to be the character's flaw. And, yet… even that doesn't seem quite right.

Hey, wait a sec…

Snakes.

Why'd it have to be snakes?

Ever wonder? Could it be that many people are afraid of snakes? Perhaps THAT should be Indy's <u>humanity</u>. It's relatable if not quite universal.

And, maybe we should break up those two passions. After all, Indy's passion for archeology causes conflict in his relationship with Marion. All she wants is a drink, not these bits of junk. While we're at it, that passion for Marion causes Indy to be captured in the film's climax. That sounds like a <u>flaw</u>. It temporarily keeps Indy from achieving his goal – to retrieve the ark. Then again, what if Indy is defined by his passion for Marion? Would that make it his <u>defining characteristic</u>?

Well, crap.

You know, I picked Indy because he seemed like a fairly simple, straightforward character. Yet, even with this simple character, discerning what he's made of seems rather complex. And, therein lies the beauty of Hollywood Character Design. It may seem to simplify characters, but in fact it creates something else entirely – a character who is simple on the surface, allowing audiences to understand them, yet the combination of these simple elements creates something far more complex, something larger than the sum of its parts. This combination yields sufficient complexity to keep the audience engaged as they discover more layers to the character, not because we've put them there, not because we've explored them in long dramatic scenes. No. The layers exist because the design creates the conditions necessary for the audience to begin to create them.

Put another way, the four attributes of Hollywood Character Design are built to allow you to choose an intriguing mix of four attributes, designed to work together by opposing each other. Oxymoronic, I know, but think about it – Indy's passion for antiquities creates conflict with his passion for Marion. Likewise, this obsession has led Indy to be the best archeologist, which is why the FBI agents come to him, saving you the need for exposition to explain it, thus providing the movie with built-in motivations for the characters. And best of all – the audience begins adding layers to the character themselves based on the combination of characteristics you chose.

With that in mind, perhaps we should try to define Indy yet again.

Third time's the charm (hopefully)! Actually, scratch that. Not hopefully. This time I **know** we'll get it right. Because, this time, I'm not doing it – you are.

Tell you what, just to hedge our bets, let's list all the possibilities for each design paradigm, so you can **circle** which one you believe is accurate for each category. Sound like a plan?

Instructions:
In each category, circle the one trait you feel most accurately reflects the character design.

3. _____Indiana Jones_____ _____Raiders of the Lost Ark_____
   (character)   (movie)

Defining Characteristic		**Humanity**	
Archeologist	Adventurer	Archeologist	Adventurer
Professor	Afraid of Snakes	Professor	Afraid of Snakes
Passion for Antiquities	Passion for Marion	Passion for Antiquities	Passion for Marion
Determination	Other (specify)	Determination	Other (specify)
Archeologist	Adventurer	Archeologist	Adventurer
Professor	Afraid of Snakes	Professor	Afraid of Snakes
Passion for Antiquities	Passion for Marion	Passion for Antiquities	Passion for Marion
Determination	Other (specify)	Determination	Other (specify)
Paradox			**Flaw**

Finally! We got it right! Well, you got it right. Congrats!

And, how do I know it's right? For that, let's check out the next page.

Just to compare, here are my selections:

3. _____Indiana Jones_____   _____Raiders of the Lost Ark_____

Defining Characteristic			**Humanity**
Archeologist	(Adventurer)	Archeologist	Adventurer
Professor	Afraid of Snakes	Professor	Afraid of Snakes
Passion for Antiquities	Passion for Marion	Passion for Antiquities	(Passion for Marion)
Determination	Other (specify)	Determination	Other (specify)
Archeologist	Adventurer	Archeologist	Adventurer
(Professor)	Afraid of Snakes	Professor	Afraid of Snakes
Passion for Antiquities	Passion for Marion	(Passion for Antiquities)	Passion for Marion
Determination	Other (specify)	Determination	Other (specify)
Paradox			**Flaw**

Hey, what do you know – I'm right, too!

And, therein lies the power of character design. For even if our answers are different, they each work for us. In other words, you filled in what works for you. I filled in what works for me. This goes for every other member of the audience as well. Obviously, audiences aren't telling themselves, "Check it out. There's Indy's defining characteristic." But, they will subconsciously say something to the effect of: this character is _____, then they'll fill in the blank with whatever content you've provided that confirms their opinions.

Notice Indy is extremely well put together, with most of his characteristics designed to oppose each other AND fit together simultaneously, creating irony and conflict. The plot of the film then bangs these attributes off each other to create various scenes and sequences. So, Indy's passion for antiquities both reunites our would-be lovers and drives them apart. Being an adventurer is at odds with Indy's role as a professor, as evidenced by the throng of students jammed in his office with questions and issues he's obviously been neglecting while off on his adventures. Had you chosen those pesky snakes, they oppose the adventurer characteristic.

The technique the tool uses is a form of <u>Binary Opposition Pairing</u>. While this approach was intended for creating protagonist-antagonist pairs, the tool applies it to character design as well. At the heart of this technique is the idea that elements in the story are created to both oppose each other and fit together in intriguing ways. So, in story terms, Indy and Belloq are the main binary opposition pair. Notice each are archeologists. This is how they fit together. But, while Indy works hard to find relics for a museum, Belloq is willing to steal what he wants, as shown at the end of the film's opening sequence. Later, both characters want the ark. This is how they're opposed in tangible terms of plot. But, Belloq is also shown to be in it for himself, willing to help even the Nazis for personal gain. This is how the characters are opposed on a more thematic level. This aspect of binary opposition pairing pits the VALUES of the characters against each other. This concept is vital to understanding how cinematic narrative works, for in it, we see the basic mechanisms of story. Both characters are archeologists, so these two elements effectively cancel each other out, leaving only their methods as a point of comparison. These methods are visual representations of the characters' values. As a result, the film achieves greater universal appeal because it's no longer a story about two archeologists in a race to find the Ark, but rather, it's a story about basic human values – in this case, selfishness versus selflessness. Because these values can apply to the pursuit of virtually ANY goal, the story takes on more universal appeal. If the movie was simply about two people wanting some ark-thingy, it would feel like it's missing something. And, that's because it is. It's missing the component that enables an audience to apply what they're watching to their own lives; their own passions; their own, personal arks, which is how a very specific story, with unique characters pursuing a unique goal also has universal appeal.

Hollywood Character design also employs the idea of <u>Matched Dramatic Potential</u>. This aspect is more about the actual choices you make for each design paradigm. So, if you choose characteristics with the potential for life-altering conflict, you maximize your chances for entertaining your audience because, if the character makes a mistake or simply doesn't succeed, the consequences will be dire. Similar to Binary Opposition Pairing, the elements you choose should also fit together logically so that a character somehow just makes sense.
Put another way – the character feels 'right'.

If you're curious about the difference between Binary Opposition Pairing and Matched Dramatic Potential, let's go back to those snakes from earlier. The Binary Opposition Pairing here is a person afraid of snakes must face snakes. The Matched Dramatic Potential portion lies in the types of snakes. Notice they weren't a bunch of harmless garter snakes. They were asps, very dangerous. And, a few cobras, just for eye-candy. So, if Indy doesn't successfully navigate the snakes, he could be bitten and die. The potential for drama is huge.

Tying all of this back into character design – when choosing characteristics, think about the specific ways these characters can both fit together and oppose one another. Then consider the universal values you can explore through these opposition pairs. If you design your characters well, with strong ties that bind yet also separate, you have a shot at creating something that's both unique yet familiar, specific yet universal. This approach also yields an interesting side effect. If every detail you choose has this opposition pairing effect, the actual categories aren't significant. Yes, you'll have to know what YOU chose for each to inform your writing, but for the audience, they'll pick whatever they wish to assign (from the choices you show them) for a character's defining characteristic, flaw, humanity and paradox. And just as before, when both of us were right even if we assigned different traits to the categories, the character still works. Actually, in some ways, the characters work even better because we've personalized their attributes, tailoring the character to our individual perspectives. Implicit in this notion is an important consideration: in order for this approach to work, you'll have to take these four characteristics and play out each. In other words, each design category would have to play out as though it were functioning in any of the design categories. So, what you choose for the character's paradox should also work if an audience member were to make it the character's defining characteristic, or the character's humanity, or, even the character's flaw. Flaw might be the big exception to this, because that ties into the character's arc. So, usually flaw is much more clearly defined (hence story beats like the Birth of the Flaw), while the other paradigms you can leave for the audience to define for themselves. Essentially, this means our four categories are interchangeable, giving each audience member different ways to establish personal connections to the characters, and by extension, to your story.

To illustrate the points in this section, let's revisit our character design chart for Indy, and highlight the opposition pairing and values to see how nearly every aspect is designed to work together to maximize conflicts, create irony and ultimately, entertain an audience.

Tying it All Together : Character Attributes, Opposition Pairing and Values

For this chart, we'll examine the connections between the design elements, looking specifically at how they're linked through opposition pairing. To determine the values being explored in a connection, simply examine the potential conflicts from this pairing and ask what core values are at stake from conflicts created by connecting these elements. For these, distill the conflict into broad terms.

To read the chart:

Arrows show the connections. **Thick arrows** mark story-critical connections necessary for the narrative to function. **Callout boxes** denote the universal or relatable values explored in these connections.

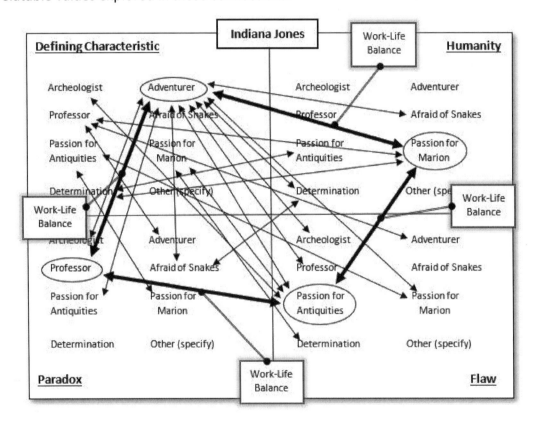

Oh, what a tangled web we weave!

It's important to note that these are my personal connections from the film. Your results may vary. Actually, they should vary. The film is designed to accommodate differing perspectives by providing viable alternatives for each design paradigm. Ever wonder how Raiders was so successful? How it resonated with so many different people? You're looking at it. Well, a big part of it.

The movie was successful because it was **designed** to succeed.

Before we move on, let's make some sense out of that mess of arrows.

Determining the Critical Path
The **thick arrows** represent the story's Critical Path from a character-based perspective. Simply put, a critical path is a combination of connections between elements that shape the plot. As you explore character through the unfolding of plot events in your screenplay, the traits you've picked for your character influence these events, helping you create scenes and beats that ultimately fuse character and plot into this little thing called story.

In the chart, we're only examining character, but we could have added plot elements designed to explore the highlighted characteristics. For instance: in the scene where Marion appears to have been killed when the basket she was hiding in is presumably put on a truck that explodes, we are shown Indy's **Passion for Marion**.

Determining a critical path is interpretive and subjective, dependent on your perception of the movie. This is by design in a well-crafted film, allowing for multiple interpretations by providing content to support viable alternative paths. But, to get at the filmmaker's intended path, examine:

1. Number of Connections
   The greater the degree of connectivity, the more the story depends on these elements, increasing the likelihood that this is the intended critical path.

2. Dramatic Potential
   Look for connections that maximize the potential for drama and conflict. Savvy filmmakers will construct stories around these.

3. Strength of Interconnectivity
   Examine the strength of connections and their importance to the character. So, for Indiana Jones, that **Passion for Antiquities** is his obsession, heavily impacting *every* connection.

Connections in your movie are established by the nature of a character trait as it relates to other character traits. This means you need scenes or beats that are intentionally designed to reveal and explore these traits to communicate them to your audience. Remember: a critical path is simply the way a filmmaker intends the audience to experience the story. But, intention and results can differ depending on individual interpretation, and how well the filmmaker guides this process. Implicit in making connections are the content created to support the connection and the design that informs the content – that's where you come in!

Design your characters well, and chances are we'll follow your suggested path through the story. But, for poorly thought-out characters, with traits that lead nowhere because they're not designed to fit together in entertaining ways, the result is a host of unintended connections that tend to undermine the story, or at the very least – leave lots of dramatic potential unexplored. For an audience, this is like asking them to put together a jigsaw puzzle in which the pieces don't fit together. Not exactly fun.

Speaking of fun... I just realized I'm having all the fun with the analysis. Don't worry – your turn is coming up!

But, before we get to that, we should probably delve into the decision-making process for choosing Indy's critical path because subconsciously your audience will be doing this with your characters in your movie.

My Indy

Hopefully you see why I chose **Adventurer** as Indy's Defining Characteristic. Based on the sheer number of binary pairings flowing from this attribute, it seemed like the logical choice.

Defining Characteristic and Flaw are closely related. Based on its interconnectivity, I chose **Passion for Antiquities** for the Flaw. Second in terms of connections is **Passion for Marion**, so that could be considered a Flaw for this character as well – especially given Indy's goal of acquiring the ark.

Paradox was a bit trickier as a strong case could be made for **Afraid of Snakes**; however, the **Professor** attribute has more binary opposition pairings, so the larger number of connections was the determining factor for this choice.

Humanity was another tricky one, but given the number of connections, **Passion for Marion** seemed appropriate. This one also impacts the story more than the others.

Defining Characteristics and Flaws are prime movers of story, so we should expect to see more connections flowing from these categories given their greater importance to the narrative. Humanity and Paradox are more about bonding the audience to a character, so fewer connections from these categories often occur simply because these parameters typically serve fewer story functions.

Okay, so that was my Indy. What about yours?

SET 12: *Character Analysis*   CRAFT   **Total Reps: *2***

Using the character chart for Indiana Jones on the next page…

Step 1: Make Your Connections by Drawing Arrows between Character Traits
In each category, use the trait as its intended function. In other words, if you chose **Afraid of Snakes** as the character's Defining Characteristic, then the Paradox might be **Adventurer** because we'd be surprised to discover our brave adventurer has such a fear. Feel free to connect as many attributes as you can.

Step 2: Examine the Interconnectivity
Traits with more connections are likely candidates to be the ones the filmmaker intended you to follow. Note the attributes with the greatest number of connections – these are likely to be the critical traits the filmmaker intended.

Step 3: Pick a Starting Point
Identify what you believe is either the character's Defining Characteristic or Flaw. We start here for the reasons mentioned earlier – these two attributes contribute the most to the narrative design. Pick a trait in either the Defining Characteristic or Flaw category to begin **your** critical path through the story. CIRCLE these traits as you identify them.

Step 4: Create Your Critical Path
Once you've identified a starting point, work your way around the chart from trait to trait, examining each for the greatest potential impact or entertainment value. These do accumulate. For example: I started with the Defining Characteristic of **Adventurer**, which led to choosing **Professor** as the Paradox. Being an archeology professor who likes adventure led to **Passion for Antiquities** as the character's Flaw, or in this case, a Strength-Flaw – the character's passion led to this career and also brings the wrath of the antagonists. With **Passion for Antiquities** as a Flaw, this made **Passion for Marion** the only real choice for our remaining category, **Humanity**, because this combination created the most conflict for the character. Once you've defined your Critical Path, be sure to fill in the Values explored in these connections using the callout boxes.

And, that's it! Simple, huh?

Your Indy:

Some points to consider as you complete the analysis:

1. The <u>Defining Characteristic</u> often determines how characters solve problems or resolve conflicts.

2. To determine values underlying a connection, look at the specific conflicts this pairing creates, then broaden them out to something more relatable to an audience.

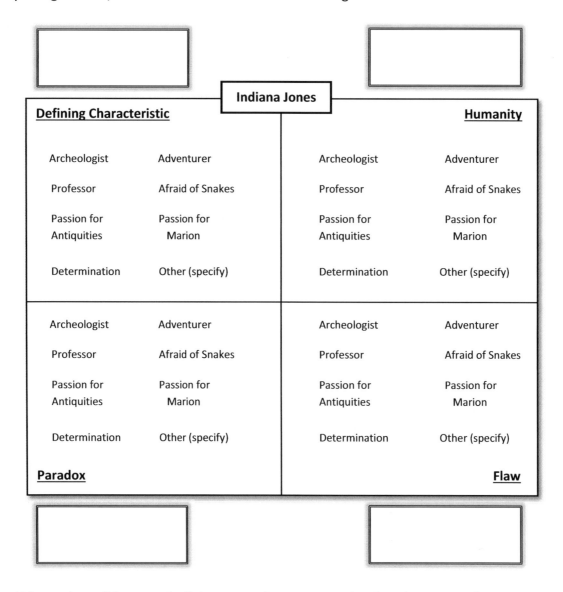

What values did you assign? I was torn between Work-Life Balance or Balancing Passions, but either way look at how relatable each of those are. You don't have to be an archaeology professor fighting Nazis to relate to the core values at stake – they literally can apply to almost anyone, even a kid juggling school and hobbies.

Okay, so that was my choice – now it's your turn!

Same deal as before, only this time, you assign the characteristics.

If appropriate, you can choose more than one characteristic in each design category as I did with Indy, just make sure there's enough content to support it. So, while Indy is an **Adventurer** to me, solving problems with action, that **Professor** trait is also on display throughout the film. Feel free to analyze one of your own characters if you like, or you can choose one from another movie.

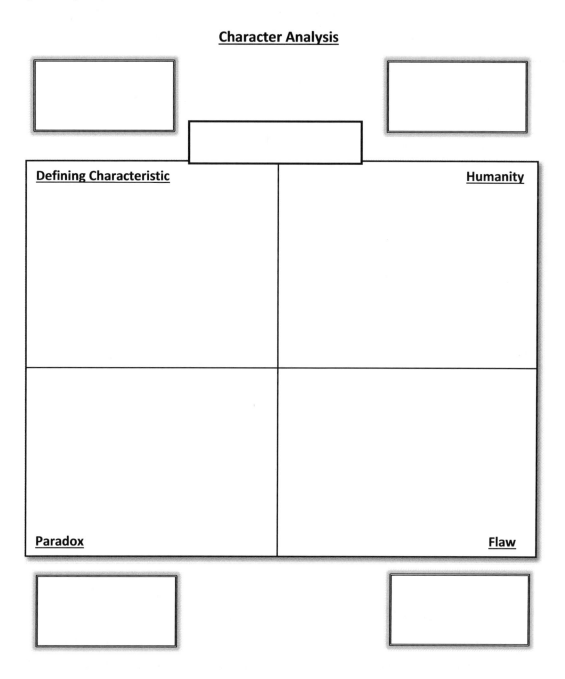

Character Analysis

Defining Characteristic	Humanity
Paradox	Flaw

That's enough analysis for now. We can create characters using this tool as well.

Creating Hollywood Characters

The process of creating characters using the four facets of Hollywood Character Design involves the following:

1. <u>Pick Specific Traits with Relatable Core Conflicts</u>
   Think of these as specific to the individual character but with relatable motivations or broader applications. Sticking with Indy, while members of the audience might not share the same passion for archeological relics, chances are they have their own passions, which helps bond the audience to the character by creating empathy – imagine if your own passions were threatened by hordes of Nazis, snakes and ruthless competitors.

   Relatability comes from the audience making connections between traits and plot, allowing individual audience members to personalize the story. To help your audience start the connection-making process, read on...

2. <u>Connect Four!</u>
   Once you pick a trait (typically starting with Defining Characteristic or Flaw), then either choose complementary traits that create interesting combinations with your starting trait and the plot of your film, or examine the connections between the qualities you've already chosen to see if this creates the most intriguing connections between the four facets of character design and the overarching plot or genre of your film.

   The connections between aspects of character and elements of plot are the key to this toolset because they provide opportunities for the audience to make and test predictions based on what they've seen, how you presented the material, their interpretation of what they're seeing, and their own, personal views and feelings regarding the characters and subject matter.

   Choose your combinations with great care. They're often the audience's initial point of contact with the characters and the story, providing opportunities for you to teach the audience that you can and will create opportunities for interaction with your film, which leads us to one more consideration, involving a little math. Wait. Math? Say it ain't so!

3. <u>Movie Math</u>!
   Finally! We get to do some math! Exciting, I know. But, before you bust out that old graphing calculator, it's not actual math -- it's movie math!

   This one originates with some advice from Ernst Lubitsch to Billy Wilder that supposedly goes something like this: "Let the audience add up two plus two. They'll love you forever"

   Okay, it's more of an analogy than actual math, but at least it's not Algebra 2.

   Continuing with the analogy -- don't give the audience four. Give them two and two and let them come up with four. In other words, don't spell everything out. Hint at it. Show them two. Show them another two. Then, let the audience put them together. This gets audience members actively writing the film with you, which has numerous benefits:

   - Creates a personalized group experience
   - Makes the film feel like more than the sum of its parts (because it is – it now has contributions from the audience)
   - Saves time. No need to show them 'four', just two and two
   - Engages the audience through interacting with the material
   - Can cover up logic holes. Each audience member can now fill in the gaps with what works for that individual.

   So, what happens if the audience adds two and two and gets three?

   That's the inherent risk in this technique. Audience members can put things together incorrectly. To account for individual perception in assembling the characters and narrative, a well-designed film has viable alternatives for differing ways a particular 'two' and 'two' can be added (and defined). Put another way – you have story elements that allow the audience to add up two and two to get three, five, eight, and of course, four. We touched on this technique in our Indiana Jones example -- character traits could be defined in multiple ways that worked no matter how you assembled them.

   This degree of craft is difficult and can impact the overall complexity of the film. The more complicated you make the script, the greater the odds we cannot assemble it in the intended way. Also, you'll have less time to build in those alternative paths through the narrative. It's a trade off to be sure, and one you'll have to define for yourself. But, don't underestimate the simple power of two plus two.

Now that we have a few important considerations out of the way, let's design some characters!

SET 13: _Character Creation_   CRAFT   _Total Reps_: _13_

For this exercise, you'll brainstorm some intriguing combinations of traits using our four design paradigms. To refresh:

<u>Defining Characteristic</u> – main trait displayed by this character. In previous examples, we've stuck to single-word descriptors; however, you don't have to. So, an adventurer archeologist is fine. So is a jerky professor, female firefighter, etc.
<u>Humanity</u> – helps bond audience to character typically through relatability
<u>Paradox</u> – given the defining characteristic, we'd be shocked to discover this aspect
<u>Flaw or (Strength-Flaw)</u> – something typically internal that the hero needs to address to truly solve the plot, often attracting the antagonist, creating conflict.

Okay, let's brainstorm some character traits. Although it's recommended to start with Defining Characteristic, feel free to vary it. Each row represents a different potential character design for a character. Do not duplicate any traits!

Defining Characteristic	Humanity	Paradox	Flaw or Strength-flaw

Examine the combinations for potential conflict inherent in your design. This is that <u>Dramatic Potential</u> we discussed earlier. If the combinations seem uninspiring, play around with the traits until you come up with more intriguing combinations. Once you have a combination you like, you're ready to move on to the next part.

Before we go to the next activity, here's some food for thought:

If you followed directions (always a big if for filmmakers), you should have 16 different traits listed on the previous page. Congratulations! Using just those traits, you could recombine them to create a total of 256 different characters (4^4 for you math fans.) So, while the tool may seem simple, it's extremely robust.

Okay, now take one of the combinations you picked and pair this character up with an antagonist. Alternatively, you can use a character you've previously created, or create a new one. Remember, we're trying to create a Binary Opposition Pairing with plenty of Matched Dramatic Potential.

	Protagonist	Antagonist
Defining Characteristic		
Humanity		
Paradox		
Flaw (Strength-Flaw)		

Typically what unites these two characters is the pursuit of a goal. Each wants it, or each has a goal that opposes the other. Either way, what would be some logical goals for these characters to pursue? Jot some potential goals below.

> Goals: (Ex: Indy wants the ark, so do Belloq and the Nazis. Also, Indy and Marion's relationship)

Remember: a good goal both unites and divides characters, creating conflict between them. Also, often heroes believe solving the goal will solve their issues; however, it's actually the pursuit of the goal (want) that exposes the need to address the flaw, which is what a flawed hero actually has to do.

A character's flaw is often born from a painful event earlier in the character's life. As a result, the last thing a characters wants to do is bring up all the pain and fear resulting from the flaw, so typically, they must be forced to do this. What forces their hand is the plot of the film, which is designed to expose the flaw and make the hero to confront it. Only then can the character change – the character's arc.

In the previous exercise, you were asked to create complementary characters with traits designed to oppose yet fit together. Depending on your design, you may have noticed the protagonist and antagonist possess many of the same characteristics. Makes sense; after all, why else would they be pursuing similar goals?

While heroes and villains are often similar, varying in motivations and methods of obtaining goals, in terms of story, the real difference lies in the character arcs.

<u>Heroes change</u> as a result of plot events, learning the lesson of the movie, its theme.

<u>Villains typically do not change</u>, do not learn the lesson of the movie, and as a result, they go down in defeat.

Obviously there are exceptions.
Examine some movies with 'down' endings (*Se7en* comes to mind), and see how often you find a hero who didn't learn the lesson of the movie, who didn't arc, didn't change, and as a result, did not succeed. Even Jack in *Titanic*, a very clear protagonist, did not change (because he didn't need to), and thus (spoiler); he dies in the end.

Implicit in this design is a need to change. This is why the hero has a flaw. It gives the character some aspect to change.

Back to the last exercise, something else to note is that you were asked to create the four facets of character as an integrated whole. Put another way – how the traits work together is just as important as what the traits are, if not more so.

While these traits are designed to function as a single whole embodied by a character, let's examine how to introduce a single trait and communicate it to an audience. We'll use Defining Characteristic as our example, but the other traits use a similar process. Remember: because these are story critical details, you draw more attention to them.

Good Cop, Bad Cop and The Case of the Defining Characteristic

As mentioned earlier, a Defining Characteristic doesn't have to be a one-word descriptor. In fact, you could make a case that using an adjective-noun pair to define the character aids in the overall design paradigm.

In this example, let's choose 'Cop' as our Defining Characteristic. That's a bit too vague to define the character on its own, so let's add a detail to make it more useful.

Meet the 10th Precinct!
Lots of officers on duty tonight, so this should be easy. There's:

    Good Cop   Bad Cop   Bitter Cop   Jaded Cop   Aging Cop
                                    And…
    Your Cop as defined here: _____ Cop
                                (put your own adjective here)

Now, let's design characters using each of these fine officers. Complete the activity below by filling in the blanks (hey, just like your audience!)

Given the Defining Characteristics below, fill in the rest of the designs to create the most intriguing combinations of character traits.

Defining Characteristic	Humanity	Paradox	Flaw or Strength-Flaw
Good Cop			
Bad Cop			
Jaded Cop			
Bitter Cop			
Aging Cop			
_____ Cop			

Hopefully, you've created some interesting combinations full of dramatic potential! To explore how to communicate a specific trait, let's pick one and run it through the process. I'll go with our Aging Cop (Defining Characteristic.)

The process of delineating a character trait and clearly communicating it involves a series of steps designed specifically for this purpose. To do this cinematically, you simply create scenes or beats in which this trait is on prominent display.

Step 1: Introduce it
Usually occurs upon meeting a character for the first time (more on introducing characters later), but for now, when we meet a character, have them engaged in a character defining activity designed to display the Defining Characteristic you chose.

Step 2: Reinforce it
Because character actions are often dictated by their surroundings, we can't be sure of the character's Defining Characteristic by showing it once. So, you show it again…

Step 3: Further Reinforce it
… and again. Not always necessary, depending on how well you did the first couple times, but hitting this trait again creates a pattern that the audience will lock in on. In other words, this is the third different situation in which you've displayed the trait – must be part of who the character is.

Step 4: Muddy it
Remember that Paradox? Let's use it to keep the audience on their toes, and more importantly, give the audience the illusion that this is a three-dimensional character by providing some aspect of the character that's unexpected, yet believable. A well-designed Paradox works great to hint at additional character layers without having to devote precious story time showing the audience those aspects. In other words, we show one unusual side, and let the audience fill in the others.

Step 5: Change it
If this is the character's Arcing Trait (the one you've chosen to demonstrate change in the character), you'll need to show us this in a scene designed to do so.

Step 6: Test it
After you've shown the character change, now you test this change to show the audience the change has stuck or is now permanent. This test provides proof of the change and is implicit to the film. To get at this notion, simple ask yourself – what can my character do at the end of the film they couldn't do at the beginning?

And, that's it!

The last two steps are typically reserved for flaws as that's the aspect of a character most likely needing to be changed. But, the process works for Defining Characteristic as well. Our other traits, Paradox and Humanity, don't have to run through the entire process because the story doesn't rely on these as heavily to function.

Graphically representing this step process and the effects it has on the audience for Defining Characteristic could yield something like this:

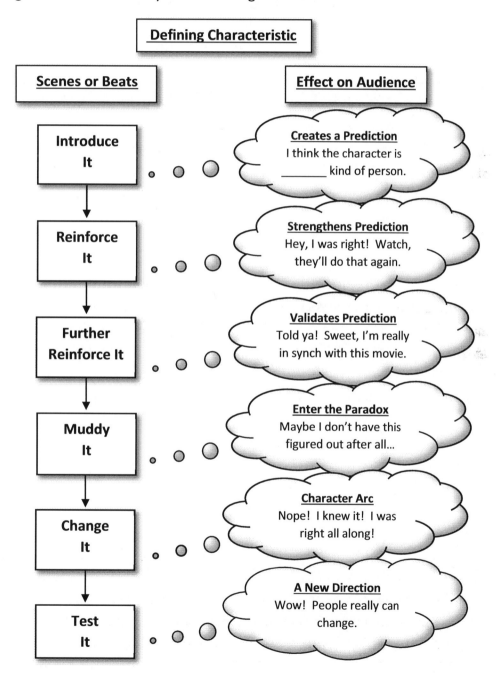

Let's use our Aging Cop to see how this system works, what effects each step has on the audience, and how you can create story starting from a single design element.

Suppose I should fill in the rest of the design first.

Hmm… Let's see. Aging… That could be considered the character's flaw – especially if our cop is having a tough time with growing old and not being able to do what he used to. So, perhaps an outward manifestation of this characteristic is stubbornness. The character refuses to admit he's getting too old for this line of work. So, one possible combination could look something like:

<u>Defining Characteristic</u>: Aging Cop.
<u>Humanity</u>: Likes cartoons (doesn't want to grow old)
<u>Paradox</u>: Plays the guitar just like he's ringing a bell.
<u>Flaw</u>: Stubborn – let's use this as a strength-flaw. A stubborn person doesn't give up – a good trait for a cop. This tenacity led the character to excel on the police force. But, if he's fighting growing old, or if tenacity became obsession, he's doomed to fail.

That'll do for a start.

Notice that the design suggests several ways the story could flow:

Perhaps our cop is about to retire, so he's been asked to train his replacement.

Perhaps he wants to solve one last case, one that's been haunting him for years, but he's running out of time to go by the book with his investigation.

Perhaps he regrets not following his musical talent. So in the end, he retires and becomes head of security for a rock band. Then, when the lead guitarist suffers an injury onstage, he finally gets his dream of playing on stage.

Lots of possibilities.

To narrow them down into something more manageable, let's focus on that flaw (stubborn) and ask yourself the magic question: why?
Why is our cop so stubborn? What happened to cause him to be this way?

Asking why for each trait, especially the flaw, opens up even more story possibilities. Each why can essentially become a scene, part of a scene or a scene's subtext. By showing us the why, you teach the audience your character's motivations, allowing us to go 'inside' the character, understand who they are. Once we do that, typically we're also informed of what the character needs to do to make things right.

For our Aging Cop story, let's choose a 'training his replacement' storyline. It's been done to death, so we'll have to address that, but it'll provide a solid launching point. We can easily change it if we need to, which is one of the strengths of approaching story through design – rather than write the screenplay and discover its issues after all that work, you can do it up front and save yourself time and effort.

All right, so back to our stubborn, Aging Cop and why he's this way.

Perhaps, early in his career he was more laid back (kinda fits the guitar player vibe), trusting that things work out if you just go with the flow. And, perhaps this attitude caused the death of his partner, so our hero developed a fear of letting things go, which led to his stubbornness. Letting go also factors into aging – retirement means letting go of how this character defines himself.
Okay, I think we can do some things with that.

Running with stubbornness a bit – notice that asking why also leads to the relatable core conflicts. Essentially, we can explore two competing philosophies of life – going with the flow or wanting control. Or, perhaps we explore trusting in fate versus defying it. Whatever you choose, this core becomes a thematic aspect of the story, indirectly informing your scenes, the conflicts between characters and even smaller details that all subtextually hint at the same message – your theme.

Perhaps it could be as simple as doing your own thing versus doing what's expected.

Now, to convey 'stubborn' you turn this trait into character-specific behaviors that either directly or indirectly point at stubbornness as their motivation, depending on the degree of nuance you wish to employ. The more subtle you wish to be in conveying story critical details, the more you'll need to rely on the design, so that all these smaller, nuanced moments are informed by, and lead the audience to, the statement you're trying to make. Think of it as giving directions – you can take us straight there, or you can provide plenty of hints as to which way to go. The choice is yours.

Back to our cop. Let's make him a stickler for the rules, a total by-the-book kinda guy. Rules provide stability, consistency and for our character, something rock solid he can attach his stubbornness to. And, if his lack of following procedure caused the death of his partner, it's understandable he'd take refuge in following rules – they'll keep that traumatic event from happening again.
Or, so the character believes…

So, our basic story design is as follows:

We'll open on our cop, much younger. We'll see that laidback, rules are for wimps attitude – a cocky rookie. One night on patrol, he trusts his gut rather than follow the rules, even though his partner warned him that's not what good cops do. He gets his partner killed – dies right there in his arms. This is our Birth of the Flaw.

Now, we move forward to present day. Our cop is much older, set in his ways. Dreams long behind him. His stubborn devotion to procedure has led to a successful career (after all, government agencies love their policy procedures) AND in the eyes of his superiors, this makes him the perfect candidate to train new officers. Which, of course, constantly reminds him of what happened all those years ago. This is the character's Strength-Flaw. It's made him an excellent cop, but it also causes conflict.

Enter the new rookie our hero must train. The rookie reminds the hero of his younger self – right down to the laid-back attitude, and the 'rules are for suckers' swagger. Great. Just great. Imagine the conflicts to come from this pairing. This creates the Matched Dramatic Potential from a Binary Opposition Pair. They're similar, yet different at the same time, and these differences lead to conflict along this story axis. Notice that the differences were created from the character traits, which serves to focus the conflict on the personal philosophies informing these traits. In other words, this is what makes the conflict thematic and relatable, allowing the audience to understand the lesson of the movie and apply it to instances where they may have faced similar situations.

Okay, now we're getting somewhere. But, something's not quite right…

Yes, the design works, but it seems like every buddy cop movie ever. When you encounter a cliché as a result of your design, you can change the design or change the outcome from the design. The design seems pretty solid and hides its cliché somewhat in the uniqueness of the character – how many cartoon-loving, wannabe rockstar cops do you know? But, it's still a weakness in the story that needs to be addressed. Hmm… What if, the rookie cop just doesn't remind us of our hero, what if he turns out to actually BE the hero's younger self?

We'll save that for a reveal, but it could be interesting. Not sure I've seen that before.

And, what if the partner who was killed all those years ago, is none other than our hero. Could be an intriguing twist in a pretty standard genre. Certainly opens up some serious dramatic potential -- if our hero doesn't solve the plot of the movie, he could be killed, and the cycle could start all over again. Definitely has stakes.

As outlandish as that idea is, ironically it also provides another point of relatability – who wouldn't want to go back, clock your younger self in the head and say, "You fool! Do this, not this!" Obviously, people deal with regret as the individuals they are, but if there was something in your past, even something minor, that you could change, and suddenly you had an opportunity to do so, it occurs to me that this is extremely relatable for many members of the audience, or at minimum, intriguing enough to pique their curiosity.

Okay, we've addressed a potential cliché and built a basic story starting with character. I think we're ready to put it all together.

We'll start with the character design, then add the layers necessary for the story to function at its full potential.

Character Design: Aging Cop

Aging Cop **Defining Characteristic**	*Stubborn* **Flaw**
Likes Cartoons **Humanity**	*Plays Guitar* **Paradox**

Now that we have our hero, let's add our step process, and another wrinkle... Introducing, the one, the only, the official...

What in the World is This Thing Chart

Okay, so the title is a work in progress, but just as the name implies, this chart is whatever you wish to make of it. Each circle represents a layer of the story, starting with your **Artistic Goal**, then to character, then to... wherever you wish to take it. However, the idea is that each inner layer informs the content in the next ones out, representing a combination of the inner 'pieces of the pie' to which it belongs.

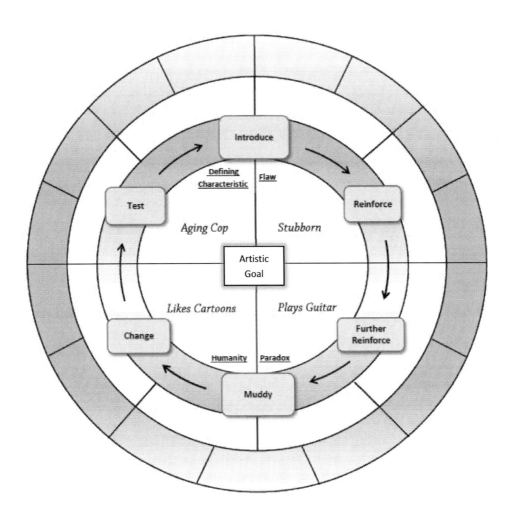

The **Artistic Goal** is your clear goal for the project (which is why it's not as blurry on the chart.) It can be thematic, the message or lesson of the film, or perhaps it's just to entertain; to get a laugh, to get a good blub, whatever. This central idea to your story <u>focuses your content</u> so that it forms a cohesive whole, held together by your intent.

If all the elements in your screenplay point to or are informed by your Artistic Goal, you can be far more indirect with your storytelling while simultaneously keeping the audience engaged and grounded in the movie. This, in turn, serves to focus your audience on what you feel is essential to the story.

Some possibilities for story/character layers using this chart include:

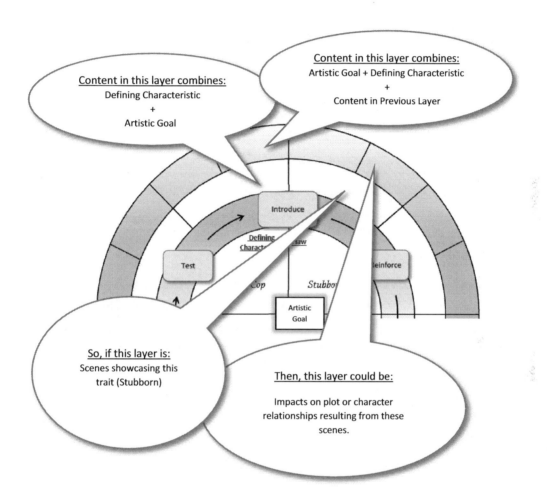

Notice, at the very center, informing every layer, is your artistic goal. So, if your goal is to get laughs, then your content should convey aspects of character and be funny. Another way to look at this chart can be through audience impact. Here's the content layer, then here are the effects you plan for this combination of layers to have on your audience. However you choose to use it, the chart is simply a visual planning space for the design of your story.

The chart is circular because, rather than thinking of your story as a linearity, think of it as a continuous whole. While technically, you control the audience's entry point into the story, in actuality, you never quite know what the audience will prioritize, despite your careful arrangement of story information. It's also difficult to gauge what an audience will gravitate toward or pick up first, how they will weigh the information you're providing, or how they will combine elements.

By designing your script as a series of integrated layers, you provide a way for the audience to make sense of the barrage of information being presented. This also mirrors the audience's journey into your story. Remember, the outer layer typically represents very specific combinations of elements. These can be specific scenes, beats within scenes and so forth. Your audience combines these specific images and sounds to create a narrative whole. The chart helps to ensure that these specificities all point in the same direction – toward your characters and toward your intentions as a writer.

The importance of character cannot be understated. If you've ever heard the analogy that a film is like a rollercoaster, then think of a character as the car we hop inside to enjoy the ride. Without it, we're simply trudging up and down hills.

Focusing Your Audience
Just as cinematographers use composition, color and light to focus an audience's attention on certain parts of the visual frame, as writers we must do the same with the story-critical elements of your movie. We do this not with a camera, but rather through the tools of our trade – words. Shocking, I know. But, think about it. Certain details must be understood for the audience to understand the story, so we give them a bit more screentime, make them more memorable, more impactful, more intriguing to draw attention to themselves, or we have a process for conveying story-critical details through an interwoven design built to take into account the many different ways individual audience members combine and interpret what they're experiencing. The chart represents one way to ensure that the specific details you choose focus the multiple perspectives an audience brings toward the direction you wish to take them. If EVERY detail points to your film's core ideas, then the story can be assembled by your audience in multiple ways.

Bonus Set: Character Design Tool   CRAFT   Total Reps: 5
Use the following template to design your own character or analyze one from an existing film. Most dividing lines are removed, so you can subdivide layers as you wish. Also, the tool really needs a better name, so that's been left blank for you to fill in.

_____ **Chart**

Character Name: _____ **Title of Work:** _____

Main Character Design

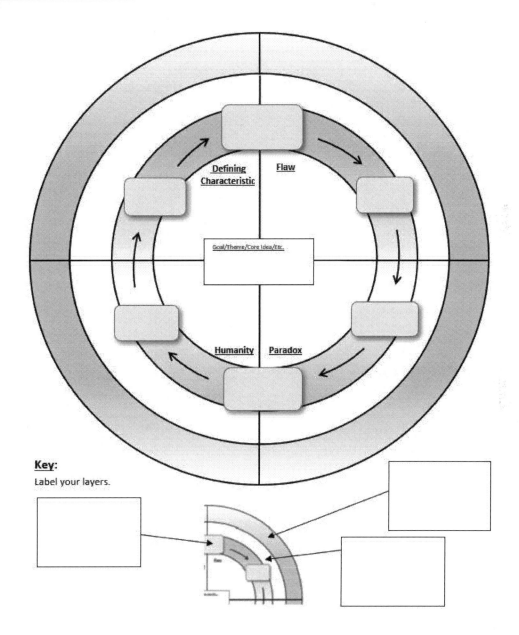

Key:
Label your layers.

75

Hollywood Character Tendencies

Check all that apply, then describe how you'll show them and/or how they apply.

- ○ Underdog
  How?

- ○ Best/Worst/Both at what they do
  How?

- ○ Larger than Life
  How?

- ○ Obsessed
  How?

- ○ Active and Driven
  How?

- ○ Choices Under Pressure
  How?

- ○ Elicits Emotion
  How?

- ○ Identifiable/Universal
  How?

- ○ Flaw/Strength-Flaw

What caused this flaw?

Problems from flaw:

Want

Need

Goal

Based on your main character design and concept, design the Antagonist here. Remember our Matched Dramatic Potential and Binary Opposition Pairing!
Also note: it may be tempting to omit this character's Humanity; after all, a hallmark of villains is inhumanity, but doing so can lead to a two-dimensional character.

Antagonist Name: _____

Character Design

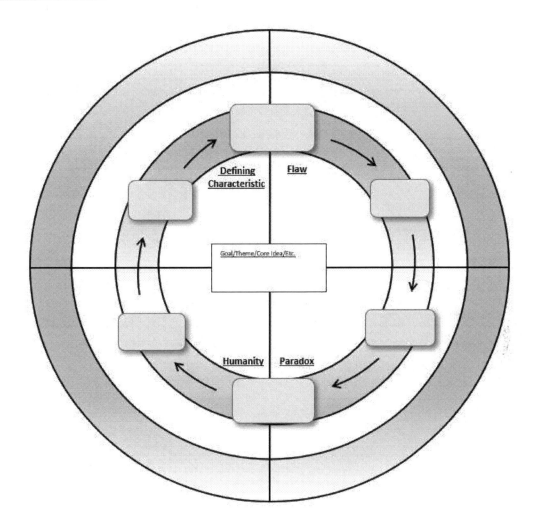

What unites AND divides these characters? How?

Putting it Together

Let's bring your characters together to see if you have a combination of character elements that will yield intriguing dilemmas and compelling conflicts. Or, if you're analyzing rather than creating, you can identify the design elements.

On the left is your protagonist. On the right is your antagonist. You'll need to re-list some traits (sorry!), but we need to see these two together to explore potential conflicts in this combination. Once you've filled in the traits, look for possible combinations that will create the most intriguing interactions. This is a sandbox of sorts, so feel free to alter traits if necessary to create more interesting dynamics.

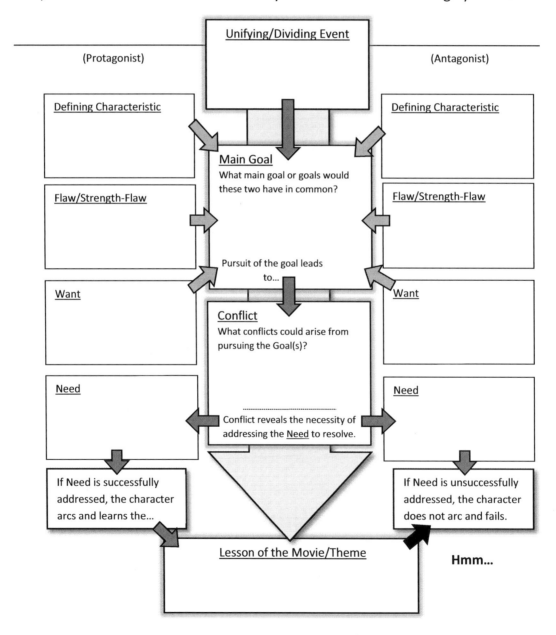

At the bottom of the chart is a little black arrow. Unlike the others, it points back. Let's explore why. The black arrow represents an idea fundamental to how cinematic storytelling works:

> Story is the <u>external force of plot</u> pitted against the <u>internal force of character</u>.

Simple principle really. But, once again, don't let the simplicity fool you. This idea is at the heart of cinematic storytelling. Think about it. Even for stories in which the conflict is primarily internal, plot events seem to actively conspire against the hero. Makes sense. Utilizing this approach maintains high conflict levels and puts the main character in peril, which, if you've bonded us to the hero, has the effect of putting <u>us</u> in peril. And, for the cinematic medium, which must externalize conflict to communicate it to an audience, this blend of external and internal conflict provides your audience with the tools they need to understand what's occurring within a character and the consequences or the stakes should our hero not succeed.

In this way, story becomes a conflict between <u>self</u> (as represented by character) versus <u>plot</u> (external forces trying to destroy self.)

Gotta admit, I was tempted to say ALL stories follow this pattern; however, declaring something as all-inclusive – especially when it comes to storytelling, is problematic to say the least. And, while one exception doesn't necessarily disprove the rule, a single exception hints at more – much like the audience effect created by the Paradox. So, with that in mind, I need your help…

Think of a narrative film that's an exception to our external force of plot versus internal force of character paradigm, and note it in the box below:

Interestingly, that last task is a small example of this principle. Something external to you tried to get you to do something. Now, obviously, there was no malicious intent, but rather, it's simply an example of internal and external forces at work. I suppose we should refine this idea a bit: story pits the elements you intend us to internalize with the elements you intend us to externalize. Yes, this does create a Boolean polarity of sorts, an us versus them mentality, and yes, those grey, ambiguous areas can be, should be explored in cinematic storytelling, but the key to successfully exploring them in story starts with that simple polarity.

By inviting the audience to choose sides between those they externalize versus those they internalize, you can now keep the audience bonded to characters while simultaneously having these characters engage in behaviors that are not bondable. It does this by creating a form of confirmation bias in the audience. How it works is relatively simple: once the audience is rooting for one side and against another, you've created the conditions necessary for confirmation bias to kick in. Confirmation bias means that once we've formed an opinion, we tend to ignore facts that don't support our opinion in favor of those that do. In cinematic terms, this means once you get us rooting for a character, we tend to dismiss aspects that don't fit our opinion. Now you're free to present those not-so-bondable aspects while maintaining the audience's bond to the character. The key to this technique is you must form the bond before you muddy it. Please note that you're not forcing the audience to do any of this – you're simply letting the craft do the work. The audience may choose to bond with your villain, and that's fine because it still creates that external versus internal, us versus them dynamic. If you've ever found yourself rooting for the villain, you've probably just experiences this technique in action.

Oh yeah, weren't we supposed to be talking about that little arrow?

The arrow represents the plot emerging triumphant over the character. So, in terms of what we just discussed, that external force of plot is shown to be successful against the internal force of character. Psychologically, it's the lesson of the movie saying -- pay attention to me or you'll be sorry! Okay, maybe that's a bit melodramatic, but think about it – characters are designed to be audience surrogates for experiencing the plot of the movie. So, in a subtle way, by demonstrating what happens to characters who don't learn the lesson, you're also subtly telling your audience to pay attention to your film.

Ultimately, this is what Hollywood Character Design is built to do. It's a system for bonding audience to character to create the conditions necessary for the story to operate cinematically. Once your audience is pulling for one side or another, confirmation bias can help you add complexity and ambiguity if you like while simultaneously helping to keep your audience grounded and thus engaged. In other words, Hollywood Character Design allows your audience to interact with your story, which in turn, helps create a personalized group experience – a lethal combination.

While Hollywood Character Design provides a way to create characters built to fit into the story, what is the story designed to fit into?

Why, our next section, of course!

But before we get to that, let's track your progress.

WORKOUT PROGRESS – CRAFT
Compile your workout totals for this unit.
Be sure to fill in the Action section of the last exercise with your choice of Application (if you used the tool to create) or Analysis (if you analyzed a work.)

EXERCISE	SKILL GROUP			TOTAL REPS	
	SET #	TYPE	ACTION	AVAILABLE	COMPLETED
Underdogs	1	Craft	Analysis	8	
Best/Worst/Both	2	Craft	Analysis	6	
Larger than Life	3	Craft	Analysis	3	
Obsession	4	Craft	Analysis	4	
Applied Obsession	Bonus	Craft	Application	4	
Active and Driven	5	Craft	Analysis	2	
Choices Under Pressure	6	Craft	Analysis	3	
Elicits Emotion	7	Craft	Analysis	2	
Identifiable and Universal	8	Craft	Analysis	4	
Identifiable and Universal	Bonus	Craft	Application	4	
Flaws and Strength-Flaws	9	Craft	Analysis	4	
Putting it All Together	10	Craft	Analysis	2	
Character Design	11	Craft	Analysis	2	
Character Analysis	12	Craft	Analysis	2	
Character Creation	13	Craft	Analysis	13	
Character Design Tool	Bonus	Craft		5	
			TOTAL REPS		

CRAFT — TOTAL REPS AND BONUS — 68

The 8-Turn Structure

Special Note: To fully complete this module, you'll need the movie *Twister*.

We ended the last section with a question – what is story designed to fit into? Well, as you can probably guess – structure. Movie structures are a bit like air, you don't notice when it's there, but if it's not, it gets your attention. There's no magic formula when it comes to structuring your screenplay. There are plenty of poorly written movies that are exquisitely structured. The reverse doesn't hold as true – chances are if a movie resonated with an audience, it placed its content in some sort of structural paradigm. The reasons for this are varied. If you were to think of your movie as a car with an automatic transmission, then imagine what it would be like if you're driving along and suddenly, the car gets stuck in second gear. Normally, when everything's operating properly, the car shifts smoothly as it gets up to speed, and this shifting goes largely unnoticed. It's only when something's off that it draws attention to itself. Now, rather than enjoying the ride and the lovely scenery, you're left wondering what's wrong. Likewise, as your movie gets up to speed, if something's off structurally, the audience senses it. The story feels slow. Or, it feels rushed. Whatever it is, something just doesn't seem 'right'.

Another way to look at structure is through its relationship with content. For our purposes, content consists of the specific details of your story – the unique characters you've created, the dialogue, the plot – essentially all the aspects of your story that make it yours. Structure is separate from content in that it's more functional in nature. In other words, it's designed to do, rather than be. Think of it like an airport. All airports have runways, tarmacs, luggage movers, etc., but each has its own style, different murals, different layouts and so forth. Structure in this example refers to the elements that make an airport an airport – those runways, holding areas and so forth that make it possible for planes to take off and land.

The more subtle you are with your storytelling, the greater the need for structure to help tell your story. Nuanced content is like a liquid. It's fluid, harder to pin down. In this analogy, structure is a cup designed to hold content and keep it from becoming a mess all over the floor (in our case, the cutting room floor.) A cup is also designed to do something else – make it easier to drink. Likewise, movie structures make it easier for audiences to consume the content you're serving. Continuing the analogy, there are different cups for different kinds of liquids. Coffee cups are insulated, designed to keep the beverage hot and your hand cool. Water bottles, gas cans, toothpaste tubes -- each is designed to hold (and dispense) specific types of content. So too are movie structures, including the one we're about to examine.

The 8-Turn Structure
Of the vast array of structural paradigms out there for movies, this one beats them all in terms of effectiveness, flexibility, precision and versatility. At its core, 8-turn structure represents the major turns in your story – the big story beats. Certain beats happen at certain times in the movie, representing the basic flow of narrative.

As with any structure, 8-turn is designed to hold content for audience consumption. This one in particular is built to fit with Hollywood Character Design – specifically characters who have flaws to overcome. For flaw-based stories, this is the structure for you. Character design and structure go hand in hand, so whenever possible, we'll present them together.

The 8-Turn Structure calls for certain story events to occur at certain times in the movie. So, while it will be presented to you in terms of pages, the page counts correspond to times in the movie. Because a typical script page represents a minute of screentime, if a beat occurs on page 10, this would be the 10-minute mark in the film.

Most film structures are a distillation of Aristotle's three-act structure, breaking it down into smaller, more manageable sections, and 8-Turn is no exception.

Our main story beats and where they go in your screenplay/movie:

P. 1 – 5: Hook
Establishes tone and genre. Think of it as a pre-story beat, Act Zero of a three-act play. It's called the hook because the content within this beat is designed to engage the audience – to grab them by shirt and make them watch the film.

As you may recall from our character design section, one type of hook is the <u>Birth of the Flaw</u>, in which we see an event, typically in the character's past, that scarred the hero. Don't underestimate the need to establish tone and genre early in the film – it helps the audience know how they should react to your content.

P. 10: Inciting Incident

This is the action that launches the story. A good way to look at this beat is: your story would not take place without this scene. Often this beat is the event that throws the hero's world out of balance. Your hero will then spend the rest of the movie trying to restore this balance. Along the way to fixing this imbalance, heroes often learn something about themselves and come to the realization that to truly fix the imbalance, they must change something about themselves, which in turn creates the hero's character arc. This aspect of the hero that he or she must deal with is often (but not always) brought to light in our next story beat…

P. 17: The Central Question

Probably THE most important beat in your story. This scene establishes what your story it really about. What occurs here varies, depending on your particular story, but the simplest way to look at this beat is: this is the main question driving the story. When it's definitively answered, one way or another, the movie's done. Roll credits. Yes, you can have a brief denouement, but after answering the central question get out and get out fast – the audience will sense that the movie is over and will typically not be pleased if you hang around.

Some ways to look at this vital beat are:
The 'meet cute'. In a RomCom, the lovers meet. The rest of the movie then explores the question: will they or won't they get together? In a buddy movie, this is usually the formation of the team.

The Central Question can be plot-based, character-based or thematic, but whatever you choose, this beat establishes your story's central dilemma.

In the ensuing pages you should be busily establishing your sub-plots, getting them set up for exploration in Act 2.

P. 30: Reaction to the Central Question

This is your hero's first real attempt to answer the central question posed on your page 17.

This beat is your First Act break, marking the end of Act 1. We have now crossed over into Act 2.

P. 45: The Next Big Hurdle
Sometimes called The First Big Hurdle.

This beat is a major complication toward solving the Central Question. Often the stakes are raised – sometimes broadened to affect more people, or heightened to affect someone more severely, but either way, here heroes discover the problem driving the story is bigger than they originally thought.

Sometimes a new character is introduced at this point to further complicate solving the central question or simply adding increased stakes if the problem is not solved.

P. 60: Apex
This is the BIG TWIST. It rivals the Central Question in its importance to your movie. In this beat our hero shifts from <u>PASSIVE to ACTIVE</u> along each major axis of your storyline – particularly in relation to his or her EMOTIONAL DILEMMA.

One of the design paradigms of the 8-turn structure is that your hero has a WANT that differs from his or her NEED. For example: the hero wants money, but what he or she really needs is love. This scene represents the hero's realization of this difference, effectively changing the direction of the story – essentially flipping the narrative to refresh it. Prior to this beat, the hero often pursues his or her want. After this beat, the hero may start to pursue his or her need. This scene can be called the MIDPOINT CRISIS REALIZATION as a result.

Often this moment represents the hero dealing with his or her flaw or inner wound – the realization of which occurred as a result of trying to achieve his or her external goal in the previous sections of the movie. How it works is simple: in Hollywood Narrative, typically we have a hero wanting some tangible thing he or she thinks will solve the imbalance caused by at the Inciting Incident. Through the pursuit of this thing (the Object of Desire), the hero realizes he or she must overcome an inner wound, a flaw, to restore balance to the world. The Apex beat is this realization.

P. 75: False (Happy) Ending
The hero thinks he or she has achieved the goal. It looks like we've solved our page 17.

However, the solution is not permanent or is somehow not quite 'right'. This can be an 'up' moment where the hero appears triumphant, but what it often really does is simply make the antagonist realize the hero has grown powerful and must be dealt with swiftly and harshly.

P. 90: Low Point
We are now the furthest away from solving Page 17. All appears lost. The imbalance seems permanent. The lovers break up. The team is in disarray. All appears lost.
<u>This marks the end of Act 2.</u>

How can our hero possibly succeed now? That's what Act 3 is all about…

The 8-Turn Structure doesn't map out your third act because this part is dependent on the specific content leading up to it, but essentially, Act 3 is all about coming back from that low point.

Here's how the beats could work in a typical romance film.

1-5 Hook
We meet Lover 1.

10 Inciting Incident
We meet Lover 2.

17 Central Question
Lover 1 meet Lover 2. This forms the fundamental question driving most romances – will they or won't they get together. Be on the lookout for this beat to occur at the 10-minute mark. If so, then look at the 17-minute mark closely. It may be that the story is really about something else.

30 Reaction to the Central Question
In romances, this is often the first date, representing the first attempt at answering the central question.

45 First Big Hurdle
For our romance, this is a complication. Perhaps an ex shows up, threatening to ruin the budding relationship between our would-be lovers.

60 Apex
Something changes in the relationship. Previously, if Lover 1 was pursuing Lover 2, the movie flips that, and suddenly, Lover 2 is pursuing Lover 1.

75 False Happy Ending
Looks like nothing will stop the lovers from getting together.

90 Low Point
The Big Breakup – didn't see that coming! Here the lovers separate, never to reunite, or so it seems…

Some Notes on the 8-Turn Structure

For movies with runtimes shorter than two hours, watch for compression between later structural beats – particularly between the False Happy and Low Point. Placing these beats closer together heightens the contrast between them, making the low point seem that much lower because we just came off the high of the false happy. We typically don't see compression between the earlier beats of the film because setting up a story cinematically takes time – in this case approximately 17 minutes of efficient storytelling to set up a central question with enough complexity to power an entire film – and make the audience care about it.

Notice this structure is really organized around a character's flaw. If we were to examine 8-Turn through *only* this lens, the structural beats would look something like this:

1-5 Hook
Birth of the Flaw – a Scar is Born.

10 Inciting Incident
Plot event occurs that will eventually force our hero to deal with the flaw.

17 Central Question
This is a tricky beat. Sometimes it directly involves the flaw. Sometimes it's presented as a plot question. Sometimes it blends both.

30 Reaction to the Central Question
Still the first attempt to answer the central question. If the central question is plot-based, the hero heads out to solve the plot. If it's flaw-based, the hero still sets out to solve plot, BUT our intrepid hero probably did this five minutes earlier in the film.

45 First Big Hurdle
The plot thickens. Notice how many of these early beats are still focused on solving the problem presented in the plot. This is the hero pursuing the WANT storyline. The NEED, which is often rooted in the flaw, will begin to take over the story, right around the...

60 Apex – The Big Twist
The hero's flaw is brought up to the surface. This adds yet another layer of complications for the hero to overcome. Here the hero is made aware that to solve the plot, they're going to have to do something about that flaw. Of course, flaws are often a source of pain for the hero, or at least a very touchy subject. And, dealing with the flaw would require the hero to change, and who wants to do that? Especially with such a sore subject, so the hero redoubles the effort to solve the plot WITHOUT changing, leading to...

75 False Happy Ending
The hero's extra effort has paid off, and it looks like the plot has been solved. Sweet! And, it was done without changing, or bringing up that pesky flaw. Mission accomplished. But, it's a false victory because what the hero really needs to do is come to terms with the flaw.

90 Low Point
Utter defeat. Crap. Just when things were looking good, too. The low point forces the hero to address the flaw. Makes sense in a way, you have to hit rock bottom to be willing to change, or so the theory goes.

This change fuels the third act. Whatever change occurs in the hero is now tested in this act, and is used to solve the plot question once and for all.

Structural Analysis
Analyzing the structure of a film provides excellent insight into how the filmmakers conceived the story. Thus, a story that appears to be about chasing tornadoes on its surface, when analyzed structurally, could reveal that it's actually about a couple trying to mend their relationship.

While the 8-Turn Structure can be used to organize (and analyze) plot, it's actually more of a character structure, designed to explore the character's internal storyline. Obviously, there's considerable crossover between plot and character, so pay close attention to the central question to see if it's plot-based, character-based or both.

If you have trouble identifying the central question, examine the ending of the film. Typically, the central question is answered at the very end, or shortly before the end if the film employs some sort of denouement to wrap up any loose ends.

Structural Outlines
You can also use the structural beats to outline your screenplay. Think of them as lighthouses, designed to help prevent you from getting lost at sea. In other words, by using a structural outline, you know you have to be at a certain place in the story by a certain time. How you get there and what you do in between these major story beats is up to you, but having milestones helps keep the script from meandering too much, forcing you to be disciplined in your craft, while still allowing for considerable freedom between the beats – a powerful storytelling combination.

We'll use this structure for outlining later, but for now let's focus on analysis and see how a film is put together.

For this first analysis, it may be helpful to work through a movie together. Unfortunately, this means I'll have to pick the film.

8-Turn Analysis of *Twister*

Yes, the 1996 tornado movie starring Helen Hunt and Bill Paxton.

Because of the complexity of this task, each structural beat counts as a rep.

***SET 1**: Let's do the Twist(er)!*   **CRAFT**   **Total Reps**: **9**

For this analysis, you'll need:

- o Well, *Twister*, of course :)
- o A timer (to note the times when beats occur)
- ✓ This book
- o The writing implement of your choice
- o Popcorn (optional)

Once you have the movie and a way to measure when the structural beats occur within the movie's timeline, you have three options:

Option 1: analyze the movie, then compare your analysis to mine, which will be on the ensuing pages.

Option 2: watch the movie and follow along with analysis provided.

Option 3: analyze a different film.

Your call. If you choose Option 1, don't peek at my analysis until after you're done!

I'd say you can opt out of this one entirely, but we'll use *Twister* as a baseline movie for some exercises, which you'll miss if you don't watch it. Once again, your call on this, but doing this analysis is highly recommended. Oh, and no I don't get royalties on sales of *Twister*. Just thought I'd mention that. :)

Once you have everything you need, sit back, fire up the film and analyze!

For Option 1: your analysis form is on the next page. Watch the film, note the timings, then compare to the completed analysis following yours.

For Option 2: you'll find the completed *Twister* analysis immediately following the blank form on the next page. Feel free to skip the blank form and go straight to the analysis that follows. Then, either analyze *Twister* for yourself or see Option 3.

For Option 3: analyze a movie of your choosing. You'll analyze another film later, but it would be a shame to waste a perfectly good analysis form, now wouldn't it?

8-Turn Structural Analysis

Title of Film: _____ *TWISTER* _____

Identify and describe these elements/scenes in the film (if applicable):

1. **Hook (1-5)**   Time this beat occurs: _____

   Describe:

2. **Inciting Incident (10)**   Time this beat occurs: _____

   Describe:

3. **Central Question (17)**   Time this beat occurs: _____

   Describe:

4. **Reaction to Central Question (30)**   Time this beat occurs: _____

   Describe:

5. **Next Big Hurdle (45)**   Time this beat occurs: _____

   Describe:

6. Apex (60)   Time this beat occurs: _____

> Describe:

7. False Happy Ending (75) Time this beat occurs: _____

> Describe:

8. Low Point (90)   Time this beat occurs: _____

> Describe:

Ending

While this structure doesn't delve into the third act, just for fun, examine the ending to see if the central question is answered. Note what happens at the end of the film here:

>

Does the ending somehow address the central question? (y/n) _____

Let's compare!
Here's my analysis of *Twister*...

8-Turn Structural Analysis

Title of Film: *TWISTER*

Identify and describe these elements/scenes in the film (if applicable):

1. **Hook (1-5)**   Time this beat occurs: 0:00 - 4:57

   Describe: The movie opens using two of our techniques for hooks – The <u>Birth of the Flaw</u>, in which Jo witnesses the tornado kill her dad, and the <u>Power of the Antagonist</u>, in which we see what tornadoes can do. Tone and genre established – this is a movie about tornadoes, and Jo dealing with the death of dad. Hook ends with transition to present day, and the start of the story.

2. **Inciting Incident (10)**   Time this beat occurs: 10:06

   Describe: After a brief intro of the main characters, Jo and Bill, this beat occurs when Jo asks Bill about the divorce papers. The reason Bill is in the movie (and goes on the adventure) is because he needs to get the divorce papers signed so he can marry Melissa. Without this beat, Bill is not here, and the movie doesn't happen.

3. **Central Question (17)**   Time this beat occurs: 16:46/16:56

   Describe: The team has just received notification there's a tornado they can chase. Bill's invited to go, but refuses. As he and Melissa walk back to their truck, she pops the central question, actually two of them that are closely related:
   1. Are you sure you don't want to go along?
   2. Did she sign the papers?
   Combining these questions into one, we get the movie's central question:
   <u>Will Bill go back to his old life with Jo?</u>

4. **Reaction to Central Question (30)**   Time this beat occurs: 29:08-32:40

   Describe: As noted in our examination of romance movies, Jo and Bill are on their first 'date', chasing a tornado We also see evidence of Jo's flaw -- she stares at the tornado, forcing Bill to drag her to safety. This hints at the issue Jo's flaw caused.

5. **Next Big Hurdle (45)**   Time this beat occurs: 44:27-45:18

   Describe: Another two-part beat.
   Part 1: Jo, Bill and Melissa chase two tornadoes (three briefly). This is up from one tornado previously (an escalation.) Melissa is visibly upset, which ups the stakes in the character story – if Bill wants to go back to his old life, Melissa is clearly not okay with this. So much for metaphors…
   Part 2: A new character, Aunt Meg, is introduced, who will add later complications.

6. Apex (60) Time this beat occurs: 58:00 – 64:00

> Describe: Jo and Bill try to deploy a Dorothy device, but fail. This is the most intense tornado scene yet. But, the actual apex is the aftermath in which Bill confronts Jo – "Killing yourself won't bring your dad back!" "Look at you, you're obsessed!" (THAT sounds familiar…) Here is Jo's flaw, brought to the surface. This scene tells us – if Jo doesn't deal with her flaw, she and Bill cannot be together. Also, the story flips in this scene. Up to this point, Bill just wanted to get divorced, now he expresses his desire to be with Jo. Melissa overhears this, adding another layer.

7. False Happy Ending (75) Time this beat occurs: 77:00

> Describe: This scene doesn't exactly feel happy – a tornado just wiped out a drive-in theater, nearly killing everyone. In the aftermath, Melissa tells Bill she's leaving. Least she says it with a smile – does that count as happy? Structurally, nothing now stands between Jo and Bill getting back together except – you guessed it, Jo's flaw, which remains unresolved. That's why it's a false ending.

8. Low Point (90) Time this beat occurs: 84:00/91:00

> Describe: This one's tricky. Jo's character low occurs at approximately 84 minutes in the ambulance with Aunt Meg, where she admits she doesn't know how to solve the problem. The plot low point, which is related to the Jo's goal, occurs at 91 minutes, where Jo and Bill fail to plant the Dorothy device yet again. And, to make matters worse, it now appears Jonas will succeed. Definitely a low point for our heroes.

Ending

Note what happens at the end of the film here:

> Jo and Bill, smiling and together, deciding what to do with the data they collected from successfully placing Dorothy in a tornado. This resolves the plot storyline (will they plant a Dorothy device?) and the character storyline (will Jo and Bill get back together?) A member of the team casually asks if Jo wants to check out the sky. No – she's had enough. This seemingly casual remark denotes the change that's occurred in Jo. Earlier she couldn't tear herself away from staring at the sky (remember that Reaction to the Central Question beat?) Now, she can. She's addressed her flaw, and now can get on with her life.

Does the ending somehow address the central question? <u>Yep, sure does</u>.

Okay, now that we've spent some time with Bill and all the gang, YOU pick the next movie to analyze!

SET 2: Structural Analysis   **CRAFT**   **Total Reps: 9**

Watch a <u>major</u> Hollywood film from the last 40 years with a timer. Find the structural beats and briefly describe each, noting the times they occur. If your film varies wildly in the timing of the beats, note what does occur at the structural times to see if there's something else going on in the film underneath the surface.

8-Turn Structural Analysis

Title of Film: _____

Identify and describe these elements/scenes in the film (if applicable):

1. Hook (1-5)   Time this beat occurs: _____

> Describe:

2. Inciting Incident (10)   Time this beat occurs: _____

> Describe:

3. Central Question (17)   Time this beat occurs: _____

> Describe:

4. Reaction to Central Question (30)   Time this beat occurs: _____

> Describe:

5. Next Big Hurdle (45)   Time this beat occurs: _____

> Describe:

6. Apex (60)   Time this beat occurs: _____

> Describe:

7. False Happy Ending (75)   Time this beat occurs: _____

> Describe:

8. Low Point (90)   Time this beat occurs: _____

> Describe:

Ending
Note what happens at the end of the film here:

Does the ending somehow address the central question? (y/n) _____

If the question is answered negatively (a down ending), note the placement of the False Happy and Low Point. These are often reversed for movies with tragic endings.

So, got the hang of it? If so -- great! Now do it again with a different film.
If not -- great! Well, okay, not great, but at least you get to try again.

BONUS SET**: Structural Analysis*   ***CRAFT   ***Total Reps*: 9**

Same deal, different film. This time you can choose any film from the last 40 years. Or, if you like, you can analyze a movie/script you created. Remember – for scripts, these would be page numbers rather than minute counts.

8-Turn Structural Analysis

Title of Film: _____

Identify and describe these elements/scenes in the film (if applicable):

1. **Hook (1-5)**   Time this beat occurs: _____

   > Describe:

2. **Inciting Incident (10)**   Time this beat occurs: _____

   > Describe:

3. **Central Question (17)**   Time this beat occurs: _____

   > Describe:

4. **Reaction to Central Question (30)**   Time this beat occurs: _____

   > Describe:

5. **Next Big Hurdle (45)**   Time this beat occurs: _____

   Describe:

6. **Apex (60)**   Time this beat occurs: _____

   Describe:

7. **False Happy Ending (75)**   Time this beat occurs: _____

   Describe:

8. **Low Point (90)**   Time this beat occurs: _____

   Describe:

Ending

Once again, examine the ending of the film to see how it's related to the central question and note your findings below.

Does the ending somehow address the central question? (y/n) _____

Please note: while you were asked to analyze big Hollywood films, this structure is not used on only these types of movies. Usually, but certainly not always, the beats are a bit more on the surface in these films, making the analysis easier.

Also note: if the movie you picked didn't hit these structural beats at all, examine the character design. Remember, this structure is built for characters with flaws to overcome. If the main character doesn't have a flaw, the filmmakers may have chosen a plot structure to organize the story rather than a character-based structure.

If you've never analyzed movie structure before, I hope you found this to be an interesting way of seeing how feature narrative is constructed. Remember, structure is just a cup designed to hold content and make it easier for the audience to consume. And, while I suppose a collector's cup or something of that sort may hold some appeal, people buy a drink because they're thirsty for its content, not because of the cup.

Structure is similar. People don't watch films for the structure – they watch for the content the structure holds.

Correction.

<u>Most</u> people don't watch films for structure.

Hopefully now, you will!

WORKOUT PROGRESS – CRAFT -- Structure

Compile your workout totals for this unit.

EXERCISE	SKILL GROUP			TOTAL REPS	
	SET #	TYPE	ACTION	AVAILABLE	COMPLETED
Let's Do the Twist(er)!	1	Craft	Analysis	9	
8-Turn Structural Analysis	2	Craft	Analysis	9	
8-Turn Structural Analysis	Bonus	Craft	Analysis	9	
				TOTAL REPS	

CRAFT — TOTAL REPS + BONUS — 27

Ancient Greek Hero Design

Let's travel through time, back to the days of Ancient Greece – the birthplace of Western thought, and as it turns out, a few things we might need to know when it comes to story. For you see, in addition to giving birth to democracy, the Olympics, elements of modern science, philosophy and all sorts of other big ticket items, Ancient Greece also gave birth to a rich dramatic tradition – the roots of which are still with us to this day.

So, strap on your sandals and let's take a walk into ancient Greek hero design. Oh, and just for the record, many aspects of this design pre-date the Greeks; they're simply the ones whose legacy passed it down to modern times.

Help Wanted. Hero. Apply Within.
To become an Ancient Greek hero, you typically had to meet certain qualifications – like a job application of sorts.

Just for fun, let's see if you qualify to be an Ancient Greek Hero. Gotta warn you though, it usually doesn't end well...

Okay, let's start the application process.

SET 1: It's All Greek to Me   **CRAFT**   **Total Reps: 1**

For this exercise, place a check by the following attributes if they apply to you.

Greek Hero Attributes

- **Hero's Mother is a Royal Virgin**
  Not a dealbreaker, but you might be surprised how often this one crops up.

- **Hero's Father is the Real King**
  If mom wasn't necessarily virginal, then at least dad was a king – or was once the king. Usually, someone else had taken over in dad's place – a usurper.

- **Hero's Father is Related to his Mother**
  A bit awkward by today's standards, but back in the day, intermarrying was common among the rich and famous – it kept all the riches and fame in the family.

- **Unusual Conception**
  There's something unusual about a hero right from the get-go – as if destiny itself is choosing these folks. There may have even been a PROPHECY surrounding the birth of a hero. Can anyone say… a chosen one?

- **Child of a God**
  Doesn't get much more kingly than this. In a way, this one ties into the second qualification. Often ancient Greek heroes were demi-gods as the result of Zeus or Poseidon or the occasional goddess coming down to Earth on a lonely Friday night just to see what's shaking with the mortals. Sometimes, nine months later, a hero is born.

- **Attempt to be Killed Early in Life**
  Right from the start, the hero is different. Sometimes they'd perform some kind of amazing feat that the rest of us mortals couldn't do. But whatever it is, would-be heroes get attention, and sometimes it's of the unwanted variety – as in an attempt to take them out.

- **Spirited Away from Homeland**
  Whether abandoned at birth or accidentally separated from their parents, heroes leave home at a young age.

- **Reared by Foster Parents**
  The hero is raised by someone other than his or her actual parents.

- **Told Nothing of His/Her Childhood**
  Either the foster parents don't know or refuse to tell a hero of his or her special heritage.

- **Returns Home upon Adulthood**
  Once the hero discovers who he or she really is, they decide to go home.

- **Victory over a King/Beast**
  The hero proves his or her mettle by defeating an evil king, a beast or sometimes both – usually as part of a quest of some sort. They might even have to face their own mortality in the Underworld, from which they'll emerge a true hero.

- **Marry a Princess**
  Yes, even in Ancient Greece, the hero would get it all. Except… usually the marriage was unhappy and chaotic.

- **Becomes King/Queen**
  A good gig if you can get it. Makes sense since dear old dad was either a god or the true king.

- **Reigns Uneventfully**
  All tends to be pretty quiet during the new king's rule – maybe even a bit too quiet for a hero used to battles, quests and underworlds.

- **Prescribes Laws**
  Might as well do something if you're the king/queen.

- **Loses Favor with Gods/Subjects**
  Hmm… I guess not everyone was happy with those laws you prescribed. Remember, as a hero you have larger than life qualities – including larger than life flaws. Sometimes you give in to your own greatness, which leads to getting a bit too big for your britches (the Greeks would call this hubris – excessive pride), and nothing offered a more sure way to the doghouse than getting too full of yourself. Few heroes could come to grips with their incredible gifts and mortality. Despite their success, they're still mortal and not quite gods.

- **Driven from Throne**
  Told you this didn't end well…

- **Meet a Mysterious Death**
  Heroes come into the world in an unusual way, and leave it the same way – shrouded in mystery. Sometimes their death is ignoble.

- **Die at the Top of Hill**
  So everyone can see.

- **Not Succeeded by Children**
  Usually a hero is a one-shot deal. No heirs to carry on their greatness. That job is up to us… as writers.

So, how'd you do?   Total: _____/20

Let's say anything over 15, and Olympus might be calling.

Did you qualify to be an ancient Greek hero?

Well, even if you didn't, you can still write movies about them. Many writers do without ever knowing it. That's the interesting thing about the design. It's something we in the west take for granted. A few thousand years of storytelling tradition have taught us that this is what heroes are. These are their characteristics.

Do we see variations?

Absolutely.

But the patterns are as recognizable to us as they would have been to the ancient Greeks, sitting on stone seats, watching the plays of Sophocles or Aeschylus.

But you don't have to take my word for it...

SET 2: *Grecian Formula*   CRAFT   *Total Reps*: 1

This time, rather than analyze yourself, let's identify the Greek origins, if any, for a movie hero. Check how many of the attributes apply to see if the filmmakers used any parts of Ancient Greek Hero Design.

Movie: _____

Genre: _____

Hero: _____

Attributes:

Note: You may encounter modern spins on these characteristics.

- ○ Hero's Mother is Royal Virgin
- ○ Hero's Father is the Real King
- ○ Father is Related to Mother
- ○ Unusual Conception
- ○ Child of a God
- ○ Attempt to be Killed Early in Life
- ○ Spirited Away from Homeland
- ○ Reared by Foster Parents
- ○ Told Nothing of Childhood
- ○ Returns Home upon Adulthood

- ○ Victory over a King or Beast
- ○ Marry a Princess/Prince
- ○ Become King
- ○ Prescribe Laws
- ○ Reign Uneventfully
- ○ Loses Favor with Gods/Subjects
- ○ Driven from Throne
- ○ Meet a Mysterious Death
- ○ Die at the Top of a Hill
- ○ Not Succeeded by Children

TOTAL: _____/20

How'd your hero do? Do we have a full-fledged Ancient Greek Hero or what?

Now, it's not quite fair if you chose, oh let's say, Hercules, especially the Disney animated one. But, sticking with Disney, if you chose Simba from *The Lion King* (1994), you may have seen just a wee bit of Ancient Greek Hero Design. Even more if you shift the last part of the design over to Scar.

You might even find the design in Harry Potter.

Or, Luke Skywalker. Or, Anakin for that matter. Mom may not have been royalty, but I hear there was no father. Midichlorians. Don't get me started...

Superhero stories are replete with this design. Superman, Wonder Woman, even Batman has pieces of it.

Of course, who can forget the 1982 cinematic classic, *The Beastmaster*, featuring the finest prosthetic nose ever worn by a villain?

The list goes on and on.

If the hero you picked possesses a large number of these traits, chances are the filmmakers wanted to create a MYTHOLOGICAL HERO – a person larger than life, one well-suited for epic adventures that will be talked about for ages. Hmm... Kinda like Dorothy from *The Wizard of Oz*. Perhaps she didn't return home as an adult, but she did go back to Kansas with a more mature perspective.

In modern stories, typically you'll find more of the origin portions of the list, which constitutes the left column. Makes sense, the latter portions seem a bit dark anyway. But then, it wasn't called Greek tragedy for nothing.

WORKOUT PROGRESS – CRAFT

Compile your totals for this unit.

EXERCISE	SKILL GROUP			TOTAL REPS	
	SET #	TYPE	ACTION	AVAILABLE	COMPLETED
It's All Greek to Me	1	Craft	Analysis	1	
Grecian Formula	2	Craft	Analysis	1	
			TOTAL REPS		

CRAFT — TOTAL REPS + BONUS — 2

Character Archetypes

An archetype is a model or prototype from which something specific is made. Think of it like those clay cars auto designers use. No one drives those -- they're used as the mold from which specific cars are created.

Much has been written about character archetypes, including Christopher Vogler's excellent book, *The Writer's Journey: Mythic Structure for Writers,* which itself is based on an internal memo Vogler wrote to break down Joseph Campbell's seminal work, *The Hero with a Thousand Faces*, into more practical terms for screenwriters.

Campbell's work centered around exploring the idea of the monomyth – one myth to rule them all, one myth to *bind* them. In particular, what Campbell found were patterns in the myths of various cultures from around the world, which led to the development of the monomyth – that human beings, regardless of culture, tended to create mythological stories using the same types of characters (archetypes, which themselves are derived from Carl Jung) and story stages (The Hero's Journey.)

The monomyth implies the idea of a collective consciousness, informing storytelling around the world. In other words, this approach theorizes that humans are hard-wired to think and to create narrative in certain ways. Considering the global scope of the film industry, we can see the interest in this approach – it's recognizable to people everywhere, because, so the theory goes, it represents an intrinsic aspect of simply being human. And, for nervous development execs, looking to mitigate risk, a proven storytelling model that's worked for thousands of years carries a certain appeal, especially after the wild success of *Star Wars*. Lucas was one of the first filmmakers to apply Campbell's work to create a movie. Of course, other films had used this story form before; after all, it is supposed to derive from a collective consciousness, but Lucas was one of the first to consciously apply the monomyth as a narrative structure for film.

As noted earlier, character design and structure are often built to fit together, and the mythological approach to storytelling is no exception. So, any exploration of character archetypes would be incomplete without the accompanying narrative structures in which they appear. So, we'll cover both. Because so much has been written about character archetypes, let's focus on what they truly are – story functions.

Character Archetypes

1. The Hero

At its core, the hero archetype represents the idea of going from self to selflessness. The mythological hero isn't defined by bravery, six-pack abs and a little DING sound when they smile, but rather they are marked by self-sacrifice, a willingness to die to save the group. Mythological heroes can have many different personalities, strengths and attributes. They can be good with a sword, good with their wits, good at home decorating, but the willingness to sacrifice themselves is what makes them a mythological hero. Naturally, not every hero wants to do this initially, and this forms the core of The Hero's Journey, as it tracks the progress of a hero from selfish to selfless motivations. In short, stories following this model are about heroes becoming heroes, and the journeys they must take to do so. This journey, as you can imagine, is fraught with peril as the hero must endure separation from their homes, travel to new, unfamiliar places and face challenging tests and obstacles. The difficulty of the journey forces mythological heroes to learn new lessons, new skills, new insights that enable them to overcome these challenges. Of course, these discoveries come at a price – nothing worthwhile is easy, and the hero may die a metaphoric or all-too-real death in order to succeed. But, as a result of the willingness to sacrifice themselves for the greater good, they are reborn as heroes.

Heroes aren't expected to do all this on their own. There's a whole supporting cast to help them on their journey, starting with our next archetype. But, before we go there, let's look at the story functions served by heroes.

Hero Story Functions:
Audience proxy (we experience the story through this character.)
Learn the lesson/theme of the movie (so the audience can, too.)

2. The Mentor

As the name implies the mentor is a teacher, a coach, someone who trains or helps heroes along their path. Sometimes this character can be a shaman, a wiser, older person. One who's been to the Special World before (more on this in a bit), and so this archetype knows just how difficult the task ahead will be. As a result, mentors often teach heroes new skills, or give them some form of magical equipment or assistance to help our would-be heroes succeed. Thus, we get Obi-Wan passing out lightsabers, or Morpheus giving digital kung-fu lessons.

Mentors represent the passing of knowledge from one generation to the next, and can take on many forms, depending on the story. They can be drill instructors, veteran cops training rookies, teachers, trail bosses, aged wizards, parents, coaches, etc., but whatever the specifics may be, from a storytelling standpoint, mentors serve a number of vital story functions. They often provide exposition. As they inform the hero of the task at hand, they're also informing the audience. They provide anticipation for the conflicts to come – it MUST be a dangerous journey if the hero needs all this training and magical gear to succeed. They also provide uncertainty that the hero will succeed, particularly if the hero doesn't pass the mentor's vigorous training regimen, which also provides the audience with the means of tracking the a hero's growth, as we witness the hero go from being unable to complete the mentor's tasks to being able to complete them. This introduces a very subtle story element – the idea that the hero must learn to succeed, and it does so in a relatively low-stakes environment, tests and training as opposed to actual combat (although some mentors may employ this.) Mentors may be lousy at their jobs or very effective, but either way, they pay a significant early role in the story.

<u>Mentor Story Functions</u>:
Provide exposition
Create anticipation
Demonstrate learning is the key to success.
Foreshadowing the conflicts to come.

3. Threshold Guardian

Riddle me, my questions three. Whether it's a troll guarding a bridge you need to cross, or a security guard the hero must get past to download the secret files, threshold guardians represent an early test for the hero.

Threshold Guardians are seldom the story's main antagonist. Sometimes they may work for the antagonist, or they can simply be an obstacle the hero must overcome to journey into the special world of the story. Either way, the role of the threshold guardian remains the same – to see if the hero is worthy of the perilous journey to come. Makes sense. If the hero can't defeat a threshold guardian, how can they be expected to overcome the big boss?

Threshold guardians provide conflict for the story, without resolving the main conflict, which of course, would end the story. They also help provide proof to the audience that the hero has grown, perhaps as a result of all that mentor training.

Traditional threshold guardians usually block the entrance to the special world, but you can employ them throughout the story to keep the conflict going and to demonstrate the growth of your hero.

<u>Threshold Guardian Story Functions</u>:
Provide conflict.
Demonstrate change or growth in the hero.

4. The Herald

The main function of the herald is to announce a challenge to the hero. In other words, heralds make the hero aware of a problem that must be overcome. Of course, in announcing this to the hero, they're also telling the audience about the problem, which is the main function this archetype serves.

Structurally, the herald represents the inciting incident or catalyst, making the hero aware of a problem that must be solved. As a result, the herald might not be a person at all, it could be the actual event that overturns the hero's world. Or, it might be the Bat Signal, letting Batman know there's trouble in Gotham.

Whatever form the herald may take, their function remains pretty much the same – to provide exposition to the audience. In so doing, heralds sometimes inadvertently hype the adventure to come; after all, if it's not something big, why announce it?

They also play a subtle role in bonding an audience to a hero. The bond is formed by the audience being able to identify with someone who was just having a regular day, when suddenly, along comes something to overturn it. We then watch to see how the hero handles this problem, which subconsciously teaches us how to potentially handle a similar problem. So, when a zombie apocalypse happens, you're well prepared to handle it. In a way, this is similar to the role of the mentor, and we see this reflected in the overlapping of their story functions.

Herald Story Functions:
Provide exposition.
Provide motivation to the hero.
Hype the adventure (or at least indicate its importance.)
Foreshadow later story events.

5. Shapeshifter

Shapeshifters are an intriguing archetype, introducing the idea of change as a story element while simultaneously providing additional layers of conflict, suspense and tension. Shapeshifters do this by, well, shifting shape.

As characters, shapeshifters are hard to pin down. They appear to be on the hero's side, an ally, a helper, part of the team, until... they're not. Often they change roles or personalities, keeping heroes off guard, on their toes and alert, and by doing this to the hero, their presence does the same to the audience.

Because shapeshifters represent change, other characters may fulfill this archetype, including the hero. Sometimes the change is physical. The hero must don a disguise (shapeshift) to get past an obstacle. For example, in *Star Wars*, Luke and Han disguise themselves as stormtroopers to get into Detention Block AA-23.

Sometimes, the change is mental, Cypher selling out the team in *The Matrix* for a piece of digital steak. Remember, the hero's journey is one of change, so this archetype is a way of introducing this as an important aspect of the story.

Shapeshifter Story Functions:
Introduce change as a story element.
Provide reversals.
Keep the hero and audience on their toes.
Generate suspense and tension.

6. The Trickster

Often thought of as merely comic relief, tricksters are actually far more important to the story than the name implies. At their core, tricksters are mischief-makers, often causing trouble just to see what will happen, or to get a laugh. But underneath this surface role, tricksters introduce an element of randomness to the story, a sense that anything can happen, which subtly allows you to use these same elements in the story itself. In other words, random events happen in life all the time, but in stories such events can appear to be plot contrivances – especially if we get the idea that they're coming from the writer. So, to introduce the sense that anything can happen, while simultaneously keeping the audience grounded in your story logic, you simply feed such events through a character, the trickster.

When thinking of the trickster archetype, I'm reminded of the old comedy adage, "It's funny because it's true." This statement encapsulates two of the vital story functions served by tricksters.   Funny. And, true. Let's take funny first.

Slaying dragons and defeating evil overlords can be serious business, so tricksters provide comic relief to give the audience a break from the heavy drama. Essentially, whenever the story needs to lighten up a bit or release some tension, the trickster provides this.

The other important function tricksters serve has to do with truth. And, to explore this one, we need the context of our last archetype – the Shadow.

Trickster Story Functions:
Introduce randomness as a story element.
Disguise plot holes or gaps in story logic (see randomness above.)
Provide humor.
Create complications.
Provide breaks for audience.
Provide perspective.

7. The Shadow

Often considered the villain or antagonist, the shadow is not necessarily either. Like villains or antagonists, the shadow creates conflict in the story and represents an obstacle to overcome, often embodying the same negative energies antagonists and villains represent. However, the shadow serves another important story function. And, to illustrate this, perhaps we should define the shadow archetype through the lens of the hero, because that's what they often are: a fallen hero.

A shadow often embodies many of the same positive attributes as heroes, with one crucial difference: while the archetypical hero is marked by self-sacrifice, the shadow is defined by selfishness. Put another way, when a hero gives into self, they become a shadow. Think about it. As heroes become powerful as a result of the journey, they could think to themselves – hey, I'm powerful enough to take over this place. I don't see anyone else helping out. Why should I endure all this crap to save a bunch of people just to die in the end? What about me? That temptation to give in to the self, to use those newfound powers to help yourself instead of others, embodies the shadow archetype. And, what helps prevent heroes from becoming shadows? This brings us back to the trickster.

Did you catch the last story function served by tricksters? To provide perspective? Whenever a hero starts to give into self, give in to that temptation, the trickster is there to knock the hero down a peg, to humorously provide perspective. Saving the world is serious business, and well-meaning heroes might think the way to fix things permanently is for them to take over. Gotta love ego. Tricksters are there to puncture that ego and to bring the hero back down to earth. Notice the very subtle message embedded in this design. A hero is one who listens to the trickster and takes their advice. Shadows are heroes who did not take the advice, who did not listen to others. The message implicit in this cuts straight to the heart of mythological storytelling, and you could say, story in general – listen and learn and you will succeed. Do not listen; do not learn, and you will fail. In this way, shadows serve as cautionary tales for a failure to learn, to change, to grow.

Shadows also serve another important story function – isolating a story variable. Because heroes and shadows often possess many of the same characteristics, this isolates the one aspect where they differ – self versus selflessness. By isolating that difference, this demonstrates to the audience that this aspect, and this aspect alone, is the reason the shadow fails and the hero succeeds. Therefore, if you want to succeed, don't give into self. Learn. Grow. Change. Oh, and listen to your elders, those mentors. In ways, this aspect cuts to the very origins of story – the passing down of knowledge and culture from one generation to the next by providing examples of what to do and what not to do, all wrapped up in story, an entertaining way to get the message across and to make it stick. This aspect of story highlights an interesting side effect – if you want to send a different message, you simply change the outcome of the battle between shadow and hero. So, if you wanted to say greed is good, you have the shadow win. If you want to say the opposite, the hero wins. By enacting these thematic struggles, you indirectly state your theme.

This process applies to any thematic statement you wish to make. <u>Characters represent differing aspects of the theme you wish to explore</u>, and when one side emerges triumphant, you state your theme without overtly stating it. Remember our movie math? This is letting the audience add up 2 + 2, and because the audience fills in the picture, the theme has a far greater chance of resonating. Think about it this way – when told what to do, many people's natural reaction is to rebel. So, as storytellers, we don't tell people what to do or think, we enact it, and let the results speak for themselves. Of course, we're heavily guiding this process for the audience, so to disguise this, we feed the story through its characters. Character archetypes are story functions in disguise, and they do for us what they've done for storytellers throughout the ages – make the story seem real. They accomplish this by hiding the mechanics of storytelling. Ultimately, this is the power of character archetypes, and why they're still relevant today.

<u>Shadow Story Functions:</u>
Represent theme.
Provide conflict.
Demonstrate what happens to those who don't pay attention, learn and change.

SET 1: *Finding Archetypes* CRAFT Total Reps: 14

List <u>two</u> examples of each character archetype in the spaces provided and briefly describe **HOW** each fits the archetype. If you encounter twists on the classical archetypes, be sure to mention how the original archetype was modified.

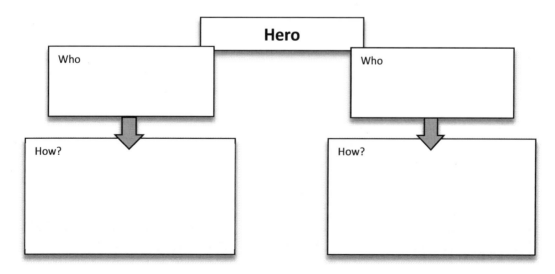

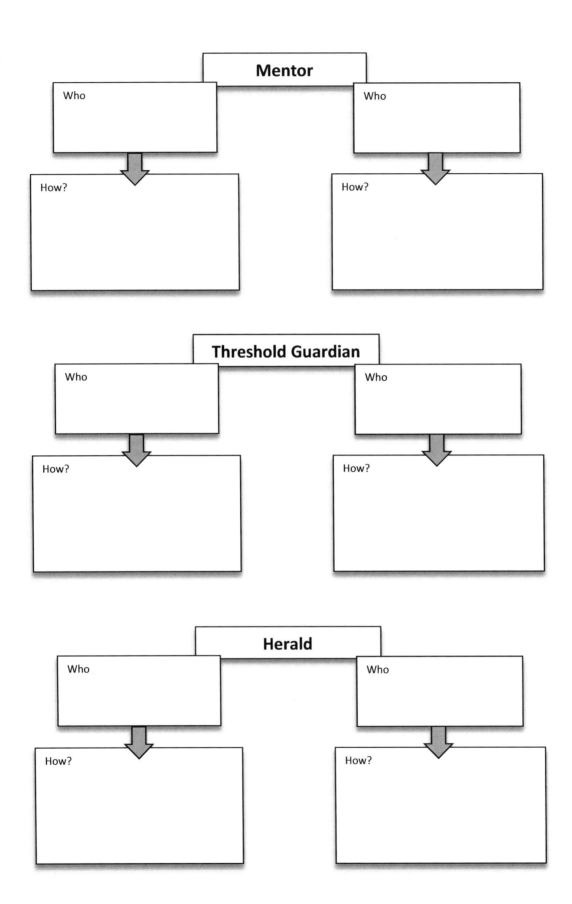

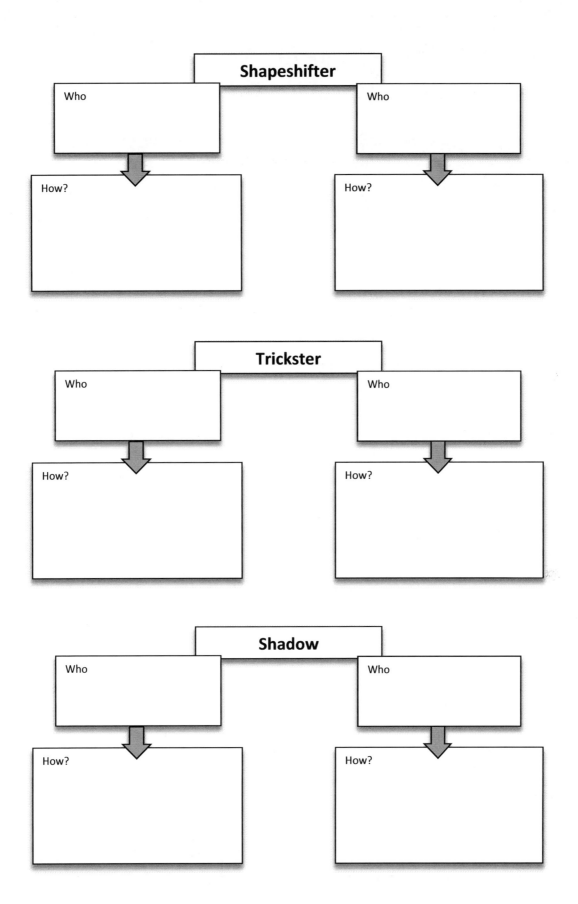

SET 2: Me and my Shadow **CRAFT** **Total Reps: 2**

Let's reexamine the heroes and shadows you picked and see if we can't have some fun with them. To do this, you should relist them here:

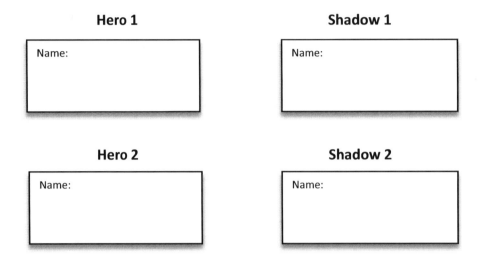

Depending on the characters and movies you chose, there should be heroes and shadows from at least two different movies listed. Your mission, should you choose to accept it – pair up a hero and a shadow from different films to see what story you can create. In a well-designed film, these two archetypes are built to complement each other. Let's see what you can create when they're not.

Pairing 1

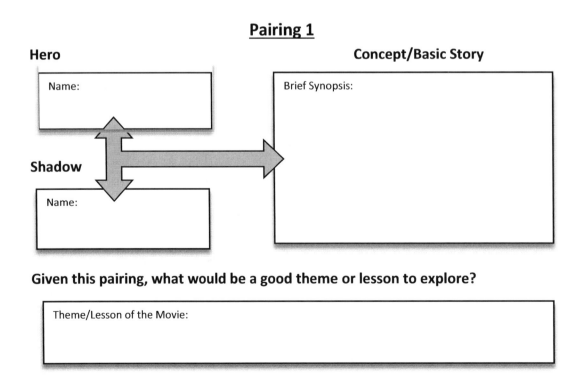

Given this pairing, what would be a good theme or lesson to explore?

Theme/Lesson of the Movie:

Oh man, that was way too easy. Let's add a wrinkle.

This time, let's switch the roles.

With your remaining hero/shadow pair, flip their roles so that the shadow is now the hero and vice versa.

Remember: there are two lines of demarcation between these characters you'll have to take into account when crafting the story:
1. Shadows are selfish. Heroes are not – at least not by the end.
2. Heroes learn the lesson of the movie and change. Shadows typically do not.

Okay, that should be enough to get started!

Pairing 2

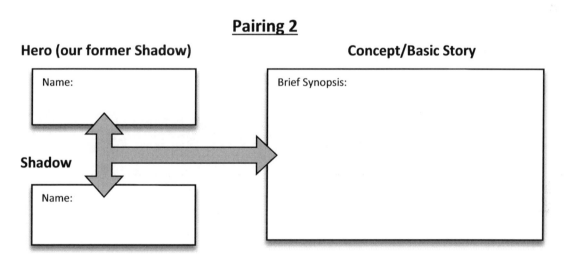

Given this pairing, what would be a good theme or lesson to explore?

Normally, this is where we'd do a structural outline for this concept. However, mythological characters are built to go with their own structure: **The Hero's Journey** aka, **Myth Structure**. So, before we can outline, it might be a good idea to explore this timeless structural paradigm. As we segue from character archetypes to their accompanying story structure, we should note that because archetypes are really story functions in disguise, a character can embody more than one archetype.

For example, Mr. Miyagi from *The Karate Kid* is clearly the Mentor (wax on, wax off, and so forth…). But, he's also the Trickster (he provides comic relief), a Herald (announcing the Tri-County Tournament to Daniel-san), Shapeshifter (Mr. Miyagi first appears to be just the apartment handyman before we discover his true identity), and in ways, a Threshold Guardian (if Daniel-san doesn't pass the Mr. Miyagi's tests, he can't go to the Special World of the film, the world of martial arts.) While the last one could also be ascribed to the role of Mentor, this highlights yet another aspect of archetypes – their flexibility. Essentially, whenever the story needs a certain function, for example, comic relief, a character may have to adopt the Trickster archetype if the film's Trickster isn't in the scene (or if the film doesn't have a 'designated' Trickster.) This is particularly useful for movies with small casts that want to tell a mythologically-based story.

Speaking of telling a story, let's get to that structure!

But first, be sure to track your progress.

WORKOUT PROGRESS – CRAFT

Compile your workout totals for this unit.

EXERCISE	SKILL GROUP		TOTAL REPS	
	SET #	TYPE	ACTION	AVAILABLE	COMPLETED
Finding Archetypes	1	Craft	Analysis	14	
Me and my Shadow	2	Craft	Application	2	
			TOTAL REPS		

CRAFT — TOTAL REPS + BONUS — 16

Myth Structure:
The 12 Stages of The Hero's Journey

The structure designed to fit with character archetypes is the Hero's Journey, derived from Joseph Campbell's book, *The Hero With A Thousand Faces*, which as you may recall from our discussion of archetypes, was adapted by Christopher Vogler as a guide for writing myth-based films. This doesn't mean that films created using this structure must contain gods and goddesses, magic swords, unicorns and other such mythological staples. You can find it contemporary stories as well. That's one of the advantages of myth structure – it's adaptable, and to a large degree, quite flexible. Because it's an established form of storytelling, in ways as old as story itself, the story patterns found in Myth Structure are instantly recognizable, which in turn, makes it easier to create variations. This combination of a different take on an established form creates a highly entertaining and dynamic one-two punch found throughout cinematic narrative – <u>unique yet familiar</u>.

The unique part comes from you. It's your original spin. The familiar part comes from the form itself, which has been ingrained for thousands of years. The one-two of this combination is that the audience can stay grounded (the familiar) while experiencing something new (the unique.) And, because Myth Structure is so ingrained, this allows you to jump straight to the unique aspects of this approach, saving you time, which allows you to devote more time to your unique characters and your original story. Put another way, if we were telling a joke, it's as though the audience already knows the set up, so all you have to do is present the punchline.

As with character archetypes, much has been written about this structure, so we'll just hit the major points here. If you'd like to explore Myth Structure in greater depth, be sure to check out Vogler's book, *The Writers Journey*, and of course, Campbell's *The Hero with a Thousand Faces*.

The 12 Stages of the Hero's Journey

1. The Ordinary World
Just another day in the life of the hero, who is completely unaware of the adventure to come. It may seem odd to devote time at the beginning of the film to something so... well, ordinary, but it's an extremely important beat because it establishes the hero as 'one of us' -- just a regular person doing regular-person things, highly relatable. Depending on your hero, you may find that this person isn't regular at all.

And, that's fine. This stage is the ordinary world for this particular character. For example, when we first meet Mr. Incredible in *The Incredibles*, it's just a normal day for a superhero, fighting crime, saving cats, uprooting trees. Now, I'm willing to bet that's not a normal day for most people. This is our unique yet familiar combination. Just another day at the office for the hero (the familiar), but this character's normal day is as a superhero fighting crime (the unique.) The relatability lies in this combination because, even though Mr. Incredible may not quite be one of us, the 'just another day' aspect is what forms the bond with the audience.

By showing heroes in their ordinary worlds, you accomplish three major things:

1.1 Reveal Character
The ordinary world of a character reveals loads of information about who they are, their likes/dislikes, wants/needs. Doing this before the adventure starts allows the audience to see how a character is in normal circumstances and then compare these behaviors to how the character acts under duress.

1.2 Establish the Stakes
We see what's threatened, what could potentially be destroyed if the hero doesn't succeed. Or, in stories where the ordinary world isn't all that wonderful, we can see what needs to be changed as a result of the hero's adventure to come.

1.3 Create Contrast
The hero's journey takes heroes to a place called the Special World, someplace unfamiliar where the rules are very different than in the Ordinary World. To show the specialness of this new environment, we need to establish the Ordinary World first as contrast. In other words, the Ordinary World establishes the baseline to highlight just how different the Special World is for our hero. Simply put, we need the ordinary to demonstrate something as extraordinary.

So, it's just another day for our hero, doing what they normally do, until…

2. The Call to Adventure
Whatever the ordinary world of your hero is, this event overturns it. The hero is made aware of a problem, a threat to the ordinary world, which must be stopped. The call can come in many forms. It can be the hero encountering the actual event disrupting the ordinary world. It can be issued by our Herald archetype (help me Obi-Wan Kenobi…), but however the hero discovers the problem, this structural beat starts the adventure – well, almost…

3. Refusal of the Call

This is an extremely important beat in which the hero resists the Call to Adventure. The resistance may be caused by doubt or fear. Think about it from the hero's perspective – here I was just doing my thing and now I have to save the world? I'm not equipped for that. And a perilous, life-threatening journey? But, my favorite show comes on tonight. I can't do this, I have plans on Friday. Whatever it is, the hero expresses reluctance to take on the adventure in this beat.

On the surface, refusing the call may seem to slow the movie down because it delays the adventure. But, it yields a couple results that make it worth the time:

3.1 Relatability
When presented with a dangerous, seemingly impossible problem to solve, a perfectly understandable reaction would be to balk, to express doubt or concern. This reaction helps bond the audience to the hero.

3.2 Builds Up the Adventure
Think about it – if the call wasn't dangerous, there'd be no need to refuse it. Having the hero refuse the call highlights just how perilous the adventure is.

In an action movie, the refusal beat may be quick – typical heroes in this genre aren't known for deeply contemplating the ramifications of their actions. For more reluctant heroes, the refusal may occupy a longer section of the script. But either way, this beat helps bond the audience to the character and foreshadow the dangerous adventure to come. It's a period of indecision for the hero, who may be unsure of what to do next. This provides another storytelling advantage:

3.3 Motivates Exposition
As our reluctant hero debates what to do next in the face of this daunting task, the problem is often discussed, which provides the perfect opportunity to reveal backstory, which can reveal character and give you some time to expand upon what we already know.

When facing a tough decision, it's only natural to seek some advice – perhaps from someone who's done this sort of thing before. Someone older, wiser, who may be able to help. This leads to...

4. Meeting the Mentor

Many of the functions of this beat were explored in our discussion of the Mentor archetype – training, teaching, testing, giving the hero some magical equipment. At this crucial time in the story, the hero may seek out guidance in the form of the Mentor.

Depending on the story, the Mentor can be a library-card-carrying Yoda of wisdom or utterly incompetent. Unwilling to help or generous in assistance. Typically, Mentors have been to the Special World before. But, that was a long time ago, and perhaps they've grown a bit too old to take on this new challenge.

The Mentor archetype is sometimes split into two specialized versions: the Donor and the Helper. Donors, as the name implies, dispense wisdom, donate magic gear or give some special insight. Helpers tend to accompany the hero on the adventure, so that they can assist along the journey. A fairy godmother is an example of this type of specialized mentor, showing up in times of need for the hero.

Because archetypes are defined by their actions and functions within the narrative, the Mentor can also be any of the other archetypes, including the Shadow. For example, in *The Little Mermaid*, Ursula is the antagonist; however, she's also the Mentor, providing magical assistance to Ariel, who wants to be human. Ursula gives Ariel legs. Of course, being an antagonist, Ursula's help comes at a price...

Magical equipment can also vary, depending on the story. It can take the form of tech, rather than magic, or it may simply be training, or even plans for battle stations the size of small moons. Whatever form it takes, the bestowing of magical gear leads us to the first of our story functions for this beat:

4.1 Build Anticipation
Magical equipment introduces a new element to the story, and your audience must watch the movie to see it in action. This new wrinkle provides something fresh for the story to explore.

Meeting the Mentor also provides other storytelling advantages:

4.2 Build Up the Adventure
We've seen this one before, but now we're getting it from an additional perspective, which helps to confirm that the adventure is indeed as dangerous as we thought. Also, because the Mentor has typically been to the Special World, this allows you to elaborate on the problem facing the Hero. By exploring the issue more fully, you can...

4.3 Provide Exposition
Which can also...

4.4 Raise the Stakes
Particularly with reluctant heroes who may need a friendly kick out the door. The Mentor often lays out the consequences of failure to the Hero in an attempt to motivate them to action, and in so doing, the Mentor is also relaying this information to the audience, letting us know precisely what will happen should the Hero not succeed.

4.5 Build Character
As our Hero struggles to complete the Mentor's tests, we can see their weaknesses, their strengths, their fears, doubts, potential, and so forth. These struggles help to plant doubt that the Hero will succeed, throwing uncertainty over the ending of the story to keep it less predictable.

As you can see, Meeting the Mentor provides numerous advantages to the story. And now that our Hero has gained some skills and gotten some goodies, they're finally ready to take the plunge.

5. Crossing the Threshold

The Hero, now ready to take on the quest, finally crosses the threshold between the Ordinary World, a place they're familiar with, and the Special World, a place of unknown mysteries and danger.

Notice at this point in the story, the audience has the same amount of information about this unknown place as the Hero. This allows the audience to explore the Special World WITH the Hero, which yields the first of several important story functions served by this beat:

5.1 Character Bonding
Because the audience and Hero experience the Special World together, and with the same amount of information, this strengthens the bond between audience and character. As the Hero explores this mysterious, new world, the audience does as well, further strengthening this bond.

In this beat, we usually encounter our Threshold Guardian archetype, blocking the Hero from entering the Special World. This provides an important early test for the Hero, yielding another story function:

5.2 Generate Conflict
Overcoming the Threshold Guardian through guile, brute force, or whatever is appropriate to the story, creates opportunities for conflict, which in turn, can highlight what the hero needs to work upon in order to succeed. It also provides the audience an opportunity to see if all that training from the Mentor has paid off.

Crossing the Threshold marks the beginning of the journey, and so usually employs a specialized function known as a <u>Beat Marker</u>. A Beat Marker is simply something that highlights a turn in the story, making the audience aware that the tale has shifted gears so to speak. For our threshold crossing, the Beat Marker often takes the form of a <u>restaurant/tavern/bar scene</u> shortly after arriving in the Special World. This scene serves several uses:

5.3 Introduces the Hero (and the audience) to the Special World
Bars, taverns and other such public meeting places provide a chance for the hero to eavesdrop and perhaps pick up useful information about the Special World, providing exposition and foreshadowing.

5.4 Provides a Break
After the excitement of defeating the Threshold Guardian and the ordeal of crossing the threshold, the hero (and audience) might need a moment to rest. Of course, this doesn't mean nothing is happening. We're picking up valuable information, and perhaps even some additional help from other travelers who've gathered here. They were in the Special World before we arrived and may have some inside knowledge to help us understand the rules of this unusual place.

One of the most famous threshold crossings in movie history comes to us from *The Wizard of Oz*, where Dorothy goes from the Ordinary World of black and white Kansas, to the spectacular world of Oz in gorgeous, three-strip Technicolor. While Dorothy doesn't land in a bar or tavern, she does plop down right in the town square of Munchkinland, a very public meeting place.

While our hero usually travels to the Special World, sometimes the Special World comes to the hero. For example, in John Carpenter's *Halloween*, the Ordinary World of the hero, Laurie Strode, is about as ordinary as it gets – a suburban home. Enter Michael Myers, who transforms the Ordinary World into the Special World of the movie. Wherever he goes, he brings the film's Special World with him. However, in most applications, Crossing the Threshold marks the hero's first step into a larger world, marking the end of Act 1 and the beginning of Act 2.

6. Tests, Allies, And Enemies
This phase of the Hero's Journey is a bit of a catchall, forming much of the movie's second act – especially its first half. In this stage our hero, finally out of the comfort zone of the Ordinary World, encounters a series of increasingly difficult challenges or obstacles. These **test** the hero's mettle, providing opportunities for conflict and growth as the hero learns to overcome each additional challenge.

Along the way, the hero may pick some **allies** to aid in the quest. So, Dorothy picks up the Scarecrow, Tinman, and Cowardly Lion to help her get back to Kansas. Sticking with *The Wizard of Oz* for a moment, we see a common variation on the Hero's Journey. Dorothy meets two mentors, one in the Ordinary World and one in the Special World. Back in Kansas, she encountered Professor Marvel, who tells her to go home. In Oz, she meets Glenda the Good Witch, who gives her the ruby slippers (magical equipment) and teaches her a bit about how Oz works.

The hero also encounters <u>enemies</u> in this portion of the story to keep the conflict going and to provide insight into the forces of antagonism the hero faces. This in turn allows the audience to track the hero's progress (and growth) toward achieving the goal. The story functions in this stage include:

6.1 Provide Conflict
Through encounters with various enemies.

6.2 Reveal Character
By enabling us to see our hero through the perspectives of other characters, all of which help to reveal the hero's personality in good times (I found an ally! Great!) and bad (I found an enemy! Great.) Interactions with allies allow you to externalize the hero's personality.

6.3 Reveal the World
Interacting with the Special World enables the hero and the audience to learn about it.

6.4 Maintain Pace
Second acts are where many screenplays sag, so the new elements and conflicts introduced in this stage of the Hero's Journey help to keep the story moving forward.

6.5 Track Character Growth
Or lack of growth, depending on the particulars of the movie. As obstacles are overcome, we can see if the hero is learning and growing. Likewise, with each setback, we may begin to doubt whether the hero has what it takes to defeat the story's antagonist.

Allies the hero may acquire in this stage include archetypes such as the Trickster, Shapeshifter and additional Mentors (if needed.)

Enemies include archetypes like additional Threshold Guardians, Shapeshifters and of course, the Shadow, whose presence begins to dominate the story.

7. Approach To The Inmost Cave
The inmost cave can represent many things in story. It can be a physical place, often the enemies headquarters. Or it can be more metaphoric, a reflection of the Hero's inner self. Whatever form it takes, the Inmost Cave represents THE most dangerous place in the Special World. Now, most people don't make it a habit of traveling to dangerous places just for fun, and our hero is no exception. There's something in that Inmost Cave the hero desperately needs, something vital to the hero's goal. That something is called the <u>Elixir</u>.

The Elixir is specific to the movie, so it can take many forms, but these forms all reflect the original meaning of elixir -- a potion, often possessing the power to heal. In terms of story function, this is what elixirs do – they heal the ordinary world. They fix the problem. So, whether the elixir is another character, a magic potion, a super-deluxe dragon-slaying sword, or simply knowledge, the hero must obtain the elixir to achieve the goal of restoring the Ordinary World back to what it was.

Often the Shadow is aware that the elixir presents a danger, so they lock it away in a stronghold, surround it with threshold guardians, and keep it close. Just as often, the elixir is something precioussss to the Shadow, if that reference *rings* a bell. ;) Sorry, couldn't resist.

Sometimes, the elixir represents the hero's Tangible Goal, something physical the audience can see the hero acquire. Tangible proof that the hero has grown. Occasionally, this tangible goal doesn't do what the hero thinks it will. It actually WON'T fix the world – only the hero can do this by growing, changing, learning, becoming a true hero, which is what the hero's journey is all about. In this case, the elixir serves as the plot device necessary for the hero to grow and learn as they pursue this object. So yes, while the ruby slippers can send Dorothy back to Kansas, what she really needed to do is learn the lesson of the movie – there's no place like home. In this way, elixirs serve to highlight a character's want and need. The Hero may want the elixir, thinking it will solve the problem, but what the Hero really needs is to change, to become a hero, to truly resolve the issue.

Let's back up a bit because this stage is actually called *Approach* to the Inmost Cave. The approach portion marks the preparation phase of entering the inmost cave. In an action movie, this is where we might find the cool, hero arming up montage in which we see the hero loading shotguns, strapping on grenades, chambering bullets and so forth.

This stage provides several important story functions:

7.1 Build Anticipation
It must be one helluva battle if the hero has to prepare this much for it.

7.2 Demonstrate Growth
Wow, the hero couldn't have done this earlier in the movie. They've really grown as a result of the journey.

7.3 Highlight Want and Need
Particularly in stories where the elixir doesn't exactly work like the hero thought it would.

7.4 Generate Conflict
Not only does this stage create conflict, it escalates it. The preparation alone indicates this isn't just another encounter.

7.5 Reveal Character
Sometimes the approach is a reflective moment before the big battle, where all the hero's doubts and fears come rushing to the surface. Can they really take on the antagonist and win?

The Wizard of Oz presents an intriguing use of an elixir to advance the story. In its most tangible form, you could say the elixir is the witch's broomstick. It certainly meets the surface requirements for elixirs. It's a physical object. Dorothy believes it will get her home, which fixes the story problem she faces. It's located in the enemy's headquarters (the witch's castle) and is surrounded by those super-creepy flying monkeys. But, in an intriguing twist, it's not the real elixir. And, as it turns out, the witch's castle isn't the actual inmost cave. The elixir in this movie is its lesson (no place like home), and the inmost cave is the wizard's chamber, where her hopes for an easy fix are dashed. There is no magic to take Dorothy home, Dorothy must learn to appreciate home before she can go, which enables the ruby slippers to do their thing. This draws out the want and need aspect of the story.

8. Supreme Ordeal

As the name suggests, this event presents an extreme challenge to the hero. It may be an external challenge, a physical battle or some daunting test. It can be internal, a deep inner crisis or mental challenge for the hero. Or, it can be both. It's not called a Supreme Ordeal for nothing.

Whether heroes are facing their greatest fears or most deadly foes, heroes must draw on all their skills, everything they've learned on the journey to this point to overcome the ordeal. Sometimes even this is not enough, and the best a hero can do is just survive.

To highlight the danger and importance of the ordeal, this beat often contains some form of death, metaphoric or literal, letting everyone know that the price of saving the Ordinary World will be high. Note how this beat presents an opportunity to show the audience whether the hero has embraced self-sacrifice yet, the hallmark of mythological heroes. In terms of story functions, this stage:

8.1 Demonstrates Growth
The hero's victory signals that they're becoming stronger both to the audience, and to a certain other character who has a vested interest in the outcome of this story – the antagonist.

8.2 Provides Foreshadowing
The brush with death in this stage introduces this story element, which will become much more than a brush later in the journey.

8.3 Motivates the Antagonist to Action
This beat will unleash the fury of the antagonist, providing justification for this character's future course of action.

8.4 Revitalizes the Second Act
The hero's actions change the direction of the story, which in turn, provides new complications to explore, keeping the story fresh and exciting.

While the hero may have experienced some form of death in this stage, by surviving the ordeal, the hero often receives a…

9. Reward

Congratulations! You've just survived a Supreme Ordeal and obtained an Elixir to heal the Ordinary World! So, here's a fabulous prize chosen just for you!

After defeating the enemy, surviving death and finally overcoming a great personal challenge, the Hero seems to be on the right track, emerging from the battle as a stronger person. As a result, the hero often receives a reward of some kind. Often this prize is the Elixir, which is why they went into the Inmost Cave in the first place. Sometimes the reward is knowledge rather than a physical object, but whatever it is, the reward usually holds the key to restoring the Ordinary World. And, the hero must now get it back there as soon as possible.

While the hero has scored a major victory, this comes with a price. Because, although the antagonist has been defeated, they haven't been beaten. If anything, all this did was enrage the antagonist. Think about it from the antagonist's perspective. They went through all this effort to protect the elixir -- hiring guards, building diabolical traps, arming their fortress, and for what? In waltzes some wannabe hero, into their house, knocking off their guards, making a mess of the place and taking, no, stealing, the antagonist's rightfully ill-gotten treasure.

Now the hero has the full attention of the antagonist. Prior to this, the hero was seen as just an annoyance. With this victory, the antagonist realizes the hero has now become a legitimate threat, one to be destroyed, utterly and quickly. Goes nicely with all that villainous rage, which is now channeled at our hero in full force, and the antagonist brings everything at their disposal to take out the hero once and for all, leading us to…

10. The Road Back

Our hero, having obtained the elixir, must now get back to the Ordinary World, often with a furious antagonist in hot pursuit. As a result, you may find some sort of chase scene in this section of the story as the antagonist goes in for the kill, and to take back the elixir.

In this stage, the hero faces perhaps the greatest challenge yet, facing an enraged antagonist and all the forces this character has. In the face of this seemingly insurmountable enemy, the hero often faces a choice between saving themselves or fully committing to returning the elixir to the Ordinary World and saving others.

This is the moment of truth. Does the hero fulfill their destiny and become a true hero, even if it means their death? Or, does the hero choose self-preservation? The antagonist may even attempt to recruit the hero, just to make the choice a little more difficult. Heroes who fail this final test by choosing self over self-sacrifice risk becoming a Shadow as the story reaches its climactic final battle.

11. Resurrection

This is the moment we've all been waiting for: the final showdown. This stage decides the fate of the hero, the fate of the Ordinary World, and in ways the fate of the story. There are no second chances. No 'live to fight another day'. This is it. Everything's on the line.

Failure here means others will suffer, all those good folks back in the Ordinary World. This puts even more pressure on the hero, which in turn, helps to invest the audience in this final battle to an even greater degree as they witness the hero struggle with fears and doubt, hope and trepidation, and a seemingly unstoppable antagonist.

It's here, in this darkest hour, that something dies or appears to die. Usually, it's the hero, demonstrating the willingness to sacrifice themselves for the greater good. This death, whether metaphoric or actual, represents the ultimate sacrifice, and from this lowest of lows, a true hero is born.

This death/rebirth beat represents the actual point of the hero's journey – the creation of a mythological hero.

Similar to our Crossing the Threshold stage, this beat employs its own Beat Markers to indicate its occurrence: <u>water</u> and <u>cleansing</u>. Be on the lookout for the presence of both, or either of these elements during the resurrection. Water is a traditional symbol of rebirth, and cleansing can be considered as both a metaphoric cleansing of evil and the hero washing away the muck of battle before returning home. Imagine what the hero's mom would say, coming in after a battle, tracking blood and guts all over her brand new carpet. It also marks a fresh, clean start for both the hero, now that they've become a true hero, and the world, now that it's been rid of the evil plaguing it.

As with our previous beat marker, the presence of water or cleansing in the resurrection doesn't define the beat, but rather, the marker merely serves as an indicator that this stage is occurring. You may also encounter variations on water. For example, in *Terminator 2*, the water element is the molten steel the Terminator is lowered into to destroy the last remaining chip, marking the hero's self-sacrifice to save the future of humanity.

When mythological heroes are reborn, they finally have the strength to defeat the antagonist and restore the Ordinary World. This beat also highlights the hero's willingness to change, demonstrating that they've learned the moral of the story. Often, it's this very lesson that provides the key to victory over the antagonist. In terms of story, this stage functions to:

11.1 Provide a Reversal
The hero appears to die and then comes back a true hero, stronger than before, creating a reversal or twist.

11.3 Entertainment
Guess we need a little of that in our story. With the stakes maxed, the conflict in this stage is intense -- and highly entertaining.

11.2 Deliver Theme
This scene demonstrates the need to learn the lesson of the movie. After all, the hero did, and they won.

Thus, our antagonist, who was unwilling to change or learn, meets with defeat, while our hero, who did embrace the moral of the story, emerges victorious. This represents the story stating its theme. All that's left now is to...

12. Return With The Elixir
The final stage of the journey marks the hero returning home in triumph, changed forever by the events of the journey. In ways this represents a back to one ending, with the hero returning to the place where the journey started; however, it's really back to a modified one. Yes, home may be the same, but the hero is now different. Or, perhaps home is better than it was before. Whatever the change, the back to one aspect of returning with the elixir enables the audience to directly compare the before and after of the journey, providing prima facie proof of the results of the adventure. In other words, we can compare the before and after to see what's changed and attribute this to the journey the hero just completed and the lesson the hero learned as a result of this journey.

In terms of story, this stage serves to impart three major ideas:

12.1 Learn the Lesson
In this way the hero serves as an exemplar and is rewarded for embracing the story's theme.

12.2 Proof of the Journey
By returning victorious, the hero has tangible proof they've been on this adventure. This proof serves to reinforce that the hero is a true hero.

12.3 Embrace Change
In stories, as in real life, it's difficult to get a person to change. But, when we're willing to change, willing to grow, the possibilities are endless…

Although the main part of the journey is over, the story may need to resolve some loose ends in this stage before the final victory celebration, which allows the audience to leave the story much like its hero – triumphant and changed, and ready for the next adventure…

Now that we've explored what the Hero's Journey is, let's delve into its why. The 12 Stages of the Hero's Journey is one of the oldest, if not THE oldest, story structures in existence. So, whether you regard it as a template, a structure, or simply a curiosity, this timeless way of telling a story does raise an intriguing question – why has it endured? What is it about this narrative pattern that enables it to be just as relevant today as it was to ancient storytellers?

In part, the answer lies in its relatability, then as now. It may seem odd to consider a structure that gives rise to the birth of a mythological hero would contain elements that are relatable to mere mortals, so to delve into this, let's change the name from the Hero's Journey to the Audience's Journey. Because if you look closely enough, you may see that the stages not only take hero on a journey, they transport the audience as well.

The 12 Stages of the Audience's Journey

We've already listed many of the specific effects each stage has on an audience, so let's keep this simple.

1. The Ordinary World
Just another day in your life, similar to our hero.

2. The Call to Adventure
Hey, there's a new movie coming out! I just saw the trailer.

3. Refusal
Wonder if I should wait for it to come out on video… Maybe I should look into it a bit more.

4. Meeting the Mentor
Okay, I've looked it up online, I even asked someone who's already seen it, and they say it's good. I think I'll go. Besides, it appears to be so well-written (okay, I added that last part.)

5. Crossing the Threshold
I'd like two tickets for [Insert super-cool movie title here] please. Notice how the ticket taker serves as a threshold guardian you must pass to enter the theater.

Guess we should stop off by the snack bar and grab some popcorn before the movie starts. It may not be a restaurant or tavern, but it'll have to do.

6. Tests, Allies, Enemies
No direct equivalent per se, although would that annoying person whose phone keeps going off count as an enemy?

7. Approach to the Inmost Cave
Jokes about the theater restroom aside, this one is more story-based for the audience. If we're pulling for the hero, the hero's peril is our peril.

8. Ordeal
Same as before, if we're still in the hero's shoes during this part of the journey.

9. Reward
Hey, that movie rocked! Glad we saw it!

10. The Road Back
Well, that was fun. Time to hit the road.

11. Resurrection
This one's a bit more metaphoric, tying back to the idea of catharsis or the cleansing of pent up emotions, that theoretically get released when witnessing a reenactment of similar feelings, but if that's not enough, let me get some water on the way out.

12. Return with the Elixir
Our audience member returns home, a better person for having gained a new insight from watching the movie.

While this comparison may seem a bit specious, consider this: what if the decision being made were far more important, life altering even (after all, movies can change lives, certainly did mine.) At its core the hero's journey is actually describing a process. And, if we recall the origins of story, as the original teaching tool for morals and culture, we might just find that the Hero's Journey isn't a story structure at all – it's a problem-solving process.

Pretend you've encountered an important problem, one you've not experienced before. One that might even threaten the safety of those around you. When we examine the Hero's Journey through this lens, we find the following:

The 12 Stages of Problem Solving

1. The Ordinary World
Just another day in your life, when suddenly…

2. The Call to Adventure
You're made aware of a problem – a big one.

3. Refusal
You may not be sure you can solve the problem, or even if it applies to you. Self-doubt may creep in. Can you <u>really</u> fix this issue? This calls for a little advice…

4. Meeting the Mentor
You seek out someone for some advice or research the problem.

5. Crossing the Threshold
You take the plunge, deciding to commit yourself to fixing the problem.

6. Tests, Allies, Enemies
You try different things to address the issue (tests), encountering setbacks along the way. Realizing the immensity of the problem, you may recruit some help (allies).

7. Approach to the Inmost Cave
You prepare to tackle the problem headlong. Hopefully, this will go well.

8. Ordeal
This problem is much tougher than it seemed, but you've had a breakthrough. All those past failed attempts have taught you a possible way to solve the problem.

9. Reward
Knowledge is its own reward, and that breakthrough is the key to solving the problem. Now, to implement it…

10. The Road Back
The breakthrough works! Now to apply it on a larger scale, which will take some effort. Done and done – well, almost done.

11. Resurrection
You've learned you really can do it, which lends a renewed sense of self. You've grown as a result of all that work. Now, it's time to…

12. Return with the Elixir
You've solved the problem. Let's celebrate and spread the word! You hero, you.

As long as people have problems and life-altering decisions to make, the Hero's Journey provides a relatable way to teach problem-solving techniques through watching them play out before our eyes. And, because the lesson being taught was presented in a fun, entertaining way, this increases the likelihood that the lesson will be passed down to future generations as well.

Working with the Hero's Journey to structure a film, there are a couple considerations to take into account.

Unlike some story structures, this one doesn't have specific times or places these events occur. Although the stages suggest an order to story events, they don't have to appear in this order. You can move them around in the story if makes more sense to do so. These beats are more about their presence, rather than their placement. That said, overlaying the Hero's Journey onto a basic three-act film structure, we can see the approximate placement of the stages in a movie.

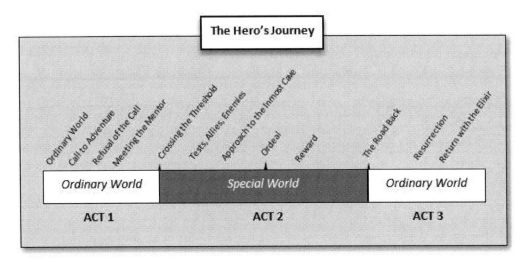

The act breaks do have corresponding stages. For myth-based stories, Crossing the Threshold marks the end of Act 1 and the beginning of Act 2 as the hero departs on the journey to address the problem they face. The midpoint of a film is reflected in the Ordeal, a moment that shifts the direction of the story. Act 3 is kicked off by the hero's attempt to get the elixir back to the Ordinary World. Notice that each of the beats occurring at major act breaks are driven by the actions of the hero.

The specific purpose of this structure is to create mythological heroes, characters who are larger than life; however, that's not its only use. As a plot structure, the Hero's Journey can be modified to fit any story that sends your characters off on an adventure to solve a major problem.

Using the Hero's Journey to analyze, we can see if a film is structured mythologically, and if applicable, how the filmmaker modified or interpreted the stages.

Similar to our last structural analysis, you'll pick a movie to analyze, and I'll pick one. You'll then have the opportunity to analyze the same movie I picked to compare our results. Unlike last time, you pick the first movie to analyze. The one I picked will come last. Each section and stage will count as a rep.

SET 1: The Hero's Analysis   CRAFT   Total Reps: 15

Using a major Hollywood film from the last 40 years, complete the analysis below. Feel free to choose any film from this era, just be aware that the structural paradigm we're studying may be more challenging to identify in smaller, independent films. Remember, the purpose of this analysis is to explore how myth-based structure manifests or is modified in modern works. Also, be aware you may choose a film that doesn't use this approach to storytelling or only uses part of it. All of this is valuable information in how the particular film you chose was built. <u>Each section and stage counts as a rep.</u>

Myth–Based Structural Analysis:
The Hero's Journey

Title: _____

Logline/Concept:

```
┌─────────────────────────────────────────────────┐
│                                                 │
│                                                 │
│                                                 │
│                                                 │
└─────────────────────────────────────────────────┘
```

What problem must the hero solve in this movie?

Is there evidence of a theme or lesson the movie intends to impart, and if so, what is it?

Archetypes

List and briefly describe the archetypes present in the film, if any. Remember, a character can be more than one archetype, depending on the needs of the story.

Hero: _____
Describe:

Shadow: _____
Describe

Herald: _____
Describe:

Shapeshifter: _____
Describe:

Trickster: _____
Describe:

Mentor: _____
Describe:

Threshold Guardian: _____
Describe:

Examine the relationship between Hero and Shadow. How are these characters similar?

How do they differ?

Sticking with the Hero and Shadow...

What are the goals of each of these characters? You may have explored these when describing the similarities on the previous page, but if not, list the goals here:

Hero's Goal: Shadow's Goal:

What conflicts arise between these characters from the pursuit of these goals?

Examining the conflicts, goals and relationship between the Hero and Shadow, how do these reflect the theme or lesson of the film (if applicable)?

Just for fun, let's see if your Hero has any of the Ancient Greek Hero qualities.

Ancient Greek Hero Attributes:

Check all that apply:

- ○ Hero's Mother is Royal Virgin
- ○ Hero's Father is the Real King
- ○ Father is Related to Mother
- ○ Unusual Conception
- ○ Child of a God
- ○ Attempt to be Killed Early in Life
- ○ Spirited Away from Homeland
- ○ Reared by Foster Parents
- ○ Told Nothing of Childhood
- ○ Returns Home upon Adulthood

- ○ Victory over a King or Beast
- ○ Marry a Princess/Prince
- ○ Become King
- ○ Prescribe Laws
- ○ Reign Uneventfully
- ○ Loses Favor with Gods/Subjects
- ○ Driven from Throne
- ○ Meet a Mysterious Death
- ○ Die at the Top of a Hill
- ○ Not Succeeded by Children

TOTAL: _____/20

Based on your findings, is the film utilizing aspects of Ancient Greek Hero Design?

The Journey

Stage 1: The Ordinary World
Most stories start off in the regular world of the hero. It's just another ordinary day. The hero doesn't yet know his/her world is threatened.

When we first meet the hero, what are they doing?

Is this a typical day in the life of the hero?
If so, how?

Stage 2: The Call to Adventure
In this stage, the hero discovers there's a problem in the world or is invited to join an adventure. Here, typically, the hero is made aware that the world is out of balance. Something in the hero's world is not right, and the hero will spend the rest of the movie attempting to fix it. In this stage we often discover what the hero's goal is.

What problem or adventure is presented to the hero?

How does the hero find out about this problem? (In other words, who or what makes the hero aware that there's an issue that needs to be addressed?)

The character archetype or device that makes a hero aware of a problem is known as a Herald. Who (or what) is the Herald in this stage? This may be same character you listed in the archetypes section.

_____

What goal, if any, is the hero presented with in this stage?

Stage 3: Refusal of the Call

Often a hero doesn't want to do anything about the problem, preferring to stay in the comfort of the Ordinary World. Let someone else fix things. The refusal is often based in fear. The hero knows it's going to be a dangerous journey and is afraid. In many movies, this moment is very fast. Almost unnoticeable. Watch for variations on a typical refusal. A common variation is to have other characters refuse the call.

How does the hero react upon receiving the Call to Adventure? Does your hero hesitate to fix the problem or join the adventure?

What decision does your hero make at this point?

Who, if anyone, helps the hero make this decision?

Stage 4: Meeting the Mentor

Once the hero encounters a problem, often a mentor is needed to prepare the hero to face the unknown (the Special World). Often the mentor character explains how the Special World works. Perhaps the Mentor has been there before, when they were younger. Sometimes the Mentor will give the hero '<u>magical</u>' <u>items</u> to help the hero on the adventure. A magical item in this instance can be anything that the hero can take on the journey that will be of assistance.

Does your hero meet someone who teaches or provides advice about the journey to come?

Who is this person? _____

Has this character been to the Special World before?

What training, if any, does the mentor provide?

What, if anything, does this person give to the hero?

Stage 5: Crossing the First Threshold

In this stage, the hero enters the Special World. The hero has decided to do something to fix the problem presented earlier in the film, and now begins the journey to solve this problem. This is typically the point in the story where the adventure gets underway. Often this moment marks the end of the First Act and the beginning of Act 2.

In many films, there will be a scene taking place in a bar or restaurant. Some sort of public meeting place. It's a crossroads where all sorts of people meet. A good place to pick up information.

What is the Special World in your movie?

How is the Special World different than the Ordinary World the hero is used to?

Is there a restaurant/eating/bar scene that occurs at or near the moment the hero enters the Special World?
If so, describe this scene:

Stage 6: Tests, Allies and Enemies

Now that the hero is in the Special World, they may meet Allies (friends to help the hero) and enemies (antagonists). The hero's skills are also tested throughout this stage. The hero often fails these early tests and must continue learning and growing to ultimately succeed.

If your Hero picks up any allies, list them here:

What enemies does your hero encounter?

Does your hero try to do something (perhaps to fix the problem presented earlier in the film) and fail miserably?

If so, what is the outcome of this attempt? Does the hero learn anything as a result of this failure?

Does the Hero continue with the original plan to solve the problem?

Stage 7: Approach to the Inmost Cave

In this stage the hero comes to the edge of a dangerous place. In fact, this is typically the MOST DANGEROUS PLACE in the Special World. Often it's the headquarters or stronghold of the hero's greatest enemy. Because of the danger, the hero often must make some final preparations before entering. Located somewhere in this place is the ELIXIR. This is the object of the hero's quest. It's what the hero seeks to solve the problem presented earlier in the film.

Does the hero go to the enemy's stronghold?

If so, why?

What preparations does the hero make before entering?

How will entering this place help the hero achieve their goal?

Stage 8: The Ordeal

This is a supreme test for the hero. Here the hero often confronts their greatest fear and is brought to the brink of death/defeat. This may not be the very end of the story, but it's the part where the hero confronts the enemy on the enemy's turf. Often the hero's values are tested in this stage as well.

What ordeal does your hero face near the midpoint of the film?

What happens to your hero as a result of this confrontation?

Does the hero take something away from the enemy?
If so, is this 'something' the elixir?

If present, describe the elixir and how it's supposed to 'fix' the Ordinary World:

Does the hero gain an insight or learn some crucial bit of information about the antagonist that may help them defeat this character later?

Does the hero conceive of a new approach or plan to achieve their goal after this encounter? If so, please describe what this is:

Stage 9: Reward (Seizing the Sword)
Having survived the Ordeal, the hero escapes the villain and takes possession of the treasure the villain once controlled. Sometimes this treasure is knowledge. Other times it's something physical. Usually the villain hasn't been destroyed at this point, just beaten temporarily.

How does the antagonist react to this confrontation with the Hero?

What plan does the villain devise to get back at the hero/get the elixir back?

Stage 10: The Road Back
Here the hero deals with the consequences of confronting the dark forces of the Ordeal. If the Ordeal did not destroy the villain, usually they come raging back at the hero, desperate to regain what the hero has taken. In this stage, the hero has angered the villain, who now brings EVERYTHING they have to bear down on the hero in a fit of rage. Sometimes this stage is omitted in modern films, but you still see various forms of it.

Is there a chase scene toward the end of the second act of the film?

Is the hero being pursued by the villain?

One point of the Road Back is to test and see if the lessons the hero learned as a result of the Ordeal were truly learned. <u>Here the hero's values are tested one last time</u>, and <u>the hero will be tempted to go back to the way they were before the journey began</u>.

What opportunity, if any, does the hero face to tempt them to go back to their old ways?

How is this tempting to the hero?

If applicable, who presents this tempting offer to the hero?

What happens as a result of this tempting moment? What does the hero realize?

Stage 11: Resurrection
Having survived the Ordeal and the temptations/trials of the Road Back, the hero is reborn. This is a second death/rebirth moment, usually at the hands of the Shadow.

In the final conflict with the villain, does the hero appear to be defeated and then finally win?

Briefly describe this scene:

Once reborn, the hero can now re-enter the Ordinary World with the elixir and save it. However, prior to this, a hero must be cleansed and purified before returning. As a result, often this stage involves WATER.

Is water (or some other form of liquid) present in this scene?   If so, describe it.

Is there some form of cleansing present?   If so, describe it.

In the final confrontation between Shadow and Hero, how does the Hero finally defeat the Shadow?

Does this action somehow reflect something the hero learned as a result of the journey?
If so, what did the hero learn to produce this result?

During which stage of the journey, did the hero learn this lesson?
and, does this lesson demonstrate how the hero has changed?

Stage 12: Return with the Elixir
In this stage, the hero returns to the Ordinary World with the something from the Special World – the elixir. Remember, an elixir can be anything, but typically it's the object that will 'fix' the Ordinary World and return it to normal once again.

What does the hero bring back from the Special World?

How does the thing the hero brings back 'fix' the Ordinary World?

Has the hero changed somehow as a result of the journey? If so, please describe.

Does this change, if present, reflect the theme of the film? If so, how?

Obviously, results vary depending on the film chosen. Sometimes, you may find bits and pieces of the Hero's Journey sprinkled throughout the film. Sometimes, there appears to be a more conscious application of this structural paradigm. And, of course, sometimes the filmmaker isn't utilizing this approach at all. But, even in films that appear to use different structures, it's amazing how often elements of the Hero's Journey appear, attributable perhaps to the collective consciousness aspects of storytelling proposed by Campbell. Or, perhaps it's the problem-solving process of the structure that lends it such universal applications. Either way, the Hero's Journey is as relevant today as it was to ancient storytellers – especially if you wish to create heroes that are larger than life, the stuff of legends, because this is exactly what the Hero's Journey is built to do. Saving the world, defeating evil, these are the byproducts of this structure. At its heart, this approach to storytelling is designed to do one thing: create mythological heroes – but not just an Achilles or a Hercules; it can apply to more contemporary stories as well. To explore this, let's apply the Hero's Journey to a modern movie, one in which the heroes weren't born on Mount Olympus…

SET 2: Dueling Structures   CRAFT   Total Reps: 15

Similar to our approach to the 8-turn analysis from earlier, because I'm picking the movie to analyze, you'll once again have a choice. Feel free to analyze the film yourself prior to reading my analysis, or you can simply read the analysis of the film.

As before, you'll have a blank analysis form first, followed by a completed one.
As for the movie we'll analyze…

Since our approach is like our 8-turn analysis of *Twister*, let's stick with that film.

Hero's Journey Analysis of *Twister*

Yep, still the 1996 tornado movie starring Helen Hunt and Bill Paxton.

For this analysis, you'll need the following:

- *Twister*, of course ☺
- ✓ This book
- The writing implement of your choice
- Popcorn (still optional)

Once again you have two options:

Option 1: Analyze the movie yourself, then compare your analysis to mine, which will be on the ensuing pages.

Option 2: Watch the movie and follow along with analysis provided.

Your call. However, if you choose Option 1, don't peek at the completed analysis until after you're done! And, as before, if you choose Option 2, feel free to use the blank form to analyze a different film.   As before, each section and stage is a rep.

Myth–Based Structural Analysis:
The Hero's Journey in *Twister*
(or the Movie of Your Choice)

Title: _____

Logline/Concept:

```
┌────────────────────────────────────────────────────┐
│                                                    │
│                                                    │
│                                                    │
│                                                    │
└────────────────────────────────────────────────────┘
```

What problem must the hero solve in this movie?

Is there evidence of a theme or lesson the movie intends to impart, and if so, what is it?

Archetypes
List and briefly describe the archetypes present in the film, if any. Remember, a character can be more than one archetype, depending on the needs of the story.

Hero: _____
Describe:

Shadow: _____
Describe

Herald: _____
Describe:

Shapeshifter: _____
Describe:

Trickster: _____
Describe:

Mentor: _____
Describe:

Threshold Guardian: _____
Describe:

Examine the relationship between Hero and Shadow. How are these characters similar?

How do they differ?

Sticking with the Hero and Shadow…

What are the goals of each of these characters? You may have explored these when describing the similarities on the previous page, but if not, list the goals here:

    Hero's Goal: **Shadow's Goal:**

What conflicts arise between these characters from the pursuit of these goals?

Examining the conflicts, goals and relationship between the Hero and Shadow, how do these reflect the theme or lesson of the film (if applicable)?

Just for fun, let's see if your Hero has any of the Ancient Greek Hero qualities.

Ancient Greek Hero Attributes:

Check all that apply:

- ○ Hero's Mother is Royal Virgin
- ○ Hero's Father is the Real King
- ○ Father is Related to Mother
- ○ Unusual Conception
- ○ Child of a God
- ○ Attempt to be Killed Early in Life
- ○ Spirited Away from Homeland
- ○ Reared by Foster Parents
- ○ Told Nothing of Childhood
- ○ Returns Home upon Adulthood

- ○ Victory over a King or Beast
- ○ Marry a Princess/Prince
- ○ Become King
- ○ Prescribe Laws
- ○ Reign Uneventfully
- ○ Loses Favor with Gods/Subjects
- ○ Driven from Throne
- ○ Meet a Mysterious Death
- ○ Die at the Top of a Hill
- ○ Not Succeeded by Children

TOTAL: _____/20

Based on your findings, is the film utilizing aspects of Ancient Greek Hero Design?

The Journey

Stage 1: The Ordinary World
Most stories start off in the regular world of the hero. It's just another ordinary day. The hero doesn't yet know his/her world is threatened.

When we first meet the hero, what are they doing?

**Is this a typical day in the life of the hero?
If so, how?**

Stage 2: The Call to Adventure

In this stage, the hero discovers there's a problem in the world or is invited to join an adventure. Here, typically, the hero is made aware that the world is out of balance. Something in the hero's world is not right, and the hero will spend the rest of the movie attempting to fix it. In this stage we often discover what the hero's goal is.

What problem or adventure is presented to the hero?

How does the hero find out about this problem? (In other words, who or what makes the hero aware that there's an issue that needs to be addressed?)

The character archetype or device that makes a hero aware of a problem is known as a Herald. Who (or what) is the Herald in this stage? Once again, this may be same character you listed in the archetypes section.

_____

What goal, if any, is the hero presented with in this stage?

Stage 3: Refusal of the Call

Often a hero doesn't want to do anything about the problem, preferring to stay in the comfort of the Ordinary World. Let someone else fix things. The refusal is often based in fear. The hero knows it's going to be a dangerous journey and is afraid. In many movies, this moment is very fast. Almost unnoticeable. Watch for variations on a typical refusal.

How does the hero react upon receiving the Call to Adventure? Does your hero hesitate to fix the problem or join the adventure?

What decision does your hero make at this point?

Who, if anyone, helps the hero make this decision?

Stage 4: Meeting the Mentor

Once the hero encounters a problem, often a mentor is needed to prepare the hero to face the unknown (the Special World). Often the mentor character explains how the Special World works. Perhaps the Mentor has been there before, when they were younger. Sometimes the Mentor will give the hero 'magical' items to help the hero on the adventure. A magical item in this instance can be anything that the hero can take on the journey that will be of assistance.

Does your hero meet someone who teaches or provides advice about the journey to come?

Who is this person? _____

Has this character been to the Special World before?

What training, if any, does the mentor provide?

What does this person give to the hero?

Stage 5: Crossing the First Threshold

In this stage, the hero enters the Special World. The hero has decided to do something to fix the problem presented earlier in the film, and now begins the journey to solve this problem. This is typically the point in the story where the adventure gets underway. Often this moment marks the end of the First Act and the beginning of Act 2.

In many films, there will be a scene taking place in a bar or restaurant. Some sort of public meeting place. It's a crossroads where all sorts of people meet. A good place to pick up information.

What is the Special World in your movie?

How is the Special World different than the Ordinary World the hero is used to?

Is there a restaurant/eating/bar scene that occurs at or near the moment the hero enters the Special World?
If so, describe this scene:

Stage 6: Tests, Allies and Enemies
Now that the hero is in the Special World, they may meet Allies (friends to help the hero) and enemies (antagonists). The hero's skills are also tested throughout this stage. The hero often fails these early tests and must continue learning and growing to ultimately succeed.

If your Hero picks up any allies, list them here:

What enemies does your hero encounter?

Does your hero try to do something (perhaps to fix the problem presented earlier in the film) and fail miserably?

If so, what is the outcome of this attempt? Does the hero learn anything as a result of this failure?

Does the Hero continue with the original plan to solve the problem?

Stage 7: Approach to the Inmost Cave
In this stage the hero comes to the edge of a dangerous place. In fact, this is typically the MOST DANGEROUS SPOT in the Special World. Often it's the headquarters or stronghold of the hero's greatest enemy. Because of the danger, the hero often must make some final preparations before entering. Located somewhere in this place is the ELIXIR. This is the object of the hero's quest. It's what the hero seeks to solve the problem presented earlier in the film.

Does the hero go to the enemy's stronghold?

If so, why?

What preparations does the hero make before entering?

How will entering this place help the hero achieve their goal?

Stage 8: The Ordeal
This is a supreme test for the hero. Here the hero often confronts their greatest fear and is brought to the brink of death/defeat. This may not be the very end of the story, but it's the part where the hero confronts the enemy on the enemy's turf. Often the hero's values are tested in this stage as well.

What ordeal does your hero face near the midpoint of the film?

What happens to your hero as a result of this confrontation?

Does the hero take something away from the enemy?
If so, is this 'something' the elixir?

If present, describe the elixir and how it's supposed to 'fix' the Ordinary World:

Does the hero gain an insight or learn some crucial bit of information about the antagonist that may help them defeat this character later?

Does the hero conceive of a new approach or plan to achieve their goal after this encounter? If so, please describe what this is:

Stage 9: Reward (Seizing the Sword)
Having survived the Ordeal, the hero escapes the villain and takes possession of the treasure the villain once controlled. Sometimes this treasure is knowledge. Other times it's something physical. Usually the villain hasn't been destroyed at this point, just beaten temporarily.

How does the antagonist react to this confrontation with the Hero?

What plan does the villain come up with to get back at the hero/get the elixir back?

Stage 10: The Road Back

Here the hero deals with the consequences of confronting the dark forces of the Ordeal. If the Ordeal did not destroy the villain, usually they come raging back at the hero, desperate to regain what the hero has taken. In this stage, the hero has angered the villain, who now brings EVERYTHING they have to bear down on the hero in a fit of rage. Sometimes this stage is omitted in modern films, but you still see various forms of it.

Is there a chase scene toward the end of the second act of the film?

Is the hero being pursued by the villain?

One point of the Road Back is to test and see if the lessons the hero learned as a result of the Ordeal were truly learned. <u>Here the hero's values are tested one last time</u>, and <u>the hero will be tempted to go back to the way they were before the journey began</u>.

What opportunity, if any, does the hero face to tempt them to go back to their old ways?

How is this tempting to the hero?

If applicable, who presents this tempting offer to the hero?

What happens as a result of this tempting moment? What does the hero realize?

Stage 11: Resurrection

Having survived the Ordeal, and the temptations and trials of the Road Back, the hero is reborn. This is a second death/rebirth moment, usually at the hands of the Shadow.

In the final conflict with the villain, does the hero appear to be defeated and then finally win?

Briefly describe this scene:

Once reborn, the hero can now re-enter the Ordinary World with the elixir and save it. However, prior to this, a hero must be cleansed and purified before returning. As a result, often this stage involves WATER.

Is water (or some other form of liquid) present in this scene?   If so, describe it.

Is there some form of cleansing present?   If so, describe it.

In the final confrontation between Shadow and Hero, how does the Hero finally defeat the Shadow?

Does this action somehow reflect something the hero learned as a result of the journey?
If so, what did the hero learn to produce this result?

During which stage of the journey, did the hero learn this lesson?
and, does this lesson demonstrate how the hero has changed?

Stage 12: Return with the Elixir
In this stage, the hero returns to the Ordinary World with the something from the Special World – the elixir. Remember, an elixir can be anything, but typically it's the object that will 'fix' the Ordinary World and return it to normal once again.

What does the hero bring back from the Special World?

How does the thing the hero brings back 'fix' the Ordinary World?

Has the hero changed somehow as a result of the journey? If so, please describe.

Does this change, if present, reflect the theme of the film? If so, how?

Turn the page to see my analysis of *Twister*.

Myth–Based Structural Analysis:
The Hero's Journey in *Twister*

Title: *Twister*

Logline/Concept:

> A divorcing couple must reconcile their differences to implement a groundbreaking system to study tornadoes.

What problem must the hero solve in this movie? Jo must overcome her obsession with the death of her father to reconcile her differences with Bill in order to place a Dorothy device into a tornado.

Is there evidence of a theme or lesson the movie intends to impart, and if so, what is it? Not a strong one, but certainly the idea of overcoming the past to work together seems to be present. Another theme the movie explores is instinct versus science. Bill represents the old, instinctual ways. Jonas represents technology.

Archetypes
List and briefly describe the archetypes present in the film, if any. Remember, a character can be more than one archetype, depending on the needs of the story.

Hero: Jo (Helen Hunt)
Describe:
Obsessed with tornadoes since the childhood death of her father during an F-5 tornado. Professor, doctor, head of a team of stormchasers.

Shadow: Jonas (Cary Elwes)
Describe:
Rival stormchaser, who copied Jo and Bill's Dorothy device for studying tornadoes. He's in it for the money and personal glory, rather than science and helping others.

Herald: Haynes (Wendle Josepher)
Describe:
She's the member of Jo's team who announces there's a tornado to be chased in the scene just after the beat where Jo and Bill explain the Dorothy device to Melissa. Bill and Jonas also serve herald functions. Bill announces the call to Jo in regards to getting divorced. Jonas indirectly issues a call to Bill in regards to a competition to see who can implant their Dorothy device first.

Shapeshifter: Jonas (Cary Elwes)
Describe:
Although the shapeshifting event occurs prior to the start of the film, because Jonas was described as being part of the hero's team before he went out to get corporate sponsors, this is how he fits the archetype. By switching sides and betraying the hero's team, he serves the shapeshifter function.

Trickster: Dusty (Philip Seymour Hoffman)
Describe:
Dusty consistently provides comic relief throughout the film befitting the trickster archetype. The clownish aspect is reinforced by his colorful costuming, which while muted, is still more colorful than the rest of the team, like a muted clown outfit.

Mentor: Jo, Bill (Bill Paxton) and Aunt Meg (Lois Smith)
Describe:
Jo and Bill serve as mentors to Melissa, teaching her about the Dorothy device. Although Jo is the hero, by teaching Melissa about Dorothy, Jo and Bill serve the mentor story functions by teaching the audience how the device works. They've also been to the special world of stormchasing, and Melissa has not. Aunt Meg serves as a mentor to Jo later in the film. When Jo and the team visit Aunt Meg, she gives some relationship advice to Jo, serving as a mentor. Aunt Meg's art turns out to be an elixir of sorts, providing Jo with the key she needs to make Dorothy fly.

Threshold Guardian: Melissa (Jami Gertz) and Jonas
Describe:
This one's tricky, but in terms of blocking the threshold to the special world of stormchasing, Jonas shows up just as the team embarks and drives Bill off the road, providing an obstacle to overcome before the heroes can enter the special world. For the relationship storyline, Melissa is a threshold guardian blocking Jo and Bill from getting back together.

Examine the relationship between Hero and Shadow. How are these characters similar? Both are stormchasers and doctors trying to study tornadoes.

How do they differ? Jo is motivated by a desire to help others (and her obsession.) Jonas is motivated by a desire to help himself. Jo's team is a ragtag affair, poorly funded and in it for the science. Jonas is well-funded through corporate sponsorship and is in it for profit.

Sticking with the Hero and Shadow...

What are the goals of each of these characters? You may have explored these when describing the similarities on the previous page, but if not, list them here:

Hero's Goal: Implant Dorothy device   **Shadow's Goal:**   Implant Dorothy rip-off

What conflicts arise between these characters from the pursuit of these goals?
Each team races to be the first to place their devices into a tornado.

Examining the conflicts, goals and relationship between the Hero and Shadow, how do these reflect the theme or lesson of the film (if applicable)?
Jonas has no instincts and relies on technology to succeed. Jo and Bill rely on instinct. These two approaches play out in how each team tries to tackle the problem.

Ancient Greek Hero Attributes for Jo

Check all that apply:

○	Hero's Mother is Royal Virgin	○	Victory over a King or Beast
○	Hero's Father is the Real King	✓	Marry a Princess/Prince
○	Father is Related to Mother	✓	Become King
○	Unusual Conception	○	Prescribe Laws
○	Child of a God	○	Reign Uneventfully
✓	Attempt to be Killed Early in Life	○	Loses Favor with Gods/Subjects
✓	Spirited Away from Homeland	○	Driven from Throne
✓	Reared by Foster Parents	○	Meet a Mysterious Death
○	Told Nothing of Childhood	○	Die at the Top of a Hill
✓	Returns Home upon Adulthood	○	Not Succeeded by Children

TOTAL: __6__/20

Based on your findings, is the film utilizing aspects of Ancient Greek Hero Design?
A bit in Jo's origin story. While we don't see the rest of her childhood, after the hook, the only member of Jo's family we see is an aunt (an interpretation of foster parents.)

The Journey

Stage 1: The Ordinary World
Most stories start off in the regular world of the hero. It's just another ordinary day.

When we first meet the hero, what are they doing?
Remember, the hook is a pre-story beat, so once the story starts, we meet Jo, all grown up, and out in the field leading her team of stormchasers. Just another day in her life.

Is this a typical day in the life of the hero? *Yes*
If so, how? *Presumably, Jo spends most of her time chasing storms.*

Stage 2: The Call to Adventure
In this stage, the hero discovers there's a problem in the world or is invited to join an adventure. Here, we often discover what the hero's goal is.

What problem or adventure is presented to the hero?
A couple, depending on the interpretation. For the divorcing couple storyline, Bill announces the call to Jo – sign the divorce papers so we can move on.

Haynes announces the call to chase storms.

Bill receives another call from Jonas – it's now a race to see who can get the devices planted first.

How does the hero find out about this problem? (In other words, who or what makes the hero aware that there's an issue that needs to be addressed?)

Haynes for journeying to the special world of stormchasing. Bill for the special world of life apart.

The character archetype or device that makes a hero aware of a problem is known as a Herald. Who (or what) is the Herald in this stage (may be same character you listed in the archetypes section.)
Bill and Haynes.

What goal, if any, is the hero presented with in this stage?
Chase storms. Get divorced.

Stage 3: Refusal of the Call
Often a hero doesn't want to do anything about the problem, preferring to stay in the comfort of the Ordinary World.

How does the hero react upon receiving the Call to Adventure? Does your hero hesitate to fix the problem or join the adventure?
Both Jo and Bill refuse their calls. Jo refuses to sign the divorce papers. Bill initially declines to chase the storm after Haynes issues the call.

What decision does your hero make at this point?
Jo stalls on signing the papers and deflects Bill's attempts to get her to do so. She decides to go meet Melissa, rather than sign. Bill hesitates to join the stormchasing adventure, but realizes Jo hasn't signed the papers. So, he follows them.
Bill answers the call issued by Jonas, and decides to join the adventure after all.

Who, if anyone, helps the hero make this decision? *No one. Although, you could make a case that Jonas' arrogance helps Bill make his decision.*

Stage 4: Meeting the Mentor
Once the hero encounters a problem, often a mentor is needed to prepare the hero to face the unknown (the Special World). Often the mentor character explains how the Special World works.

Does your hero meet someone who teaches or provides advice about the journey to come? *Melissa does, as Jo and Bill teach her about stormchasing. Jo meets Aunt Meg, who offers relationship advice.*

Who is this person? *Jo, Bill, Aunt Meg*

Has this character been to the Special World before? *Yes for Jo and Bill. Unknown for Aunt Meg.*

What training, if any, does the mentor provide?
Jo and Bill demonstrate the Dorothy device, teaching Melissa (and the audience) how it works. Aunt Meg doesn't provide training, but does offer some advice.

What does this person give to the hero? *Nothing tangible.*

Special Note: as a mentor, Aunt Meg shows up after we've entered the Special World. *The Wizard of Oz* uses a similar approach, with Dorothy meeting Glenda the Good Witch, who provides magical equipment and advice after Dorothy has crossed the threshold into Oz.

Stage 5: Crossing the First Threshold
In this stage, the hero enters the Special World. This is typically the point in the story where the adventure gets underway. Often this moment marks the end of the First Act and the beginning of Act 2.

What is the Special World in your movie? *Stormchasing is the main one.*

How is the Special World different than the Ordinary World the hero is used to?
Technically it's not for Jo, so this beat is shifted to Melissa. She's never been stormchasing before.

Is there a restaurant/eating/bar scene that occurs at or near the moment the hero enters the Special World? *Yes.*
If so, describe this scene:
The team stops off at a diner shortly after embarking on the adventure.

Stage 6: Tests, Allies and Enemies
Now that the hero is in the Special World, they may meet Allies (friends to help the hero) and enemies (antagonists). The hero's skills are also tested throughout this stage. The hero often fails these early tests and must continue learning and growing to ultimately succeed.

If your Hero picks up any allies, list them here:
The stormchasing team. Obviously this existed prior to the adventure, but they are the allies.

What enemies does your hero encounter?
Jonas and his team. Oh, and a few tornadoes.

Does your hero try to do something (perhaps to fix the problem presented earlier in the film) and fail miserably?
Yes, they try to implant a few Dorothy devices and fail each time.

If so, what is the outcome of this attempt? Does the hero learn anything as a result of this failure?
They discover Dorothy is too light to work as they envisioned. While this occurs later in the film, it serves this function. It's also alluded to in the hero's first attempt as the tornado picks up the truck and tosses it aside. Also, illustrated in the first attempt is Jo's FLAW (her obsession with tornadoes.) While the hero doesn't learn from this, the audience does – seeing how Jo's obsession could get her killed. This attempt also highlights the issue in the relationship story line.

Does the Hero continue with the original plan to solve the problem? *Yes.*

Stage 7: Approach to the Inmost Cave
In this stage the hero comes to the edge of a dangerous place. Because of the danger, the hero often must make some final preparations before entering. Located somewhere in this place is the ELIXIR.

Does the hero go to the enemy's stronghold? *The film modifies this beat, blending literal and metaphoric applications of this story function.*

When Jo and Bill enter a tornado, this is the most dangerous place in the special world of stormchasing. However, you could make a case that entering Aunt Meg's collapsing house after it was hit by a tornado, is another inmost cave. It certainly looks like a cave. Aunt Meg in this case is the elixir.

You could also make a case for the ambulance scene where Jo tends to Aunt Meg. Jo doesn't know how to solve the issue and appears to give up the chase. Aunt Meg convinces her of the need to keep trying (an elixir). This moment is followed immediately by Jo gaining a valuable insight by looking at one of Aunt Meg's tornado sculptures (yet another elixir.)

If so, why? *To implant Dorothy/to save Aunt Meg.*

What preparations does the hero make before entering?
If we consider the preparations made after Jo's insight, the team cuts up cans and makes propellers for the Dorothy sensors before entering the next tornado.

How will entering this place help the hero achieve their goal?
By entering the tornado, the heroes will be able to gain information on how tornado's work, enabling them to design an early warning system to help people.

Stage 8: The Ordeal
A supreme test for the hero. Here the hero often confronts their greatest fear and is brought to the brink of death/defeat. Often the hero's values are tested in this stage.

What ordeal does your hero face near the midpoint of the film?
This beat occurs after Jo and Bill fail to implant the Dorothy device in the 'ghost' tornado (the one that keeps disappearing on them.) In the aftermath, Jo and Bill argue. Bill tells Jo she needs to let go of her past and the death of her dad, or she'll wind up killing herself. Bill confesses he's still in love with Jo. Melissa overhears this.

What happens to your hero as a result of this confrontation?
Jo refuses to let go of her past at this point, and in the subsequent scene at the drive-in theater, signs the divorce papers.

Does the hero take something away from the enemy? *Not really. Although, if we want to get interpretive with this, you could say that saving Aunt Meg keeps the tornado from taking her (as it did with Jo's dad earlier in the film.)*

If so, is this 'something' the elixir? *Yes, in a symbolic sense. The knowledge Jo gleans from this beat will eventually serve as an elixir.*

If present, describe the elixir and how it's supposed to 'fix' the Ordinary World:
The data from Dorothy will enable the hero's to design a better warning system, 'fixing' the Ordinary World.

Does the hero gain an insight or learn some crucial bit of information about the antagonist that may help them defeat this character later?
Once again, if we go with Jo gaining an insight, then yes.

Does the hero conceive of a new approach or plan to achieve their goal after this encounter? If so, please describe what this is:
This is the propeller plan. Then, after another failed attempt, the new plan is to drive their truck with Dorothy attached to give the pack enough weight to operate the way it was intended.

Stage 9: Reward (Seizing the Sword)
Having survived the Ordeal, the hero escapes the villain and takes possession of the treasure the villain once controlled. Sometimes this treasure is knowledge. Other times it's something physical. Usually the villain hasn't been destroyed at this point, just beaten temporarily.

How does the antagonist react to this confrontation with the Hero?
If we consider a tornado as antagonist, it doesn't react. However, the film accounts for this by making the last tornado an F-5, the strongest one on the scale. In a metaphoric way, this is the antagonist sending everything it has against the heroes.

Considering Jonas as the antagonist, he keeps doing the same things.

What plan does the villain come up with to get back at the hero/get the elixir back?
Not really applicable.

Stage 10: The Road Back

Here the hero deals with the consequences of confronting the dark forces of the Ordeal. If the Ordeal did not destroy the villain, usually they come raging back at the hero, desperate to regain what the hero has taken. In this stage, the hero has angered the villain, who now brings EVERYTHING they have to bear down on the hero in a fit of rage.

Is there a chase scene toward the end of the second act of the film?
Yes. Tornados keep chasing our heroes. Jonas is lurking on the fringes as well, chasing tornadoes in an attempt to defeat Jo and Bill.

Is the hero being pursued by the villain?
Yes.

One point of the Road Back is to test and see if the lessons the hero learned as a result of the Ordeal were truly learned. <u>Here the hero's values are tested one last time</u>, and <u>the hero will be tempted to go back to the way they were before the journey began</u>.

What opportunity, if any, does the hero face to tempt them to go back to their old ways?
The movie presents some intriguing spins on this one. Jo is tempted to give up on Bill and implanting Dorothy. At the very end of the film, Jo and Bill are tempted to argue again (over who's in charge and who will analyze data). Will they go back to their old, argumentative ways? In this scene, Jo is also tempted to look at the sky by a member of the stormchasing team. Earlier in the film, she couldn't tear herself away from the sky. This time, she refuses the temptation, and instead kisses Bill.

How is this tempting to the hero?
Jo wants to be in charge. Studying the sky has been Jo's obsession since childhood, so an offer to look at it, is still a temptation.

If applicable, who presents this tempting offer to the hero?
Jo self-issues this one for the argument. A member of the team presents the other one.

What happens as a result of this tempting moment? What does the hero realize?
For the relationship, it's agreeing to disagree in a sense. A willingness to compromise, which, when Jo was in the throes of her obsession, would not have been possible. Same thing with the offer to check out the sky. Notice how both of these beats demonstrate that the hero has successfully overcome the flaw, which for Jo is obsession with storms.

Stage 11: Resurrection
Having survived the Ordeal, and the temptations and trials of the Road Back, the hero is reborn. This is a second death/rebirth moment, usually at the hands of the Shadow.

In the final conflict with the villain, does the hero appear to be defeated and then finally win?
Yes. In this case, it appears Jonas will be the first to implant a Dorothy device.

Briefly describe this scene:

Jonas races toward a tornado while Jo and Bill can only watch.

Once reborn, the hero can now re-enter the Ordinary World with the elixir and save it. However, prior to this, a hero must be cleansed and purified before returning. As a result, often this stage involves WATER.

Is water (or some other form of liquid) present in this scene?   If so, please describe.
Yes. At the very end of the film, Jo and Bill are being sprayed with water from a well.

Is there some form of cleansing present?   If so, please describe.
Yes, the water is cleaning off the muck from the tornado.

In the final confrontation between Shadow and Hero, how does the Hero finally defeat the Shadow?
With Jonas serving the shadow functions, the storm destroys him. Jo and Bill's instincts come into play as they attempt to warn Jonas that the tornado will shift and come after him. Jonas refuses to heed the warning (this is our shadow refusing to learn the lesson), which ultimately causes his demise.

Does this action somehow reflect something the hero learned as a result of the journey? Yes.

If so, what did the hero learn to produce this result?
To anchor the pack, and stop being so obsessed.

During which stage of the journey, does the hero learn this lesson?
This stage and stage 12.

Does this lesson demonstrate how the hero has changed?
Yes, when Jo is finally able to tear herself away from stormchasing to embrace her relationship with Bill.

Stage 12: Return with the Elixir

In this stage, the hero returns to the Ordinary World with the something from the Special World – the elixir. Remember, an elixir can be anything, but typically it's the object that will 'fix' the Ordinary World and return it to normal once again.

What does the hero bring back from the Special World?
Data on how tornadoes work.

How does the thing the hero brings back 'fix' the Ordinary World?
They'll be able to use the data to design an early warning system to give people more time to seek shelter when tornadoes strike.

Has the hero changed somehow as a result of the journey? If so, please describe.
Jo goes from being obsessed with tornadoes, which while driving her to excel, has also caused her marriage to fall apart to letting go of her obsession and healing her relationship with Bill.

Does this change, if present, reflect the theme of the film? If so, how?
Yes and no, depending on how we define the theme. Dealing with obsession is pretty standard fare for movie themes, and this one's no exception. While instinct versus technology comes into play a bit in the scene where Jonas is killed, this one feels more like the result of not letting go of obsession.

If you did your analysis before reading this one, how'd the two line up?

Hopefully, you found that analyzing mythic structure, particularly in a film with a contemporary setting, can be quite subjective. And yet, there it is.

Perhaps you found something else as well – especially considering this is the same movie in which we found another structure, in this case 8-turn. What we've stumbled upon is a pattern, one you'll find again and again in successful, well-crafted films:

> **Movies have more than one structure.**

A strong statement I suppose, and as with all things film, you'll find exceptions. Actually, correction: this approach IS the exception -- because with it, you have the framework to create exceptional films. Ones that resonate. Ones that last. And, ones that sell.

We'll explore how this system works in our next section, but for now I suppose it could use a name.

Hmm…

How 'bout we call it: Dual Structure Screenwriting.

Not exactly catchy, I realize, but there's something to be said for the understated utilitarian aspect. Makes it low key. Like a secret almost. And, while the name doesn't involve saving cats or any of that, I think you'll find it will save you something else – time.

And, who knows?

You may just find the Dual Structure approach to be the only one you'll ever need.

WORKOUT PROGRESS – CRAFT
Compile your workout totals for this unit.

EXERCISE	SKILL GROUP		TOTAL REPS	
	SET #	TYPE	ACTION	AVAILABLE	COMPLETED
The Hero's Analysis	1	Craft	Analysis	15	
Dueling Structures	2	Craft	Analysis	15	
			TOTAL REPS		

CRAFT — Total Reps + Bonus — 30

Dual Structure Screenwriting

What we observed in *Twister* is an example of our Dual Structure approach at work – two structures, working together, side by side, to tell a single, cohesive story. We've already examined how each structure works independently. Now, let's examine how they work together. Placing 8-turn structure alongside its mythological counterpart, we can see where these two structures interact.

8-Turn and Hero's Journey Structural Overlay

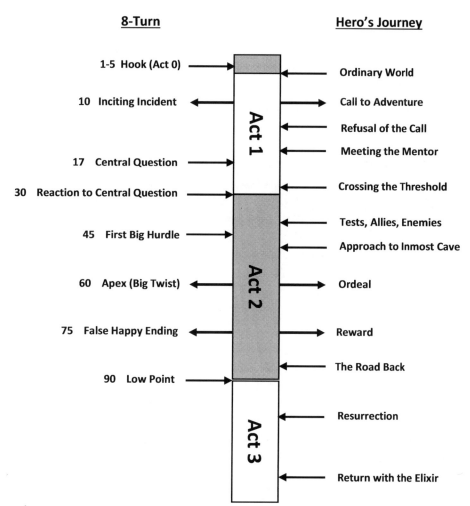

Remember:
Hero's Journey beats can occur in different places depending on the needs of the story.

167

From a narrative perspective, this structural overlay yields a story that flows something like this:

We begin with the *hook*, a pre-story beat designed to live up to its name and hook the audience into wanting to watch more. While this beat may contain story elements, the actual tale hasn't quite started yet.

We then see the *ordinary world* of the hero, where we learn about our main character and see what's at stake. The juxtaposition of ordinary world and hook should create anticipation for what's going to happen when these two story elements collide.

The *inciting incident* and *call to adventure* are similar both in intent and function. Each is designed to bring the main character into the story by making this person aware of a problem. Occasionally, for the inciting incident specifically, a subplot is launched here.

The next couple mythological story beats occur to highlight the adventure to come. The *refusal* plants a bit of doubt that our would-be hero can actually solve the challenge presented in the call. *Meeting the mentor* allows for the challenge to be further delineated for the audience, while our hero acquires information, skills and equipment necessary for the journey ahead. Because these beats explore the main issue facing the hero, you'll often find the *central question* being presented here.

This leads us to the first act break, which in both 8-Turn and the Hero's Journey, represents the hero's first attempt to solve the central question. Notice on the timeline these two beats are slightly staggered. This is to reflect the two differing storylines these structures organize. It also reflects the key difference in these approaches to storytelling.

The 8-Turn structure is a <u>character structure</u>, designed to explore a character's internal storyline and is based around the character's flaw. As such, it represents the 'need' a character must address to successfully solve the problem presented in the central question.

The Hero's Journey is a <u>plot structure</u>, used to organize the plot events the hero will encounter. It's primary purpose is to provide the 'want' storyline. So, our hero thinks getting the elixir will solve their problems, but in actuality, what the hero discovers through the pursuit of the elixir is that it's not enough. The problem is so difficult it will require the hero to address their own shortcomings (flaw) to prevail.

The slight staggering of these beats serves to highlight two different stories being presented to the audience. The 8-turn is the character's internal story, what they must do to fix themselves. The Hero's Journey is used to organize the external storyline, what the hero must do to fix the world. In this model, the plot serves as the motivation to finally address what's been eating at this character for a long time.

For flaw-based stories, in which a character must arc or change in order to succeed, you'll find this structural overlay to be a way to explore the character's internal world, while simultaneously showing the external, tangible events necessary to keep the audience engaged. In these stories, we may find the hero's actual journey launches at approximately 25 minutes into the movie with the *crossing of the threshold*, while the 8-turn equivalent (the *reaction to the central question*) maintains its hold on the film's 30-minute mark.

For stories in which the character does not have an internal flaw or wound to overcome, you may find the *reaction to the central question* and *threshold crossing* to be the same. Because there's no flaw to overcome, there's really no need for the 8-turn structure, so typically the story omits the overlay.

The next Hero's Journey sequence is our *tests, allies and enemies* phase, which builds to the *hurdle* beat in 8-turn, marking a major complication or test for our hero to overcome.

The *approach to the inmost cave* leads to an *ordeal* for our hero as they attempt to get the elixir. The ordeal and *apex* are closely related. Notice how the ordeal often marks a direct blow to the antagonist, which is reflected in the passive to active aspect of the apex as the hero takes the battle to the antagonist so to speak. The ordeal is so tough that our hero may realize the elixir is not enough to succeed. This realization is also a hallmark of the apex. However, at this point in the story, our reluctant hero may need a bit more convincing that the key to success really lies in changing themselves; after all, they haven't even had a chance to try the elixir. However, the victory here marks an upswing for the hero, leading to both the *False Happy Ending* and the *Reward*.

Our antagonist, now outraged, pursues the hero during the *road back*, bringing everything they have against the hero. The antagonist's renewed efforts to destroy the hero lead to the *low point* of the 8-turn structure. Here the hero learns that while the elixir might just fix the ordinary world, the hero will have to grow by addressing their flaw in order to implement the elixir. Making the low seem that much lower, our hero may appear to die. Game over, man!

Whether this death is literal or metaphoric, in the hero's journey it's followed by the *resurrection* beat as the protagonist is transformed into a mythological hero. The 8-turn structure approaches the beat in a similar fashion, only, instead of the main character growing to become a hero, their growth is measured simply by addressing the flaw. It's a slight difference to be sure, but if we examine this section of the story through the lens of internal versus external storylines, we see the 8-turn is focused more internally, designed to fix what's holding our hero back, while the hero's journey is more of an external manifestation of this change, in which the protagonist becomes something greater than themselves -- a mythological hero.

Both approaches mark a change for the better in the hero. However, one addresses a negative character trait (8-turn), while the hero's journey is more aspirational in nature, representing change in a positive character attribute. In keeping with our workout theme, think of the difference between these two approaches like so: 8-turn could be losing 25 pounds through diet and exercise; whereas, the hero's journey would be using diet and exercise to gain 25 pounds of muscle, becoming stronger and more fit in the process.

The 8-Turn structure ends at the low point, so we'll end our examination here. But, now that we've explored how these structures work together, it's time for a little work of our own.

SET 1: *Dual Structure Analysis*   CRAFT   Total Reps: 21

Analyze a major film from the last fifty years for the presence of both the 8-turn and Hero's Journey structures and their accompanying character design paradigms.

On the left, briefly describe each 8-turn structural beat. In the center, note the times these beats occur. Just for fun, feel free to include the timings of the Hero's Journey beats if you like. Describe the Hero's Journey beats on the right.

As with all of our analyses, the goal is not to make the movie fit the tool – the goal is to use the tool to help figure out how the movie is constructed. However, do be aware that you may encounter variations on each of these story beats, which can require a high degree of interpretation to make the beat 'fit'. In these cases, use your best judgement. <u>Each stage of both structures counts as a rep</u>.

Dual Structure Analysis

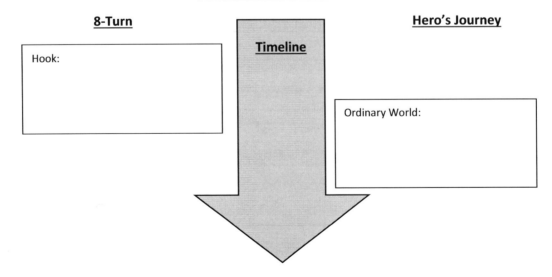

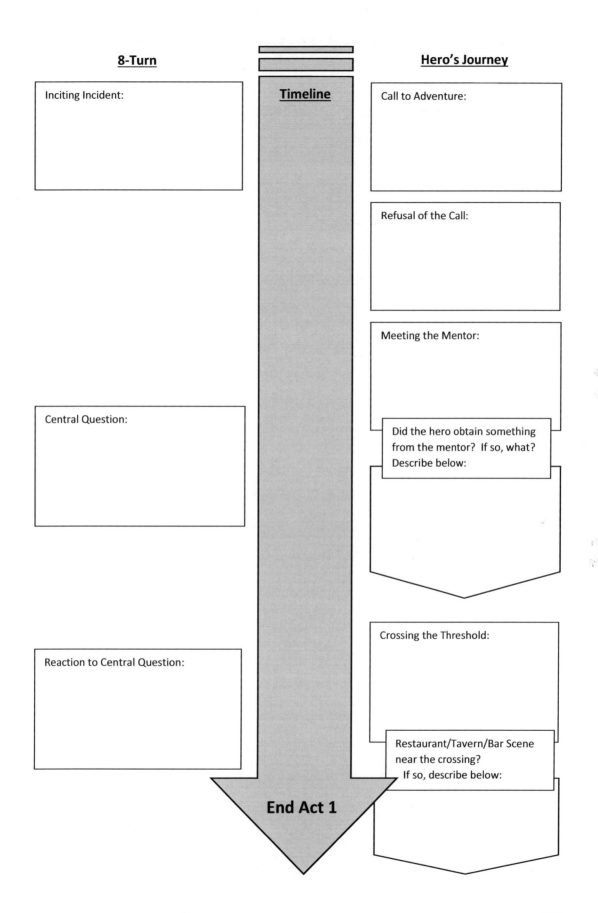

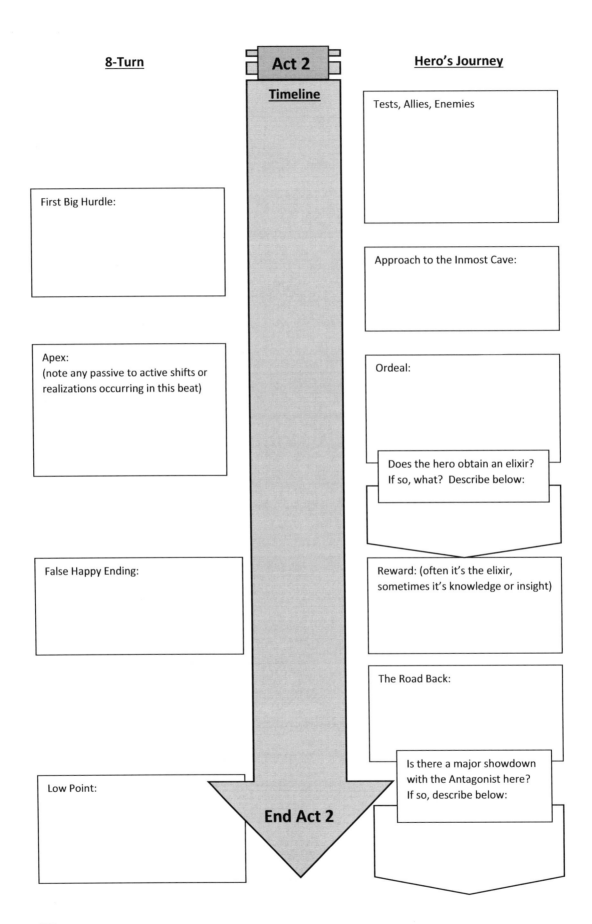

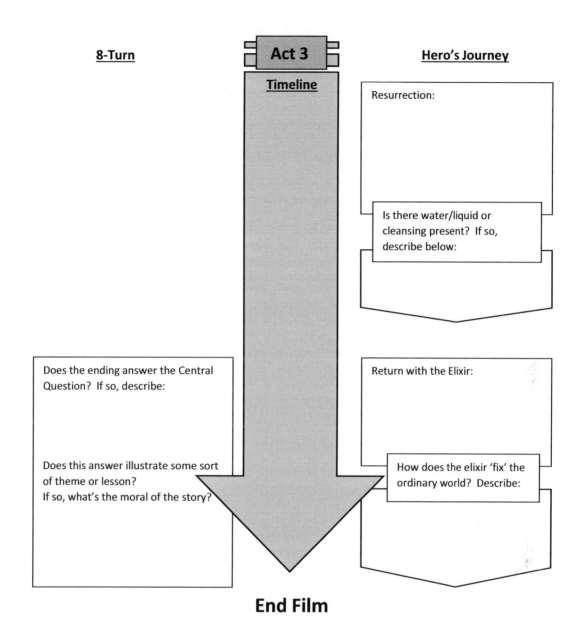

End Film

So, how'd your movie do?
Were you able to locate the structures? Or, did you find that the film is using some other form of organization?

Obviously, your results may vary, depending on the film. And, while this analysis is designed to explore how a movie is constructed, it does yield some intriguing insights into the filmmaker's approach to telling this story. These insights are broad, and once again, highly subject to interpretation, but we may find some clues embedded among the story beats that give us a glimpse into how the movie was written.

Interpreting the Results

Here are a few possible interpretations based on your findings:

If you found both structures in their entirety, chances are the filmmakers were consciously using these structures to organize their approach to telling the story.

If you found some of the 8-turn beats hit their timings, while others were way off, reexamine what occurs at the approximate times the beats should have happened to see if there's something more subtle underneath the surface serving the story function of the beat.

If you found the film leaned more heavily on one structure while the other was more hit or miss, you may have discovered that the filmmaker consciously used one structure to organize the film, and the other structure was not a conscious choice. This combination usually occurs with 8-turn being the primary structure and the Hero's Journey as the inadvertent one. That said, you may discover just the opposite. Either result indicates an important aspect of these structures – as filmmakers, we, just as our audience, subconsciously understand story structure; after all, depending on the number of films we've watched, we've seen it dozens, hundreds, thousands of times. These beats and their placement are second-nature to filmmakers and audiences alike. As filmmakers, sometimes we simply include beats that somehow feel right, without knowing why. The process of moving this instinct into conscious manipulation helps you master your craft, enabling you to find holes in the story (or perhaps even in our story instincts) and to do this without all the cumbersome, trial and error rewrites and clunky table reads. Okay, perhaps we can't do away with all that. What would screenwriting be without awkward table reads? But, when trying to discover why a story doesn't work, it might be nice to have a flashlight to go searching in the dark. How much time could you save? Time you can devote to your next project.

How liberating it would be to move this largely subconscious process into conscious choice? To no longer have to rely purely on instinct or the muse to descend upon your keyboard. But rather, to rely on your knowledge of the craft to help inform that instinct and to help you consciously integrate all the elements of your story into a cohesive, tightly-constructed whole.

Imagine the effects you can achieve on your audience – the conscious, purposeful effects that come with a command of the craft.

Actually, you don't have to image it.... :)

SET 2: Dual Structure Outline   CRAFT   Total Reps: 24

For this exercise, use the Dual Structure approach to outline a feature film you plan to write.

To utilize this approach, we'll need a main character with a flaw to overcome, as well as the other design parameters that going along with the 8-turn structure. From a Hero's Journey perspective, at minimum you'll need the following archetypes:

Hero, Shadow, Herald, Mentor, Threshold Guardian.

Feel free to include the others, but these are the key ones that affect structure.

You can start with a basic premise, plot or characters. Then, think about how to integrate these elements into the structure of your screenplay. Revise as needed until the story is where you want it. That's one of the advantages to this approach, you can check the story design BEFORE you write. Also, feel free to jot additional notes in the spaces between major story beats. These can be scenes, thoughts, genre conventions, etc. <u>Each section and stage counts as a rep</u>.

Dual Structure Outline

Title: _____

Genre: _____
         (can be a blend)

Concept:

Theme/Lesson of the Movie:

Main Character Designs:

Hero Name:	Design	Shadow Name:
	Defining Characteristic	
	Paradox	
	Humanity	
	Flaw	

Archetypes:
Name and describe each.

Herald: _____
Describe:

Mentor: _____
Describe:

Threshold Guardian: _____
Describe:

Shapeshifter (if applicable): _____
Describe:

Trickster (if applicable): _____
Describe

Outline

8-Turn   **Act 0**   **Hero's Journey**

Timeline

Act 1

Hook:

Inciting Incident:

Ordinary World:

Call to Adventure:

Refusal of the Call:

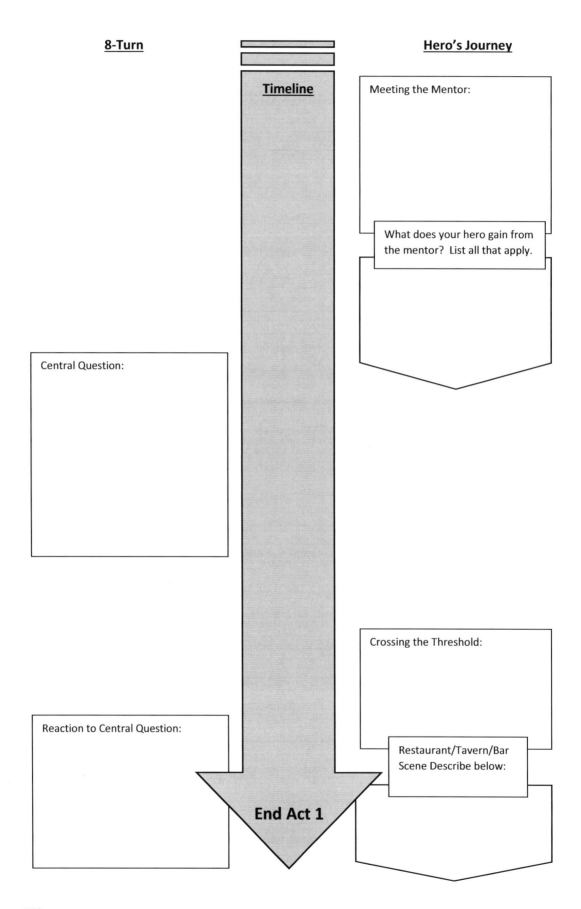

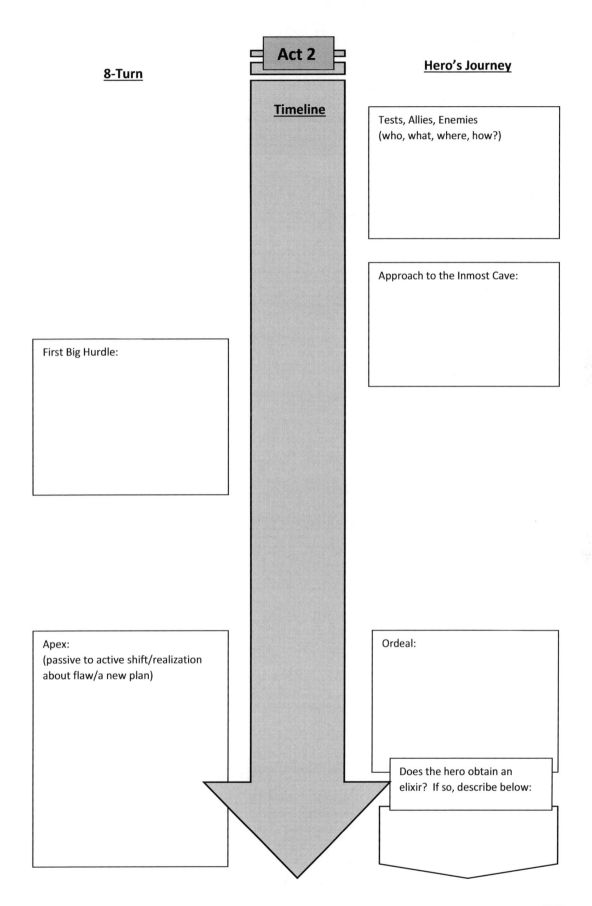

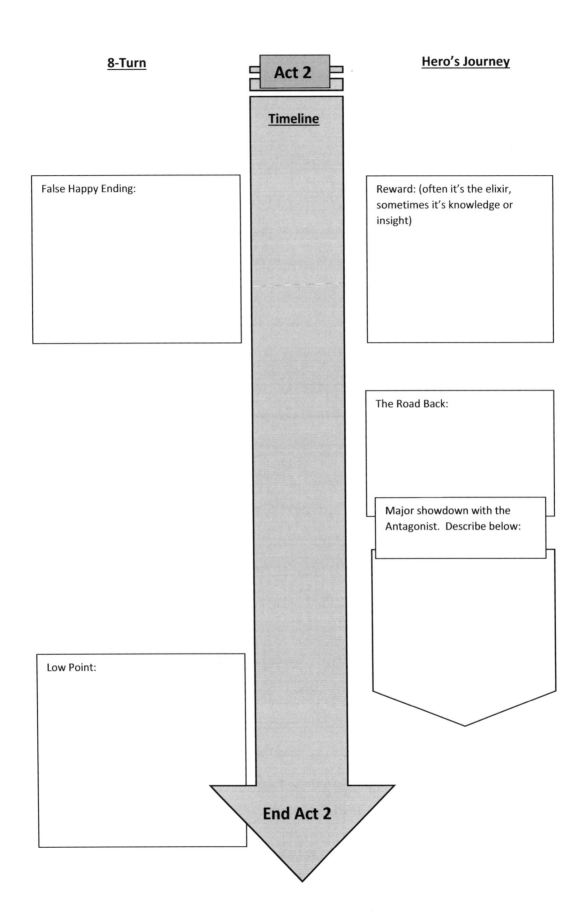

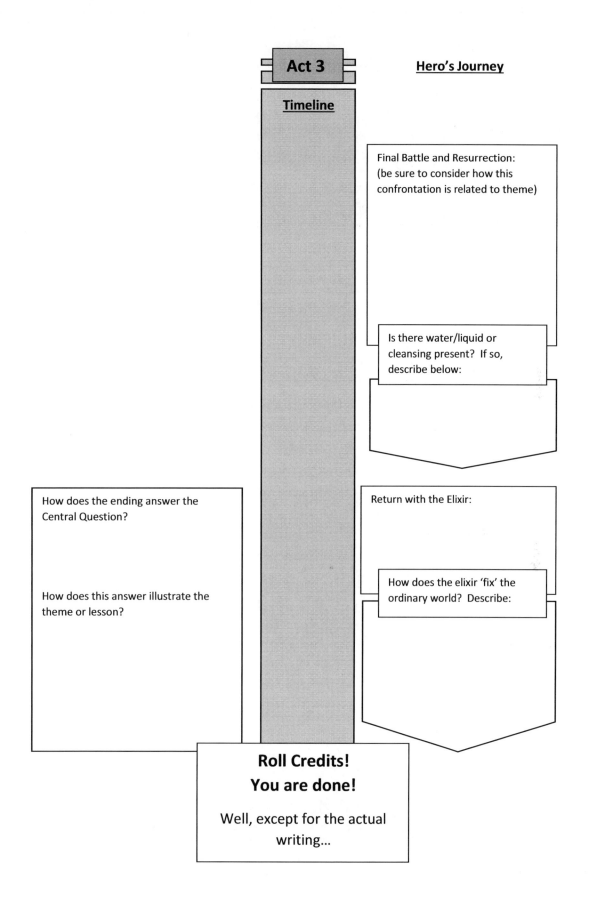

While the boxes on the outline suggest placement and length of certain major story beats, these are approximate, depending on the needs of your story. You may find it makes more sense to arrange your story differently to achieve the effects you want. Structure shouldn't dictate content, but rather, content dictates structure. That said, structure can provide the familiar part of 'unique yet familiar', allowing you to devote your creativity to your unique characters, plots and so forth.

Remember: structure is just a container to hold story content, like that coffee cup holding coffee. That's all it does. There's no magic in any structure -- it's merely the stage on which you perform your magic.

But, I would ask you to consider this...

Every screenplay is written one word at a time. All of them, including yours. One single, sometimes maddening, word at a time. Each word is a step on your journey from FADE IN: to FADE OUT. What the structural outline does is provide a set of mile markers, guide posts, lighthouses in that sea of words to help you know what direction you're headed, to help you know which way to step, to keep you from wandering around, lost, adrift, unsure of where to go or what to do next. By knowing where you're going, you can now focus all your creativity on getting there. Which just happens to be the focus of the next part of this book. :)

WORKOUT PROGRESS – CRAFT
Compile your totals!

EXERCISE	SKILL GROUP		TOTAL REPS	
	SET #	TYPE	ACTION	AVAILABLE	COMPLETED
Dual Structure Analysis	1	Craft	Analysis	21	
Dual Structure Outline	2	Craft	Application	24	
			TOTAL REPS		

CRAFT — TOTAL REPS + BONUS — 45

182

Act 2

The Workout

Sticks and Tomes:
The Origins of Story

Let's travel back in time, shall we? To a time before writing. Because, believe it or not, that's where the craft of screenwriting was born.

To activate our time machine and go back to the days before the written word, simply turn the page...

Okay, maybe traveling back to The Land Before Writing wasn't the best idea for a book. Least it was a quick read. Guess we should find a use for those blank pages.

Hmm…

Kind of a quiet time before writing. And, to fill that time, humans did what humans throughout history have done when they had a little downtime all to themselves…

No, not that.

Well, okay, yes, that. But, they did something else, too.

They told stories.

But, why? Ever wondered? A case could be made for entertainment I suppose. But then as now, there are plenty of forms of entertainment. And, that doesn't really address the question – why story in particular? Before we dive into that, we should make a distinction. Yes, the origins of story predate writing, but that doesn't preclude the use of words. They were just spoken, rather than written.

Story didn't begin on the page, it began on the stage – whether that stage was by a campfire, in a cave, or on the hot, sandy floor of the Coliseum, story was first communicated by the spoken word – oral storytelling. Even the word 'story**tell**ing' hints at the origins of our craft.

The first stories were told in two primary ways – through sound (spoken language) and image (cave paintings and such.) Hey, wait a second…

Sound? Image? Story? That's a movie! It may seem ironic, but ours is not a written craft; it's an oral one. More specifically, screenwriting is the art of oral storytelling communicated through the medium of writing.

Not to bring Marshall McLuhan into this, but in our case he's got a point – while our medium may not be the message, it does shape everything about how we communicate our message. Because the challenges faced by those oral storytellers ten thousand years ago are the exact same challenges faced by screenwriters today. And, in the pressures faced by those early storytellers and their attempts to overcome them, is where we'll find the tidal pool in which the craft of screenwriting spawned. To dive into the pool however, we need a story.

SET 1: _Novel Ideas_　　　　　　　　**CRAFT**　　　　　　　　**Total Reps: 1**
On the first partially blank page (page 185), write a simple short story in prose form about two people falling in love . Time to break out your inner novelist. Oh, and be sure to have a moral to the story – some sort of message or theme.

Once, you've written your novella (novelita?), proceed to our next activity.

SET 2: Telling it Like it Was   **_CRAFT_**   **_Total Reps_: 5**

On Page 186, write the same story as though you were telling it to someone during a morning commute. Gotta love carpooling. The important thing here is to write down the story <u>exactly as you'd say it</u> -- pauses, ums, and all. Then...

On Page 187, examine the first prose story and the oral version, then draw images that tell the exact same story in pictures. No words. Just images. No art skills required. But think about what images, whether literal or metaphoric, would communicate the story you just told. A challenge, yes, but third time's the charm.

On Page 188, examine the best aspects of the prose version, the oral version and the visual version and combine these to write the screen version as it would appear in a screenplay. No need to print in 12-point courier, but kudos if you can.

Oh, and no worries if you don't get to the end of the story. Just fit as much as you can in the space allotted. After all, you have told this story three times already.

<u>When you're done with those, check back in on the next page (p. 191)</u>. But, only after you're done. Deal? Hope so, because you have some writing to do...
See you back here in a few.

Was it possible to fit the entire prose story into your screen version (P. 188)? I should think that version may have required more space to convey the same amount of story as the original.

The same could be said for telling the story with images. It may have even been possible to fit even more story onto the page depending on image size and so forth, but that story in images also requires the most audience input and the highest degree of interpretability, making it much more difficult to recreate the prose story with any degree of precision.

As for the oral version… It's possible for this one to have captured all of the initial prose version's details. I do wonder if that approach would be as entertaining. Examine your oral version. Did it use more time transitions? These are phrases like – 'and <u>then</u> she….' or '<u>suddenly</u> they…', and so forth. If so, then what you found in those transitional words was an attempt to account for the experiential nature of oral storytelling. In other words, the oral version includes aspects to describe the experience of the story.

Ah, now we're getting somewhere…

As soon as time becomes a factor in conveying the story, it alters HOW the story is told.

The reader of a novel can pause, reread, or read at a personal pace. The reader controls the flow of information. Same with still art. You can ponder a painting for weeks or just give it a glance. For oral storytellers and screenwriters, this is not the case. *We* control the flow of information. And, if our audience misses something, they've missed it. Yes, the reader of a screenplay could go back and reread something, but that isn't desirable. We have to make it stick the first time. What does this imply about the complexity of what we can communicate cinematically? Let's come back to that because we have one more space to fill.

<u>In the blank space on the previous page</u> (you didn't think we'd waste that, did ya?), take the best of all the previous versions and combine them to tell as much of the original story as possible. If you have to jettison some of the nuance, that's okay, but the story itself should be a complete retelling.

Then, once you've done that – continue reading on the next page…

Examine this last version closely and ask yourself a few questions:
What did you cut?
What did you keep?
Did you leave any parts open to interpretation?
What sort of blend did you employ between visual, prose and oral?
On a related note – which story elements did you choose to communicate with each of these three approaches and why?

You don't have to write the answers -- just think about your process and why you made each decision. For our next question, please do write a response.

What was the theme or moral to your story? _____

_____

Wait. That's the point? That short statement?
If the moral is the actual point of the story, our takeaway, why not just say it then? Why go through all the trouble of creating characters, writing dialogue, coming up with visuals, plots, subplots, settings, subtext and conflicts? Why not just state your theme and be done. Think of the time savings alone. But, would it be effective? Would it be memorable?
Would it stick?

This was the problem facing those oral storytellers in the days before writing. The only way to pass down knowledge and culture from one generation to the next was through the spoken word. Art could do this, but it's too abstract to convey specific thoughts and communicates with a higher degree of subjectivity than words.

But, if you just say it – "blammo, there it is", would anyone listen? Would they even care? Or remember? After all, what's the point of passing down knowledge and culture to the next generation if they don't remember it well enough to pass it along as well? Of course compounding this is the fact that people, then as now, typically don't appreciate being told what to do, much less what to think.

How do you make thoughts and ideas permanent without a permanent way of recording them?   Simple. You had to make it stick in the only recording device available – the human mind. Okay, not so simple.
What they created to accomplish this task was story.

Interactive classrooms, touch screen desks, Smart Boards, forget about it. The original technological breakthrough for teaching was, and is still, the most effective: story. In short, story is what keeps the lesson from becoming a lecture.

Story is a form of technology, and as with any technological device, it's constantly being updated, modified, improved. But at its core, story still does what it was originally designed to do -- take some point, some statement, some *thing* some *one* wants to say and connect this statement to an audience.

Those early storytellers quickly realized they weren't in the storytelling business, they were in the connection business, and they made connections for audience members using story as the tool to do so.

As members of an audience, your audience, when you allow us make a connection for ourselves, we create meaning. Meaning that's relevant to us as individuals, our own personal connection to the material, the story, the characters, their struggles, their desires to overcome. This personal meaning creates resonance. And, ironically, a desire to do what the original purpose of story was -- pass it along. Think about it, when you like a movie, really like a movie, what do you want to do?
      "Hey, you gotta check this out!"
      "You really ought to see this!"
      "I don't want to spoil it for you."

In this way, story takes a thought and reproduces it, replicates it in the minds of others. Sounds like a virus, and in a way it is, but a good one.

What we're discussing here may seem obvious, but sometimes, in these very basics, lie aspects of our craft that can be easily overlooked -- especially as you master the finer points of storytelling. When we examine these basics, always it's with an eye toward taking these aspects of story we can sometimes take for granted, and making sure we're accomplishing them. We're also bringing those elements up to the surface so you can consciously manipulate them to ensure that every part of the story is supporting your goal in writing it.

Ultimately, we're still in the business of making connections in the minds of others. And, our tools to do this are more advanced than ever. But the oldest tool is still the most advanced, and perhaps, the most powerful -- story.

With this in mind, let's examine the various modes of communication you were asked to work with in this section through the lens of connectivity. Each medium creates slightly different types of connections for your audience. And, because cinematic narrative is comprised of many forms of communication, we can use these varying types to create different ways for an audience to connect to your story.

Prose and Cinematic Narrative

To convey a lot of story quickly, nothing beats prose. Novelists can go inside the minds of the characters at will. A character can be sitting on a bench doing nothing, and the novelist can take us on a brilliant 40-page flashback, to provide necessary exposition on the spot. In a way, the aspect of prose that allows this degree of storytelling freedom lies in how it connects to its audience, the reader.

The reader has direct control over the pace of the story, which frees it from time as a parameter in conveying information. As such, we can get that 40-page flashback and not blink an eye, because time is not a storytelling element influencing the connection to the audience. Make sense?

If we compare prose to cinematic communication, we find another profound difference: prose gives you the story and asks you to help provide the images. Film gives you the images and asks you to help provide the story. Obviously, novels can tell beautifully visual stories, and graphic novels can give you the images, too. But in its purest sense, the fundamental difference between media (in this case prose versus cinema) lies in what each form asks the audience to bring to the table; i.e., what parts of the story does the audience provide? It's these two parts, your content and the audience contribution that help form the connection. Visually it looks something like this:

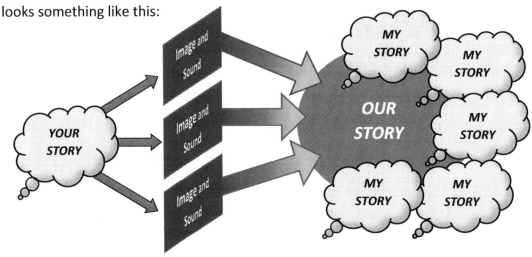

Notice that the imagery and sound act as an intermediary between your story and the stories assembled by the audience. Because the means of communicating story cinematically is indirect and highly interpretable, the content you create to tell your story must account for the varying connections created by the form. Implicit in this relationship between audience and content is how movies actually entertain. Movies engage audiences by providing them with content to interpret and assemble. The audience then subconsciously makes predictions based on how they interpreted the content and put it together. They then check to see if their predictions are accurate. This subconscious process of making and testing connections is how movies create an entertaining experience, which story tangentially feeds by providing the motivations to want to make connections. In other words, film uses story as a means to reward the audience for interacting with the content as well as giving the audience a reason to do so. Ever wonder why your climax has to be worth the wait? Why it has to outdo the scenes that precede it? In part, it's to reward the audience for their contributions.

The cinematic equivalent to telling stories in prose form is dialogue. While good movie dialogue tends to be subtextual and elliptical, you can use on the nose passages when you need to communicate an idea with greater clarity. Notice this last technique goes against how cinematic narrative generates entertainment, which is why it should be used sparingly. Watch a poorly made film and typically you'll find lots of characters belting out story in dialogue. With the interpretability removed, successful dialogue passages of this type usually find other ways to entertain -- humor, irony and so forth.

The indirect way cinema communicates story carries a heavy implication:

> **Movies are built to tell simple stories in a complex way.**

This doesn't mean movies are incapable of telling a complex story, but the form isn't built to do this with any degree of accuracy, without resorting to less cinematic ways of communicating story information with greater precision.

Examining the different components of cinematic storytelling by degree of interpretability can enable you to consciously manipulate how you deliver story to your audience, which can help you create the most entertaining experience while conveying the story you intended to tell.

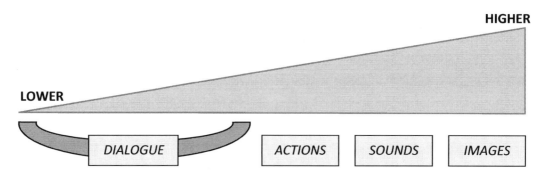

Obviously, each of these components can have a greater or lesser degree of interpretation depending on how you handle it, but in general, the ranges depicted in the graphic are how audiences are accustomed to processing story information. Using a blend of these varying means to communicate story allows you to control the flow of information and the degree of interpretation you wish your audience to engage in.

So, you want to hint at a story point without directly expressing it? You may wish to use image to convey it.

Want a stronger hint? Use sound or character actions.

Need to clarify a plot element to keep the audience grounded? You may use dialogue to convey that.

To manipulate the flow of story, you then mix these elements.
So, you may hint at an idea with an image, follow it up with a sound effect to reinforce (or obfuscate), then follow that later with dialogue to confirm the audience's hunches from the first two.

The more you rely on imagery to tell the story, which is both highly interpretable and entertaining, the more content it takes to convey an idea with clarity; thus, imagery does best when communicating simple ideas. The more complex the idea, the more images needed to communicate it. Yes, a picture can say a thousand words, but are those words accurate depictions of what you, the filmmaker, are trying to say?

Want to cover a lot of story ground quickly and accurately? This might call for a dialogue driven scene. For example, in *Raiders of the Lost Ark*, after the opening action sequence and a quick classroom scene to establish Indy's character, there's a long dialogue scene with the FBI agents in which the plot of the movie is laid out. Indy provides a couple images, one from a book and one he draws on a board to provide visuals to reinforce the dialogue and to foreshadow the concrete visuals that come later in the film so that in these moments the audience understands what they're watching.

These techniques are ways cinema handles the same challenges faced by oral storytellers long ago. By enacting themes and messages, you allow the audience to connect what they're watching and hearing to the ideas informing these actions. By providing content for the audience to connect, and then simply allowing them to make those connections, you create memorable, entertaining experiences that also have something to say. In this way, you guide the audience to draw the conclusions you wish them to have. And, because the audience makes the conclusions, they're more likely to stick and have meaning. So, while telling a story cinematically may take more time, it also yields a much more impactful result. Impact is why story was invented -- to teach lessons and to pass them down to future generations in ways that were engaging and memorable, making them more likely to be passed down again. After all, what are you more likely to pass along? Something that made an impact on you, or something that didn't? And, by continuing to learn about your craft, hopefully your stories will be the ones passed down to future generations.

WORKOUT PROGRESS – CRAFT
Compile your workout totals for this unit.

EXERCISE	SKILL GROUP			TOTAL REPS	
	SET #	TYPE	ACTION	AVAILABLE	COMPLETED
Novel Ideas	1	Craft	Application	1	
Telling it Like it Was	2	Craft	Application	5	
			TOTAL REPS		

CRAFT   Total Reps + Bonus   6

Building Better Loglines

Loglines. Nearly every writer I know hates these things. They're the screenwriting equivalent of filing taxes – one of those necessary evils you can't ignore. I suppose, if loglines are necessary, we should define them:

> **Logline: a one-sentence synopsis of a film or screenplay.**

Hmm… seems harmless enough. Just a single sentence. How hard can it be? Of course, how do you take an entire movie or screenplay and reduce it down to a single sentence? The short answer is – you don't. You can't. And, therein lies the rub. All those cool scenes you wrote, the drama, the laughs, the thrills – all of that fun goes away in a logline – leaving just the thing at the center, the story's core.

In ways, this is what loglines are designed to do: strip away all the surface details, all those fabulous one-liners, powerhouse moments and thrilling action sequences, all those shiny distractions that can obfuscate the truly important thing – the story.

Yes, those surface details are important, but if the story isn't there, you've basically created a chocolate-covered turd. Sure, it may look good on the outside all covered in sprinkles and a tastefully drizzled raspberry reduction, but once you take a bite, you have a mouthful of crap no amount of decoration can cover.

Let's see. Turds. Crap. Filing taxes. Removing the entertainment, the fun. And people wonder why loglines get such a bum rap. From the writer's perspective, loglines can seem to misrepresent the story by removing what makes it special, your unique execution. However, once again, that's what loglines are built to do. A logline distills the story down to its essence, so that the person reading it can check the foundation so to speak. The house might look great on the outside, new hardwoods and tastefully decorated, but if the foundation is bad, no amount of sprucing up will fix it. It's the same with your screenplay – if the foundation, the concept, doesn't work, chances are the film made from this idea won't work either. Or so the theory goes.

Think about it. Would you risk buying a house if the foundation was broken? Now imagine sinking millions, if not hundreds of millions, into a script with a faulty foundation. Doesn't exactly inspire confidence.

Actually, not everyone dislikes writing loglines – especially those with high concept stories. These loglines tend to write themselves. And why? Because the core concept is intriguing enough to compel someone to want to read more. Ultimately, a logline exposes your story concept and places it in one of two categories: high concept and low concept. Let's quickly explore both because understanding the differences is crucial to writing effective loglines.

High Concept is a story premise that in inherently intriguing. The juxtaposition of elements in the concept are enough to warrant interest. High concept is not synonymous with big budget, special effects extravaganzas, explosions, car chases and the like. A low budget film can be high concept as well.

Low Concept is a story premise we may have seen many times – a love story for example. Been there, seen that. For low concept ideas to stand out in the marketplace, the uniqueness comes from the execution. So, a love story told in a unique or artfully beautiful way might qualify as low concept. The issue with writing a logline for a story like this is apparent – the logline removes the execution, leaving only the concept, which by definition, isn't the selling point of a low concept idea.

It's this execution component that the logline weeds out. Screenplays that are execution dependent are far riskier than ones in which the concept alone is enough to draw interest. This is also why we see high concept so often lumped in with bigger-budgeted films – the concept is intriguing enough to warrant the risk.

The vice is also versa. Low concept tends to garner lower budgets simply because more things can go wrong. Even at the professional level, execution-dependent scripts are more difficult to pull off successfully – so many things can go wrong and take the movie down with them.

Okay, so now that we have a little background on loglines, ready to file those taxes? Who knows, maybe this year we'll get a refund.

Elements of a Logline
Depending on your concept, at minimum a logline contains the following:

- The Main Character (HERO)
- This character's FLAW
- This character's GOAL
- The ANTAGONIST or obstacle opposing the Main Character
- The BIG PROBLEM or catalyst that forces the hero to conceive a GOAL
- The BIG BATTLE (what brings the hero and antagonist into conflict)

Some of these are more applicable than others; for example, perhaps your character doesn't have a flaw, but these are the core elements of a logline.

Notice the list suggests a basic flow to the story:
> our HERO must overcome a FLAW to defeat an ANTAGONIST in a BIG BATTLE to achieve the main character's GOAL of solving the BIG PROBLEM.

Also notice, this can suggest how to approach writing a logline. For example:

An overprotective father, who's afraid to leave his home, must travel across the ocean to save his only son from captivity.

Or, how about this:

A boxer who believes he's a loser is given a chance by the heavyweight champion to fight for the title and regain his self-worth.

Not exactly Shakespeare, but if you recognize the movies, we got *something* right.

Logline Tips
Some things to remember when writing loglines:
- No names. Use titles instead: teacher, cop, billionaire playboy philanthropist
- Keep it to a single sentence. Or at worst, no more than two.
- Use an adjective or two to describe the main character and antagonist.
- Do not give away the ending. Just set up the main conflict to come.
- Do not sell. A solid concept doesn't need hype.

That's it, really. Just a simple breakdown of the core elements of your story.

Our third tip, the adjective one, requires extra scrutiny because it's the key to understanding how to craft effective loglines.

Going back to our overprotective dad trying to save his son from a certain dentist in Sydney, notice how the adjective describing dad (overprotective) suggests the character arc. In other words, being overprotective is the internal flaw the hero must overcome. Also notice how the flaw and the hero's fear tie into the plot, implying some of the conflicts this character will face. In a logline, the descriptors you choose for your hero should imply this character's arc.

Thinking back to our Hollywood Character Design, we find two aspects of the design lead directly into formulating a logline – the Defining Characteristic and Flaw. Defining Characteristic can be used for the character, with the flaw as the adjective describing the character. If you're curious, the remaining two aspects of Hollywood Character Design, Paradox and Humanity, are used to pique audience interest in the character.

To understand how vital those adjectives are in creating loglines, let's play around with them to demonstrate their impact. First, we need a logline. How about this:

While exploring a legendary shipwreck searching for treasure, a deep-sea diver falls in love with the ghost of a passenger roaming the sunken ship, kept alive by the very treasure he and a rival treasure hunter seek.

Okay, so the merits of the film are debatable, but this will get us started.

Now, let's examine that deep-sea treasure hunter and add a descriptor to see the different effects this lone word can have on the potential story. But, before we do this, we need to work out the story from the current logline.

SET 1: Water Logged   ***CRAFT***   ***Total Reps: 1***

Outline a basic story using the logline above. For this one, since the logline doesn't indicate a clear flaw, let's use the hero's journey for our outlining guide.

<u>Briefly describe each stage:</u>

1. Ordinary World

2. Call to Adventure

3. Refusal of the Call

4. Meeting the Mentor

5. Crossing the Threshold

6. Tests, Allies, Enemies

7. Approach to the Inmost Cave

8. Ordeal

9. Reward

10. The Road Back

11. Resurrection

12. Return with the Elixir

Hopefully, the story should have come pretty easily. Although, I could see the Call to Adventure presenting an intriguing choice. Given the logline, that beat could go at least a couple ways: one could be the treasure hunter being made aware of the treasure -- the other, finding the ghost.

Now, let's change things around a bit with a few choice words...

Suppose we made the hero a <u>lonely</u> deep-sea diver. What effect would this have on the story? Might amp up the choice the character faces. Certainly could help explain how this living, breathing person could fall for a ghost. But, aside from that, making our hero lonely doesn't seem add much.

What if we made the hero a <u>widowed</u> deep-sea treasure hunter? How would this story play out? Let's find out!

SET 2: Sunken Treasures   **CRAFT**   **Total Reps: 1**

Outline a screenplay for our modified logline. This time our hero is a <u>widowed</u> deep-sea diver. Now that we have the makings of a flaw, let's switch to the 8-Turn Structure, since it's designed to explore character flaws. Write your outline below:

Hook (5)

Inciting Incident (10)

Central Question (17)

Reaction to Central Question (30)

Next Big Hurdle (45)

Apex (60)

False Happy Ending (75)

Low Point (90)

Ending:

What changes, if any, occurred once you made the character widowed? Did it add any extra layers to the conflict? Several possibilities emerge. Perhaps our hero feels guilty about falling for someone else. Perhaps the ghost can talk to our hero's former lover – might be interesting. Or perhaps, any relationship between a ghost and living person is doomed, just like the hero's previous relationship, so the journey is about the hero learning acceptance. Whatever it is, notice how adding that one word, widowed, could have a tremendous effect on the story. To explore just how much, let's do this again, this time with <u>divorced</u> rather than widowed.

SET 3: Underwater Angel   **CRAFT**   **Total Reps: 2**

Outline a screenplay for our modified logline. This time our hero is <u>divorced</u>.

Hook (5)

Inciting Incident (10)

Central Question (17)

Reaction to Central Question (30)

Next Big Hurdle (45)

Apex (60)

False Happy Ending (75)

Low Point (90)

Ending:

So, how did THAT one turn out?

Several new story possibilities should have opened up by choosing 'divorced' to describe the hero. Perhaps the encounter with the ghost turns into a form of marriage counseling. Perhaps the rival treasure hunter is our hero's ex – that could be fun. Perhaps the hero comes to realize his obsession with treasure ruined his/her marriage. Lots of possibilities. But, the real key is choosing descriptors that imply the main character's arc, and thus the overarching flow of the story. The secret to writing effective loglines lies in choosing story and character elements to create intriguing combinations that suggest how the story will play out. They also imply the genre of the screenplay through language choice and the elements selected. So, for our original deep-sea treasure hunter story, what genre does the logline suggest?

Genre: _____

Hard to pin down exactly, but for me, the logline implies some sort of drama – either a straight up love story or perhaps a romance with action elements. Whatever the specific genre, the tone set by this logline suggests a more serious treatment of the subject matter. It's good that the logline isn't too specific -- this allows for a bit of flexibility, which in turn allows for a degree of interpretation. In this way, the logline guides its reader to a narrowed down list of genre possibilities, creating a number of interpretations that can vary depending on the person reading it. This flexibility helps the reader personalize the story, which can broaden appeal.

Changing the elements just a bit can dramatically alter the perceived genre. What if we describe the ghost as luring treasure hunters to fall in love? What genre does this additional word now suggest?

Genre: _____

Hopefully, luring had a negative connotation for you, suggesting more horror elements to the story. If we want to hint more strongly, perhaps we could switch the ghost from roaming the sunken ship to haunting it.

Just for fun, what if we changed our lonely/widowed/divorced treasure hunter to a clueless/goofball/amateur treasure hunter? What genre does this change imply?

Genre: _____

Feels more comedic to me. But, once again, you may need to alter the descriptor for the ghost to drive that one home.

Whatever direction you decide, notice just how important a single word, or the interpretation of a single word, can be in the perception of the story the logline conveys. As such, when writing loglines, choose every word with extreme care and consider the various interpretations created by your choice of story elements and language. So, for a comedy, a light-hearted, flippant approach to the logline would be appropriate – for a serious drama, not so much.

High Concept Versus Low Concept Loglines
Writing loglines for high concept stories tends to be easier than with more low concept ideas. Makes sense. Loglines are written to convey the core concept of the story, and by definition, this is the intriguing aspect of a high concept script. Thus, the logline presents the most appealing aspect of the story.

Writing loglines for low concept ideas becomes a bit trickier because the concept, which loglines are written to communicate, is not the intriguing part of the story. In this way, the logline almost works against these types of stories.

One way to tackle loglines for low concept stories is to use the logline to highlight what is original about the story. Back to our underwater romance, notice the core idea is low concept – a love story. So, the logline devotes a bit more time to describing the more unique aspects – underwater, ghost, sunken ship, etc. In essence, the logline blends a low concept core with high concept execution. Put another way, for low concept story ideas try adding some high concept touches to the logline so that it does the job it was intended to do – get someone to read (and hopefully buy) your screenplay.

SET 4: *Film Out of Water*   **CRAFT**   **Total Reps: 2**
Okay, let's leave our sunken ship behind and practice a few loglines. For the first one, pick an <u>existing film</u> and write the logline below:

Title: _____

Genre: _____

Logline: _____

_____

_____

Let's play with that logline a bit!

Using the same film, reword the logline to imply a different genre. Rewrite the new logline below:

New Genre: _____

Logline: _____

_____

_____

BONUS SET: Two for the Road   **CRAFT**   **Total Reps: 2**

Now, write loglines for two of your stories. Feel free to use any of the stories you've created in your workout or an original idea. Also remember, the title helps us figure out the genre. Be sure to choose strong, vibrant language and evocative verbs.

Concept 1:

Title: _____

Genre: _____

Logline: _____

_____

_____

_____

To check if your logline is accurately conveying genre, share it and ask what type of movie your reader thinks it will be.

Concept 2:

Title: _____

Genre: _____

Logline: _____

_____

_____

_____

_____

In conclusion, loglines serve two important functions: one is as a writing guide – a single statement to focus your story. The other is to entice someone to read your script, not through hyperbole or hype, but by simply communicating just how cool and original the concept for your screenplay is. And, if it's not? Hone it until it is.

WORKOUT PROGRESS – CRAFT

Compile your workout totals for this unit.

EXERCISE	SKILL GROUP			TOTAL REPS	
	SET #	TYPE	ACTION	AVAILABLE	COMPLETED
Water Logged	1	Craft	Application	1	
Sunken Treasure	2	Craft	Application	1	
Underwater Angel	3	Craft	Application	2	
Film Out of Water	4	Craft	Application	2	
Two for the Road	Bonus	Craft	Application	2	
				TOTAL REPS	

CRAFT — TOTAL REPS + BONUS — 8

Introducing Characters

The old saying, "You only get one chance at a first impression," doesn't just apply to real life – it fits the characters in your screenplay as well. Before we get to your characters though, let's delve into the world of science for just a bit.

Background: The Science of First Impressions

In 1999, Tricia Prickett, a psychology student, collected a series of videotaped job interviews to test whether it was possible to guess the outcome simply from observing the interaction between the interviewer and interviewee. She found that an observer could predict whether or not the interviewee would be offered the job from watching just the first 15 seconds of the tape - the handshake, the "hello" and very little else. What happened in those few, brief moments was enough to determine the candidate's future. No pressure. :)

"First impressions are the fundamental drivers of our relationships," says Professor Frank Bernieri of Oregon State University, who supervised Prickett's study. "In a sense, it's a little like the principle of chaos theory, where the initial conditions can have a profound impact on the eventual outcome. A first impression is your initial condition for analyzing another human being."

The Power of 'Thin-Slicing'

Bernieri is an expert in "thin-slicing methodology". His research is based on the theory that we make a reasonably accurate assessment of a person from observing just a few seconds, or a "thin slice", of their behavior. From evidence gleaned in not much more than a few glances, we decide whether we like another person, whether they're trying to flirt with us, whether they're friend or foe.

And, whether or not we want to watch them in a movie.

The Impact of First Impressions

The early assessments we make set us on a certain course. If we've decided that a character is a certain type of person, who thinks, feels and behaves a certain way, we pay more attention to evidence that confirms our theory is correct. This cognitive phenomenon is known as confirmation bias. We seek out the information that tells us we are right, and we ignore or assign little importance to anything that might suggest otherwise.

Beyond the Script: Casting Calls...

We may be taught not to judge a book by its cover, but when we see a new face, our brains decide whether a person is attractive and trustworthy <u>within a tenth of a second</u>, according to a 2006 Princeton research study. Princeton University psychologist Alex Todorov found that <u>people respond intuitively to faces so rapidly that our reasoning minds may not have time to influence the reaction</u> -- and that our intuitions about attraction and trust are among those we form the fastest.

Back to the Script...

Okay, before we start casting, we've got to get these roles written! And, to do that we have to splatter some words around on a screen or even (gulp) paper.
And, doing that effectively is what this section is all about.

Writing Character Introductions

The same principles that apply to first impressions in the real world also apply to meeting characters for the first time, but in a slightly different way (it also means that an actor's face, demeanor or personal charisma can override a well-drawn character on the page, but that's a different story.)

Rather than drawing first impressions from faces, in your screenplay readers form opinions about characters from your words -- how well you write your characters. And remember, we're wired to evaluate people in a matter of seconds.

Words on the Page: Introducing Your Character to the World

When introducing your characters consider the following:

- Brief description of character including age and a detail or two that conveys appearance and <u>attitude</u>. Ideally we want qualitative description (qualities rather than specifics). Keep it as short as possible – we're used to gaging people quickly.

- Define the character through actions. When we first meet your character he or she should be engaged in a <u>character-defining</u> **action**.

- Don't tell everything there is to know about this character in his/her introduction. Withhold details to reveal later. This adds to the mystery.

- Character names should be in ALL CAPS when introduced. After that, handle them as regular names. Groups of people can be capped or not.

- For characters with no names, CAP their introduction and treat any later references to them as regular names. Example:

```
A BIG THUG steps into the light.  Big Thug approaches.
Menacing.  Behind him, an EVEN BIGGER THUG steps out.
Not good.  Even Bigger Thug grins.
```

Notice: the first letters are capped like an actual name.

- Try to avoid labeling characters as Cop 1, Terrorist 2, and so forth. Even a one word description helps us picture a character.

- If characters are referred to in dialogue before we meet them, do not cap their names in the dialogue text. All caps is reserved for physical introductions.

- If we hear characters before we meet them, there's no hard and fast rule for how to handle their introductions. Try to avoid these scenarios whenever possible, but if not, make sure we understand the connection between the voice and the character. Example:

```
              MAN'S VOICE (O.S.)
         It all began on the page...
The voice belongs to JACK WORDLY (55), care-worn but
meticulously dressed, like a run-down house about to
go on the market.
```

- REMEMBER: we begin to form opinions about characters almost immediately. If you establish the wrong first impression, your character may never recover from it – particularly in a short. As a result, <u>choose character descriptions, actions and first lines of dialogue with extreme care</u>!

SET 1: Character Descriptions   **CRAFT**   **_Total Reps_: _4_**

For this exercise, think of two people you know well and describe them as they would be introduced in a screenplay. Please include the **scene headings** and **brief action-description passages** below. Also, consider what character-defining actions your characters would be engaged in. If you like, name your characters differently than their real life counterparts.

1.

2.

Using the individuals you just introduced, decide what the following characteristics of Hollywood Character Design would be:

Character 1:

Name: _____

Main Characteristic: _____

Paradox: _____

Humanity: _____

Flaw: _____

Character 2:

Name: _____

Main Characteristic: _____

Paradox: _____

Humanity: _____

Flaw: _____

BONUS SET: Just for Fun!   **CRAFT**   **Total Reps: 2**

Share the descriptions from the previous page with someone and see if they can guess what your characters' main characteristics and flaws are. If the guesses are wildly inaccurate, perhaps you should modify the character's introduction, and try again.

Even More Fun!

Share your character introductions with the people who inspired them to see if they recognize themselves in the description.

SET 2: *Character Introductions*   **CRAFT**   **Total Reps: 12**

Let's give character introductions some context by creating their accompanying scenes. The characters will be provided – the rest is up to you!

Introduce us to the two characters below using tone, attitude, actions and interactions to reveal character and personality. Please name the characters within in your action-description as well. Remember, FIRST IMPRESSIONS COUNT!

Character 1:
He's a rebellious 20-something guy stuck in corporate America and wanting out. Remember he should be engaged in an action that is indicative of his character.

_____
_____
_____
_____
_____
_____

Character 2:
She's a 30-something female co-worker to our guy above. She's a real go-getter who loves her job. Her actions should convey character, too.

_____
_____
_____
_____
_____
_____

Now that we've met our characters, let's bring them together.

Instructions:

Briefly describe an encounter between these two characters at the office.

Include **dialogue** as necessary – remember, those first lines say a lot about these characters. They can (and should) reveal character.

Write this scene as you would in a screenplay in the spaces provided.

Remember that setting is also a character in the story, and should be depicted with the same care as your other characters. While the setting is a corporate office, your scene can take place in any number of locations within this space. Perhaps they meet in the breakroom, the boardroom, the bathroom – you pick!

Also, please name the scene. The name should reflect your scene's content.

Character Introduction Scene Exercise (10 reps)

Note: for this activity, please assume that you have already introduced the characters separately (the previous exercise) and this scene follows those. This space continues on the next page.

Name of Scene (be creative!):
_____

Notice when you bring characters together, you can define them simultaneously. Bonus score!

WORKOUT PROGRESS – Introducing Characters – CRAFT
Compile your workout totals for this unit.

EXERCISE	SKILL GROUP			TOTAL REPS	
	SET #	TYPE	ACTION	AVAILABLE	COMPLETED
Character Descriptions	1	Craft	Application	4	
Just for Fun!	Bonus	Craft	Analysis	2	
Character Introductions	2	Craft	Application	12	
			TOTAL REPS		

CRAFT — TOTAL REPS + BONUS — 18

Oh, the Troubles I've Scene:
The Elements of Scene Construction

The last exercise in the previous section got me thinking. Suppose if we're creating scenes, it might be useful to explore the facets of scene design – especially since scenes form the basic building blocks of film. This section pulls examples from the movie, *Raiders of the Lost Ark*, so that might be handy as you explore it.

Scene Construction Principles
Here are some overarching guidelines for building scenes:

<u>Keep Scenes Short</u>
Anything over three pages is a looooong scene. You can have these, but be aware that something major better be happening to hold our interest.

<u>Must Drive the Plot</u>
Aside from the occasional transitional scene, every scene must be fully integrated with the plot. If you can remove a scene and not change the story, the scene should probably be eliminated.

<u>Demonstrate Change</u>
Scenes that don't contain some sort of change within the character or story are typically non-events, and as such, should be removed or modified to contain some sort of change.

<u>Focused</u>
Scenes should have a primary focus, and although complications may arise within the scene, it's typically about a single thing – usually obtaining whatever goal the scene's driving force or character wants.

There's an old adage – if the scene's about what the scene's about, it's a bad scene. What this alludes to is that a good scene is…

<u>Layered</u>
Yes, a scene should be focused on the scene goal of the character driving the scene. But, underneath this is what the scene is truly about -- its **subtext**.

Subtext in scenes can take many forms. It can be character-based, revealing layers and motivations within the characters. It can be thematic, or symbolize the message of the movie. But the bottom line is if the scene is about what the scene is about, it's almost always overly-simplistic and not very efficient. As a result, scenes like this can leave the audience asking – that's it? That's all there is? And, the result typically underwhelms.

Get in Late; Get out Early
An oldie but a goodie. The idea is to begin the scene as late as possible into the main action of the scene. So if the purpose of the scene is to show two characters falling for each other, get to your point and quickly move on.

But, you may ask, what about those slow-burning scenes that build, build, build to a scintillating climax?

The 'get in late, get out early' maxim applies here too. Once you've reached that climax, end the scene. Don't hang around.

Goal Driven
Scenes, like characters, are driven by goals. Ask yourself – what is my character's goal in this scene? How are they trying to achieve this goal? What's in the character's way?

Without these basic elements, scenes tend to meander. They lack a point and a purpose. And all too typically, the scene lacks drive as a result.

The goals can be small – after all, it is but a scene, but even the smallest of goals, should have a point in the overarching story. So, in *Twister*, when Bill is trying to get Jo to sign the divorce papers, there's an overarching plot point being explored here. Likewise, in the diner scene between Melissa and Jo, Melissa is trying to order lemonade (a super simple goal) but what's being explored during this action are Jo's feelings toward Bill.

Often separate from the actual goal of the scene is its real purpose - a layer hidden beneath the surface. It can be subtextual or metaphoric, but ultimately it's like a miniature version of movie construction – the idea that through the pursuit of a goal (the 'want' story) a character learns what they need. It's this dual purpose that gives a scene depth, and makes it feel like it's part of the narrative whole.

You also need to ask, what's your goal as filmmaker in this scene? Scenes should feel organic to the characters, and yet, if you leave characters to their own devices, your story may wind up wandering around the desert, going nowhere.

The trick here is to hide your personal goal for the scene; otherwise, it can feel forced and artificial.

Conflict
Every scene must have some form of conflict. 'Nuff said.

End on Dramatic Question
A great construction device. End the scene with some sort of question to be answered later in the movie. Perhaps it's the next scene; perhaps it's later, but if the question intrigues us, it will propel the audience through the film.

The trick with this approach is that in obtaining the scene goal, this action raises a question or questions in the mind of the audience that they want to know the answer to. The desire on behalf of the audience to want to have a question answered hinges on the audience caring about the question being asked. Put simply, if we don't care about the question, we don't care to have it answered.

The idea is to always leave us in a constant state of asking – **what happens next**? Then withhold that information from this scene. Make us watch another scene to answer the question. Enough of these, and pretty soon you'll have us hanging on your every move. Which leads us to…

Arrangement of Scenes
As if knowing where to start and stop a scene isn't enough, you also need to consider how your scenes are arranged throughout your movie.

One of the most powerful of cinematic tools available to you, the order and arrangement of scenes is really a **system to control flow of narrative information**.

In ways, the main function of scenes is time management within the movie. It involves choosing the most interesting moments in the story (and in the lives of its characters) and eliminating everything else.

There's an old adage – drama is life with all the boring parts cut out. Scenes are the basic unit of cinematic narrative that enable you to do just that.

As long as your film is being driven by dramatic questions and goals, you can compress (and expand) time at will.

Ever run into the problem of having to skip to the next day in your movie?

Almost always, when you encounter issues moving through time within your film, the issue isn't time at all – it's a lack of dramatic questions. In other words, time is the only thing propelling your story – the drama is not.

To help with this issue, let's look at a simple device to chain scenes together…

The Power of But and So
But and so -- two little words with enormous implications.

In linking scenes together, and in effect your movie, one way to look at it is as a long series of sentences joined by conjunctions. Remember conjunctions? Those little words English teachers told you could be used to put together clauses? There are seven coordinating conjunctions, but when it comes to joining scenes in a movie, we'll stick with just two – but and so.

The idea here is relatively simple….

Scenes Joined with But
These are scenes in which the hero may obtain a scene goal, **BUT**, it doesn't quite work out as planned.

Or, perhaps the hero obtains the goal, BUT, the villain steals it back.

Joining scenes with 'but' leads to reversals, irony and complications.

It also keeps the audience guessing. We expect a certain outcome, get that outcome, and yet, things don't quite work out as we expected. In this way, the audience can have its cake and eat it too. We get the satisfaction of having been right, while at the exact same time the surprise that comes from the reversal of expectations – the 'but' part of the equation.

Joining scenes with 'but' also contributes to dramatic irony. Similar to a reversal, there's a sense of irony when a character accomplishes some goal, but in so doing creates complications. Or, the success somehow backfires on the character. The reverse can also happen. A character might experience a setback BUT this yields a breakthrough that leads to a successful conclusion.

To see how this works, let's examine this technique in action.

Time to break out a little *Indy* film…

Using buts in *Raiders of the Lost Ark*...

> Indy gets the Ark in one scene

BUT

> The Nazis get it back.

SO

> Indy goes after the Ark and retakes it.

BUT

> The Nazis take it back.

And, so forth...

Notice I snuck in a 'so'. Let's talk about that one a bit.

Scenes Joined with So

Joining scenes with 'so' implies the cause and effect relationship between scenes. One scene causes the next scene to happen, which causes the next scene to happen, and so forth...

Now it may seem like we're talking about things occurring between scenes, and yet you'll find that the ending of one scene leads to how you link it to the other. In other words, **the way you end one scene implies its relationship with the scene to follow**.

Also note: **you can use but and so within the scenes themselves**.

Back to *Raiders of the Lost Ark* for just a moment.

Remember the scene where Indy discovers Marion tied up in the tent?

He thought she'd died earlier in the movie, so he's thrilled to see her still alive. He goes to cut her loose, so they can escape... then stops. If he breaks her out, the Nazis will know he's there and he won't be able to go after the Ark. He puts her gag back in and leaves, promising to break her out when he gets a chance. The scene ends with Marion furious.

Let's examine this scene for its 'but and so' moments:

Indy slips into the tent disguised. Marion's momentarily frightened…

BUT

Indy slips off his disguise. Marion's relieved.
Indy removes her gag. They kiss.
Looks like Indy will free her.

BUT

Indy stops.

SO

Marion asks why. Indy reveals he knows where the Ark is.
And he can get it…

BUT

If he frees Marion the Nazis will comb the place for her,
and discover him.

SO

He replaces her gag, promising to return and free her.

SO

He scurries out before he's discovered, leaving Marion furious.

There are smaller moments of but and so within the scene, but these are the major ones. Notice how each of the beats in the scene are joined with these two powerful little words.

Also notice the scene ends on a dramatic question – actually a few…
What will Marion do after being left like this?
How will she react when she sees Indy again?
If Indy's not going to set her free, how will she escape?
Lots of good dramatic potential here.

In terms of scene arrangement, in the next meaningful scene after this one, the Nazis are discussing what to do with Marion. Belloq, the French archaeologist helping our bad guys, insists she knows nothing about the Ark. But (there's that word again) the Nazis aren't convinced. So, they've brought in the Gestapo agent from earlier in the film to interrogate her. Yikes!   Things are getting serious, which raises the stakes.

Although the tent scene between Marion and Indy is a small moment in the movie (literally it's less than one and a half pages in length), it's huge in terms of its story implications by setting up our next technique…

Scene Repetition
A subset of scene arrangement, this device is used to demonstrate character growth and change.

The idea here is early in the film you have a scene that presents a character with a choice. The character chooses a certain course of action, a certain response based on his or her personality – and often, his or her flaw.

Later in the film, the character is presented with the same choice, or at least a similar one testing the same character trait as the earlier choice. Once again the character makes a choice. If the choice differs from the first one, all things being equal, this demonstrates the character has changed. In this way, the audience can see the internal change the character has undergone, and you have now externalized the character's arc.

So, back to *Raiders*…

In the Indy-Marion tent scene we explored earlier, Indy leaves Marion behind to pursue the Ark.

Later in the movie after a brief submarine ride, Indy must choose between the Ark and Marion, only this time all he wants is the girl.

The repeated choice the character faces (and the differing response) show his change during the movie.

In its set up scene, Indy left Marion behind.

Now, he's willing to leave the Ark behind in favor of her. Notice what's repeated is the **choice** the character makes in the scene, not necessarily the scene itself.

On a side note: even this scene is driven by but and so…

> Indy threatens to blow up the Ark unless he gets Marion.
> But, the Nazis refuse. So, Indy reiterates his threat.
> But, the Nazis call his bluff by stepping back, giving Indy a clear shot at the Ark.
> All Indy has to do is pull the trigger…
> But, he simply can't destroy it.
> So the Nazis capture him.

As you can see, the repeated scene serves to demonstrate Indy has changed – he now values Marion more than the Ark. But, it also shows that he still has a passion for the Ark – he can't blow it up. This sets up the film for its big finale…

Scenic Polarity

Variety is the spice of life, and you can spice up your script by including a little variety from scene to scene. At a rudimentary level, polarity between scenes can be achieved through simple **contrast**. A loud scene followed by a quiet one. A long scene followed by a short one. Dark followed by light, and so on.

Contrast has the added effect of magnifying the polarity of both scenes. So the quiet scene seems even quieter if the scene preceding it is loud. Likewise a loud scene is recalled as being even louder because the moment following it is so quiet.

Scenic polarity works across nearly any aspect of a scene, from its emotional charge to its level of conflict – anything you can contrast to keep and maintain audience interest, as well as heighten the roller coaster ride of your film.

While polarity works across scenes, it also works inside them. Polarity denotes the change occurring within the scene. We'll examine polarity within a scene a bit later, but for now, just remember that polarity between scenes serves much like the polar ends of magnets – like charges repel, opposite charges attract, and in our case, serve to bind the movie together.

Scenic Proximity

The closer two scenes are, the more an audience will link them together. Obviously, if you're ending one act and beginning another in the next scene, the hard break between the two will override their location within the film's timeline, but, exceptions aside, placing two scene next to each other implies some sort of connection between them whether you intend there to be one or not.

The design principle here is the greater the proximity, the greater the potential for connection between the two scenes.

Depending on its length, a scene can have acts like a movie, with individual beats in the scene serving the same functions as scenes within the overarching movie itself. As a result, it may be useful to examine scenes in terms of their functionality within the overall narrative of the film. But, before we do that...

SET 1: Like Big Buts   **CRAFT**   **Total Reps: 1**

For this exercise, you'll need choose a <u>major scene</u> in a film or screenplay and list the beats or moments in the scene to see if they're joined with 'but' or 'so'. Name the scene and note its length (pages/time.) If you encounter an 'and' you can list this, too.

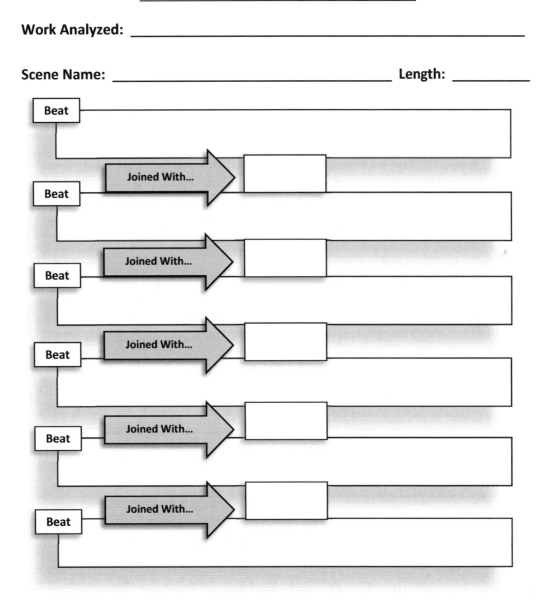

SET 2: *Even Bigger Buts*   *CRAFT*   **Total Reps: 1**

Same exercise, but rather than looking within a scene, now we're looking for But and So <u>between scenes</u> or major story beats in a film or screenplay. Once again, if you an encounter an 'and' feel free to include it.

Movie Construction Analysis for But and So

Work Analyzed: _____

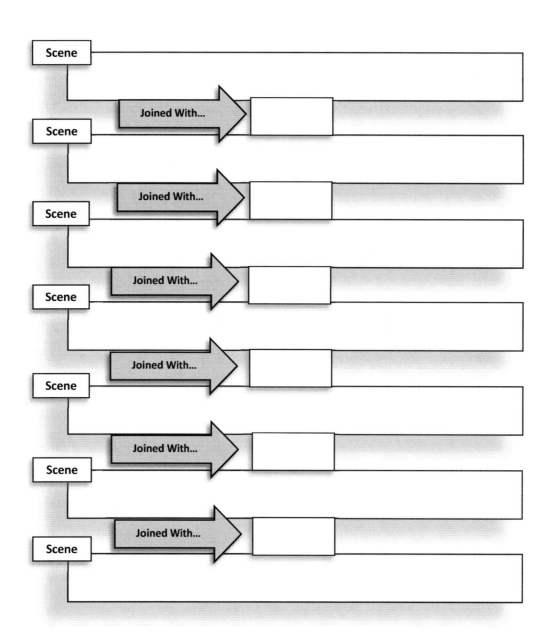

Now, let's examine <u>scenic polarity</u> between scenes.

SET 3: Opposites Attract **CRAFT** **Total Reps: 1**

Using Scenic Polarity pick a sequence of <u>at least four scenes</u> in a movie or script and examine the contrast between them. Pay attention to the emotional energy between the scenes, the levels of action (static vs. dynamic), lighting, length, basically any design element that can be contrasted.

Movie Construction Analysis for Scenic Polarity

Work Analyzed: _____

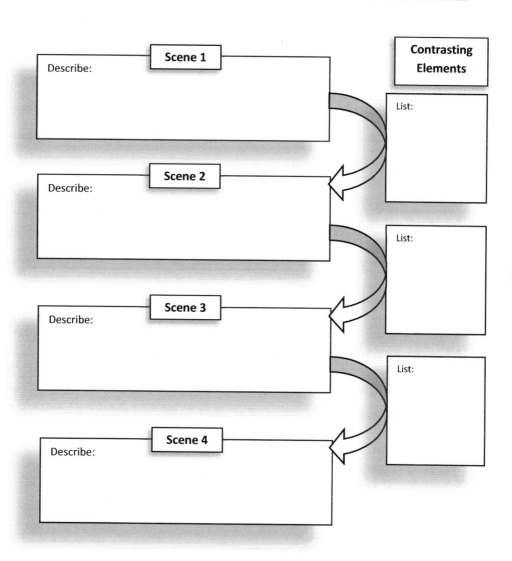

229

SET 4: *Scene Repetition*   ***CRAFT***   ***Total Reps: 8***

Pick a film or script and describe <u>repeated scenes</u> that feature a character facing choices or taking actions that test or are informed by the same thematic value. Note the locations within the story these occur, along with the length of each scene.

If the character faces a choice or does an action and the typical response changes, note what occurred in the scene or scenes prior to the one in which we see the change. Did anything happen in this scene that would have prompted the change in the character's behavior?

<u>Do this exercise for both the main character and the antagonist.</u>

Please note: you may have to watch the film in its entirety before doing this exercise to pick up on patterns in character behavior. Each scene counts as a rep.

Movie Construction Analysis for Scene Repetition

Film Analyzed: _____   **Release Year:** _____

Main Character: _____

Any observable pattern of behavior for this character? _____ (y/n)
If yes, how does this character typically react in a given situation?
Describe:

[ ]

Choice this character faces: _____

How does the character react or what choice is made?
_____

Location of Scene (page or time): _____   **Length of Scene:** _____

This will be the behavior or choice used to check for scene repetition. Now, look for scenes or beats where the character faces similar choices. Also, be on the lookout for patterns in this character's reactions to similar events.

Repeated Scene(s) that feature this choice or reaction:
Note any scenes where the choice or behavior is repeated, along with the character's reaction.

Repeated Scene 1

    Location of scene (page or time): _____   Scene Length: _____

    Choice presented: _____

    Character Reaction: _____

    Is this reaction the same or different? _____

    If different, what (if anything) occurred during the scene or in the scene prior to cause this change?

Repeated Scene 2

    Location of scene (page or time): _____   Scene Length: _____

    Choice presented: _____

    Character Reaction: _____

    Is this reaction the same or different? _____

    If different, what (if anything) occurred during the scene or in the scene prior to cause this change?

Repeated Scene 3

Location of scene (page or time): _____   Scene Length: _____

Choice presented: _____

Character Reaction: _____

Is this reaction the same or different? _____

If different, what (if anything) occurred during the scene or in the scene prior to cause this change?

Repeated Scene 4

Location of scene (page or time): _____   Scene Length: _____

Choice presented: _____

Character Reaction: _____

Is this reaction the same or different? _____

If different, what (if anything) occurred during the scene or in the scene prior to cause this change?

Usually, the change in behavior marks the end of the scene repetition, with the exception of a final test to see if the change stuck.

If you observe a change in the character's choices or behaviors, is there a follow-up scene after this change occurred that somehow 'tests' this new behavior? _____

If yes, what does the character do now instead of the old behavior?

Now, let's do this same process for the antagonist.

Antagonist: _____

Any observable pattern of behavior for this character? _____ **(y/n)**
If yes, how does this character typically react in a given situation?
Describe:

┌───┐
│   │
│   │
└───┘

Choice this character faces: _____

How does the character react or what choice is made?
_____

Location of Scene (page or time): _____ **Length of Scene:** _____

Repeated Scene 1

Location of scene (page or time): _____   Scene Length: _____

Choice presented: _____

Character Reaction: _____

Is this reaction the same or different? _____

If different, what (if anything) occurred during the scene or in the scene prior to cause this change?

Repeated Scene 2

Location of scene (page or time): _____   Scene Length: _____

Choice presented: _____

Character Reaction: _____

Is this reaction the same or different? _____

If different, what (if anything) occurred during the scene or in the scene prior to cause this change?

Repeated Scene 3

Location of scene (page or time): _____   Scene Length: _____

Choice presented: _____

Character Reaction: _____

Is this reaction the same or different? _____

If different, what (if anything) occurred during the scene or in the scene prior to cause this change?

Repeated Scene 4

Location of scene (page or time): _____   Scene Length: _____

Choice presented: _____

Character Reaction: _____

Is this reaction the same or different? _____

If different, what (if anything) occurred during the scene or in the scene prior to cause this change?

Does the antagonist have an opportunity to change? _____

Does the antagonist change behavior when presented with this opportunity? _____

If the answer to this last question is no, you've just discovered a fundamental difference between protagonists and antagonists. One changes. One does not. This aspect of character and plot design is covered elsewhere in this book. But, for some reason, it seemed appropriate to repeat it. ;)

WORKOUT PROGRESS – CRAFT

Compile your workout totals for this unit.

EXERCISE	SKILL GROUP			TOTAL REPS	
	SET #	TYPE	ACTION	AVAILABLE	COMPLETED
Like Big Buts	1	Craft	Analysis	1	
Even Bigger Buts	2	Craft	Analysis	1	
Opposites Attract	3	Craft	Analysis	1	
Scene Repetition	4	Craft	Analysis	8	
				TOTAL REPS	

CRAFT — TOTAL REPS + BONUS — **11**

Scenic Efficiency and Functionality

In ways, functionality is related to scene type. So, a 'Dazzler' scene is intended to dazzle us, to blow us away with its visual virtuosity, its side-splitting humor, its intensity, etc.

But, another way to assess a scene is through the number of functions it serves, how efficient the scene is, how densely packed it is with meaningful information.

As you can probably guess, <u>an efficient scene is one that serves many functions</u>. A well-crafted movie wastes no space – it simply can't afford to. Time is always nipping at your heels, demanding that you leave no opportunity behind to convey character and story.

With this in mind, let's examine some of the functions of scenes.

Scene Functions

- <u>Advance the Story/Plot</u>
  This should go without saying, but nearly every scene has to move the story forward.

- <u>Evoke Mood/Tone</u>
  What kind of movie are we watching? This scene function lets us know.

- <u>Bond Audience to Character</u>
  Make us care about your characters. It's oh so more than just saving cats...

- <u>Convey Genre</u>
  Some scene's main function is simply to relay genre conventions.

- <u>Establish/Heighten Tension</u>
  This scene tightens the screws on a character to create dramatic tension.

- <u>Establish/Escalate Conflict</u>
  This one should go without saying as well, but some form of conflict dominates these scenes.

- <u>Create a Setback</u>
  This is a scene in which a character's goal is thwarted.

- Raise the Stakes
  Similar to heightening tension, these scenes broaden or intensify the consequences should our hero (or any character) fail.

- Reveal Backstory/Exposition
  Challenging scenes to write, here's where we learn about things that happened before the movie started. Watch out for exposition dumps.

- Embed a Set-Up (plant)
  Set-up and payoff – a powerful one-two punch. They hold the film together.

- Reminder of a Set-Up
  If the set-up occurred a while ago, you may want to use this scene function to remind us of it.

- Payoff a Set Up
  If you're going to go to the trouble of setting up, might as well pay it off.

- Teach a Character
  This is a scene in which a character learns something or gains a new insight.

- Offer Alternative Perspectives
  An important scene function, these moments keep the movie from becoming propaganda. As such, these scenes allow opportunities for the audience to create meaning in the story.

- Display Eye-Candy
  Like the name suggests, give us something visual to dazzle our eyes.

- Establish a Character Trait
  These next three are related, and all of them have to do with character building…

- Reinforce a Character Trait
  This function confirms our suspicions about a character's personality.

- Further Reinforce a Character Trait
  Just in case we missed it. Actually, this one is less about the audience missing the trait and more about reconfirming that we were right about a character's personality.

- Portray Character
  Much like the other character functions of a scene, it's a basic function.

- Provide Irony
  How bittersweet this function is – like ray-eee-ain, on your wedding day, which technically isn't really irony, but who's counting?

- Add Humor
  All the world loves a clown.

- Raise Dramatic Questions
  These pique our interest to discover the answer, which conveniently is another function of scenes.

- Answer Dramatic Questions
  Similar to set-up and payoff. Can't have a Q&A with the audience, without the A.

- Provide Surprise
  Boo!

- Create Suspense
  When we absolutely, positively gotta know, these scenes extend the moments between question and answer to leave us begging to know more.

- Build Anticipation
  Similar to suspense, this function sets us up for the awesomeness to come.

- Get a Reaction
  One order of shock value to go, please.

- Create Contrast
  A scene function that works with other scenes or within a scene to change tempo, pace, or any other element you can contrast to generate interest.

- Transition Time or Place
  Perhaps this scene is showing time elapse, or bridging us to another setting.

- Misdirect an Audience or Character
  This function purposely misleads to create interest, proving that red herrings still taste great!

- Provide Texture
  Similar to creating mood and tone, texture refers to adding layers to the story, rounding out its world and characters.

- Develop Subtext
  This function makes us have to read between the lines.

- Create Parallel Action
  Thank you, Edwin S. Porter.

- **Explore metaphor and symbolism**
  Why should writers of literature have all the fun?

- **Explore Theme**
  With all due respect to Samuel Goldwyn, if you want to send a message, use this scene function.

Seems like a pretty good start, but we must have missed a couple along the way. That's where YOU come in!

SET 1: My Two Functions   **CRAFT**   **Total Reps: 2**

Think of **two** more scene functions to add to our list. Please elaborate on each in the space provided below each function.

- _____
  (function)

- _____
  (function)

Now that we know some of the many functions of a scene, we can begin to measure scenic efficiency. We do this by counting the number of functions a scene accomplishes.

As a general rule, the longer the scene, the more functions it needs to serve to justify its length. For the movie to be efficient enough to convey a story with any degree of complexity, each element tends to serve multiple functions. Likewise, a shorter scene can get away with fewer functions.

With this thought in mind, let's analyze some scenes to measure their efficiency.

SET 2: Scene Efficiency   **CRAFT**   **Total Reps: 2**

For this exercise, pick a long and short scene from the same movie. Then, analyze each scene by checking off the functions you find, including the two you added to the list. Please feel free to define long and short scenes by your own criteria.

Analyzing for Scene Efficiency

Movie: _____

Long Scene: _____ **Length in Seconds:** _____

(name the scene)

Scene Functions: Place a check by each function found in this scene. Then, add up your checks to get the total number of functions. Including yours, there are 37 functions.

☐ Advance the Story/Plot	☐ Add Humor
☐ Evoke Mood/Tone	☐ Raise Dramatic Questions
☐ Character Bonding	☐ Payoff to a Set Up
☐ Convey Genre	☐ Answer Dramatic Questions
☐ Establish/Heighten Tension	☐ Provide Surprise
☐ Establish/Escalate Conflict	☐ Create Suspense
☐ Create a Setback	☐ Build Anticipation
☐ Raise the Stakes	☐ Get a Reaction
☐ Reveal Backstory/Exposition	☐ Create Contrast
☐ Embed a Set-Up (plant)	☐ Transition Time or Place
☐ Reminder of a Set-Up	☐ Misdirect an Audience or Character
☐ Teach a Character	☐ Provide Texture
☐ Offer Alternative Perspectives	☐ Develop Subtext
☐ Display Eye-Candy	☐ Create Parallel Action
☐ Establish a Character Trait	☐ Explore Metaphor and Symbolism
☐ Reinforce a Character Trait	☐ Explore Theme
☐ Further Reinforce a Character Trait	Your Functions:
☐ Portray Character	☐ _____
☐ Provide Irony	☐ _____

Total Number of Functions: _____

Now, let's do the same exercise for a <u>Short Scene</u>.

Short Scene: _____ **Length in Seconds:** _____
(name)

Scene Functions: Place a check by each function found in this scene. Add up your totals at the bottom. There are still 37 functions, including yours, on the list.

☐	Advance the Story/Plot	☐	Add Humor
☐	Evoke Mood/Tone	☐	Raise Dramatic Questions
☐	Character Bonding	☐	Payoff Set Up
☐	Convey Genre	☐	Answer Dramatic Questions
☐	Establish/Heighten Tension	☐	Provide Surprise
☐	Establish/Escalate Conflict	☐	Create Suspense
☐	Create a Setback	☐	Build Anticipation
☐	Raise the Stakes	☐	Get a Reaction
☐	Reveal Backstory/Exposition	☐	Create Contrast
☐	Embed a Set-Up (plant)	☐	Transition Time or Place
☐	Reminder of a Set-Up	☐	Misdirect an Audience or Character
☐	Teach a Character	☐	Provide Texture
☐	Offer Alternative Perspectives	☐	Develop Subtext
☐	Display Eye-Candy	☐	Create Parallel Action
☐	Establish a Character Trait	☐	Explore Metaphor and Symbolism
☐	Reinforce a Character Trait	☐	Explore Theme
☐	Further Reinforce a Character Trait		Your Functions:
☐	Portray Character	☐	_____
☐	Provide Irony	☐	_____

Total Number of Functions: _____

To calculate the Scenic Efficiency for your two scenes, turn the page.

To calculate efficiency:
Take the total number of functions and divide by the length of the scene in seconds.

Long Scene:
Total Functions _____ ÷ Length of Scene _____ = _____
                  (# of functions)   (in seconds)   **Scene Efficiency**

Short Scene:
Total Functions _____ ÷ Length of Scene _____ = _____
                  (# of functions)   (in seconds)   **Scene Efficiency**

The higher the number, the greater the efficiency, so based on your findings, which scene was more efficient?

While there is no target number for scene efficiency, it can be a good indicator of how many different things a scene is accomplishing. This, in turn, can indicate if a scene is pulling its weight. Put another way, the greater the efficiency, the tighter the script is. And, a tight script, one in which every aspect serves multiple story purposes, can create a far more engaging audience experience, simply because there's more packed into the film.

Factors Influencing Efficiency
Efficiency isn't the end-all, be-all of analysis, but it does provide a useful measure of how much meaningful information a film is packed into a scene. However, sometimes a scene needs to be less efficient to serve its purpose.

For example…

Earlier we noted that our Indy-Marion tent scene was short, surprisingly short given its importance. In less than a minute and a half we see Indy's flaw, a set up for a repeated scene showing his eventual character arc, provide some nice reversals, advance the plot, etc.

With so much riding on this one scene…

A Question for You
If the tent scene in *Raiders* is really so important to the story, why is it so short?
Jot some thoughts in the space below:

243

It may seem counterintuitive at first, but the reason it's so short is because it's so important.

In other words, it's meant to do one major thing – set up the Repeated Scene that illustrates Indy's arc. As such, if the scene were attempting to do too much, this vital piece of story information may be lost on an audience – embedded in a swirl of details and nuance.

Yes, the scene does serve several functions, but none of them overshadow the scene's main goal.

The rule of thumb here is: **if you want something to stick with an audience, don't overload them with too many details within the scene**. Keep its purpose to the most important element and very little, if anything, else.

Also influencing scene efficiency is the complexity of what the film is trying to accomplish. The greater the complexity of a moment, the more time you may need to devote to this element to communicate it effectively. As such, the scene may seem inefficient, and indeed it will be, but not necessarily to the detriment of the film. <u>Increased complexity often leads to a decrease in efficiency.</u>

Counterbalancing this notion is the idea that the more functions a scene serves, the greater the complexity in the scene. It's an odd paradox, but it cuts to the heart of how movies work.

Ever wonder why so many films combine known elements in unique ways?

It's because those films achieve complexity through the efficient combination of elements that don't require much explanation. In other words, the film achieves complexity through efficiency. What this means is…

To achieve maximum complexity, every element in the film must serve multiple functions.

There's simply no time to do anything else. Or at least do it well.

<u>Remember:</u>
If you want something to stand out, you may wish to minimize the number of functions within a scene to zero in on that one, crystal clear story element that is vital for the audience to understand.

As long as such scenes are kept short, typically you're in good shape.

Playing with these elements a bit…

If you have a complex element that requires considerable explanation to function, as long as you explain it while serving many other story functions, you can maintain efficiency in the narrative, which should keep your audience from getting bored.

There are other factors at play here as well.   Perhaps a particular scene is designed to give the audience a break after a particularly exciting sequence. Perhaps it's a slow, thoughtful change of pace scene, etc.   The bottom line:

Scene efficiency doesn't necessarily mean a film is more entertaining.

It is simply a measure of how efficient you are at your craft. What this translates to is something a bit more nebulous to define -- <u>how tight the story feels.</u>

When we say something is tight, what's really being said is that nothing is wasted. Every element ties in somehow with every other element. Everything has more than one purpose.

That's where you want to be – holding a tight, efficient, entertaining, bulletproof script in your hands. Those scripts get made.

Conclusion:

Understanding scene efficiency requires you to understand what an audience wants and needs from a scene or a particular moment in your film. In most cases, efficiency is welcomed. It gives multiple members of your audience a playground in which to play. So, if some members of the audience want to play on your story's monkey bars, there they are. If others want to play on the swings or slide down the slide, efficiency ensures those functions exist in every moment to allow the audience to pull out of your scene exactly what they wish to get out of it.

However, all those rides can get distracting. Sometimes, you as filmmaker need to limit the functions, so that we, the audience, have a limited number of elements to focus upon. We may not understand why you closed some of the rides. But, if it pays off later, the audience may give you a little time if you've earned it. And, one way to earn that time is by creating a tight, efficient screenplay.

***BONUS SET: Scene Efficiency* and You   CRAFT   *Total Reps*: 2**
For this exercise, choose any two scenes from one of your screenplays or films, and analyze their efficiency. While this can be any two scenes, for fun, be sure to contrast the scenes you pick (long/short, near the beginning/near the end, etc.)

Analyzing for Scene Efficiency

Movie: _____

Scene 1: _____ **Contrasting Element:** _____
           (name the scene)   (ex: long/short, end/start)

Scene Functions: Place a check by each function found in this scene. Then, add up your checks to get the total number of functions. Including yours, there are 37 functions.

- ☐ Advance the Story/Plot
- ☐ Evoke Mood/Tone
- ☐ Character Bonding
- ☐ Convey Genre
- ☐ Establish/Heighten Tension
- ☐ Establish/Escalate Conflict
- ☐ Create a Setback
- ☐ Raise the Stakes
- ☐ Reveal Backstory/Exposition
- ☐ Embed a Set-Up (plant)
- ☐ Reminder of a Set-Up
- ☐ Teach a Character
- ☐ Offer Alternative Perspectives
- ☐ Display Eye-Candy
- ☐ Establish a Character Trait
- ☐ Reinforce a Character Trait
- ☐ Further Reinforce a Character Trait
- ☐ Portray Character
- ☐ Provide Irony

- ☐ Add Humor
- ☐ Raise Dramatic Questions
- ☐ Payoff to a Set Up
- ☐ Answer Dramatic Questions
- ☐ Provide Surprise
- ☐ Create Suspense
- ☐ Build Anticipation
- ☐ Get a Reaction
- ☐ Create Contrast
- ☐ Transition Time or Place
- ☐ Misdirect an Audience or Character
- ☐ Provide Texture
- ☐ Develop Subtext
- ☐ Create Parallel Action
- ☐ Explore Metaphor and Symbolism
- ☐ Explore Theme

Your Functions:
- ☐ _____
- ☐ _____

Length in Seconds: _____ **Total Number of Functions:** _____

Scene 2: _____ **Contrasting Element:** _____
                (name the scene)   (ex: long/short, end/start)

Scene Functions: Place a check by each function found in this scene. Add up your totals at the bottom. There are still 37 functions, including yours, on the list.

☐	Advance the Story/Plot	☐	Add Humor
☐	Evoke Mood/Tone	☐	Raise Dramatic Questions
☐	Character Bonding	☐	Payoff Set Up
☐	Convey Genre	☐	Answer Dramatic Questions
☐	Establish/Heighten Tension	☐	Provide Surprise
☐	Establish/Escalate Conflict	☐	Create Suspense
☐	Create a Setback	☐	Build Anticipation
☐	Raise the Stakes	☐	Get a Reaction
☐	Reveal Backstory/Exposition	☐	Create Contrast
☐	Embed a Set-Up (plant)	☐	Transition Time or Place
☐	Reminder of a Set-Up	☐	Misdirect an Audience or Character
☐	Teach a Character	☐	Provide Texture
☐	Offer Alternative Perspectives	☐	Develop Subtext
☐	Display Eye-Candy	☐	Create Parallel Action
☐	Establish a Character Trait	☐	Explore Metaphor and Symbolism
☐	Reinforce a Character Trait	☐	Explore Theme
☐	Further Reinforce a Character Trait		Your Functions:
☐	Portray Character	☐	_____
☐	Provide Irony	☐	_____

Length in Seconds: _____   **Total Number of Functions:** _____

My Scene Efficiency:
Take the <u>total number of functions</u> and <u>divide</u> by the length of the scene in seconds.

<u>Scene 1:</u>
Total Functions _____ ÷ Length of Scene _____ = _____
　　　　　　　　(# of functions)　　　　　　　　　　　(in seconds)　　**Scene Efficiency**

<u>Scene 2:</u>
Total Functions _____ ÷ Length of Scene _____ = _____
　　　　　　　　(# of functions)　　　　　　　　　　　(in seconds)　　**Scene Efficiency**

Now, we can compare your scene efficiency to that of the film you analyzed.

Your Scene Efficiency　　　　　　　**Their Scene Efficiency**

　Scene 1: _____　　　　　Scene : _____ (long/short)

　Scene 2: _____　　　　　Scene : _____ (long/short)

So, how'd you do?　Remember:　higher the number, the greater the efficiency.

It's important to remember that scene efficiency doesn't indicate if something's good or bad -- it's just a way to gauge if you're getting the most out of your scenes and to identify areas that can do more work for you, which in turn, can help you convey more story in less time.

WORKOUT PROGRESS – CRAFT
Compile your totals!

EXERCISE	SKILL GROUP		TOTAL REPS	
	SET #	TYPE	ACTION	AVAILABLE	COMPLETED
My Two Functions	1	Craft	Application	2	
Scene Efficiency	2	Craft	Analysis	2	
Scene Efficiency and You	Bonus	Craft	Analysis	2	
			TOTAL REPS		

CRAFT　　　　　　　　　　　Total Reps + Bonus　　6

Build-a-Tale 1
Story and Scene

This is the first of several Build-a-Tale exercises. Each of these is designed to work several skillsets, but the primary skill we're building is the ability to make connections between elements to find the story possibilities in them. This is a vital skill every screenwriter should develop and hone. To isolate and strengthen this skill, the elements will be chosen at random. You'll then have to figure out a story based on this arbitrary combination.

Your selections will be chosen on this page by picking numbers from (and including) one to ten. You'll then flip the page to see the story element that corresponds to each number you picked. The large letters you see below correspond to the different categories of story elements you'll be combining.

Oh, and don't peek at the next page to see what the options are. This should be random to really work those story chops!

Choose your Numbers!
Pick a number from one to ten for each category, and write it in the space provided. Choose wisely. You MUST include all four elements in your story.

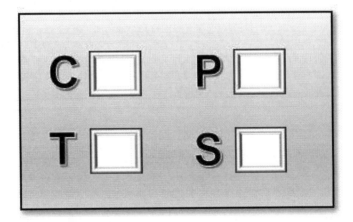

Special Notes on this Build-a-Tale:
For this particular Build-a-Tale, you'll be incorporating your random elements into a scene. Remember, you must use all four elements.
Okay, let's see what you picked!

SET 1: *Story and Scene*   **CRAFT**   **Total Reps: 6**

Write a scene with the character, setting, time period and situation chosen.

The chosen character should be the main character, but isn't necessarily the ONLY character. Likewise, most of the scene should take place in the chosen place and time, but you can elaborate on these if necessary. Most details have been left a bit vague to allow some flexibility. You may combine your chosen elements any way you wish, so long as all four are included in your scene.

Circle the numbers you chose in each category to begin.

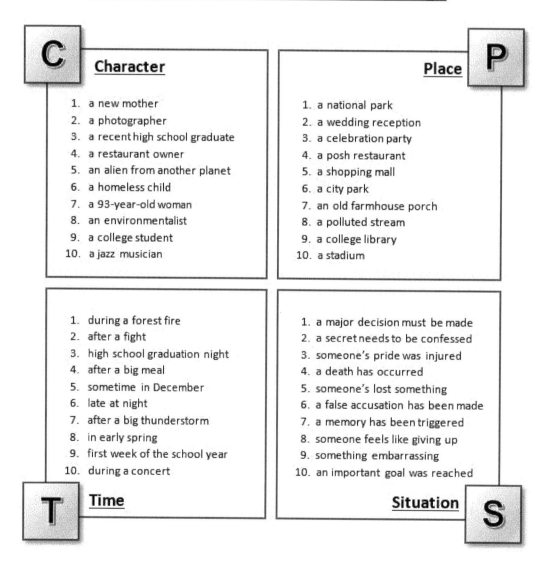

Character
1. a new mother
2. a photographer
3. a recent high school graduate
4. a restaurant owner
5. an alien from another planet
6. a homeless child
7. a 93-year-old woman
8. an environmentalist
9. a college student
10. a jazz musician

Place
1. a national park
2. a wedding reception
3. a celebration party
4. a posh restaurant
5. a shopping mall
6. a city park
7. an old farmhouse porch
8. a polluted stream
9. a college library
10. a stadium

Time
1. during a forest fire
2. after a fight
3. high school graduation night
4. after a big meal
5. sometime in December
6. late at night
7. after a big thunderstorm
8. in early spring
9. first week of the school year
10. during a concert

Situation
1. a major decision must be made
2. a secret needs to be confessed
3. someone's pride was injured
4. a death has occurred
5. someone's lost something
6. a false accusation has been made
7. a memory has been triggered
8. someone feels like giving up
9. something embarrassing
10. an important goal was reached

Using this combination, complete the following to create your scene:

Character: _____
(place your chosen characteristic here)

This will be the main character's <u>Defining Characteristic</u>. Think of complementary traits to flesh out this character and place them below. If you have a second character in your scene (and you probably should), design this person as well. Be sure to consider the design of the first character when creating the second so that they form the most intriguing combination.

Main Character: _____   **Second Character:** _____
(name)   (name)

Character Design

Defining Characteristic	Flaw/Strength-Flaw		Defining Characteristic	Flaw/Strength-Flaw
Paradox	Humanity		Paradox	Humanity

Situation: _____
(place your chosen situation here)

<u>Flesh out the character's situation</u>.
Depending on what you picked, the situation should imply a goal for our main character.

Given the situation and the character design, what would be a logical goal for the character in your scene? Please note: if your situation contains the word 'someone' this can be the main character or another character – your call.

Scene Goal: _____

If you have a second character, how do they complicate (or support) attaining the goal? Be sure to take into account THIS character's design as well.
Jot some thoughts here:

Now, elaborate on the situation by choosing <u>specific details</u> that integrate elements of the character design (and, jumping ahead, the time and place as well.) So, if a major decision must be made (Situation 1), what is the <u>specific</u> decision facing this character? <u>Brainstorm some awesome specifics here</u>:

Time: _____ **Place:** _____
        (chosen characteristic)   (chosen characteristic)

<u>How can the time and place contribute to the characters and the situation?</u> If possible, try to make these add to the conflict by providing additional challenges for the character's pursuit of the scene goal.

Jot some possible complications from the setting (time and place) in the space below.

We could elaborate further, but this should be enough to write your scene. Oh, and please give the scene a name. Be creative!

Scene: _____
                                        (scene name)

Feel free to write your scene in the space provided on the next two pages, or you can type it. Either way, please write your scene in screenplay format. <u>The scene counts as five reps.</u>

Like what you started?
Great! Outline the story! Then, write it! First, we should probably give it a title…

BONUS SET: *Structural Outline* **CRAFT** **Total Reps: 1**

Outline a script based on your combination and describe how you'll show these beats.

Title of Movie: _____

Concept:
Write your concept or logline for the movie here:

1. Hook (1-5)
Can be the birth of the flaw, power of the antagonist, creatively introduce the hero's world or all.

2. Inciting Incident (10)
Overturns the hero's world; introduces a subplot, etc.

3. Central Question (17)
The main story question that will be explored throughout the rest of the movie.

4. Reaction to the Central Question (30)
This is the hero's first attempt to answer the Central Question.

5. First Big Hurdle (45)
Stakes raise. Add a new character to the mix.

6. Apex (60)
Passive to active in relation to the FLAW.

7. False Happy Ending (75)
Looks like we've answered the Central Question in the hero's favor, without addressing the flaw.

8. Low Point (90)
Furthest from answering the Central Question. Must confront GREATEST FEAR to overcome/fix/address FLAW.

Ending:

There are more Build-a-Tale exercises throughout this book; however, if you enjoyed this one, feel free to do it again. Simply pick different numbers to create a new random arrangement of elements to challenge your abilities to find the story in virtually anything.

Now that you know the choices in this exercise, if you wish to keep it truly random, just open the book to a page and use the last digit of the page number (if the page ends in 0, this is ten) to pick what elements you'll be assembling.

If you're concerned about running out different stories with this tool, in just this exercise alone there are 10,000 (10^4) different combinations for you to explore, so get writing!

WORKOUT PROGRESS – CRAFT

Compile your totals for this unit.

EXERCISE	SKILL GROUP			TOTAL REPS	
	SET #	TYPE	ACTION	AVAILABLE	COMPLETED
Story and Scene	1	Craft	Application	6	
Structural Outline	Bonus	Craft	Application	1	
			TOTAL REPS		

CRAFT — TOTAL REPS + BONUS — 7

It's Your Own, Personal... Dictionary?

So, one day I'm watching the old, 1960's *Lost in Space* TV show with my kids – you know, the one with the big, blinky tin-can robot always saying "Warning! Danger!" And, to keep myself occupied, I started listening to the show's soundtrack. While this may seem odd, I was listening for a specific reason. You see, the soundtrack was composed by a guy named Johnny Williams. And, this intrigued me. He's the same guy who, later as John Williams, went on to compose some of the greatest movie soundtracks of all time – *Jaws, Superman, Close Encounters, Raiders, Harry Potter, Jurassic Park, Schindler's List*, and a little ditty that was named the top movie soundtrack of all time – *Star Wars*.

As I sat there watching cheesy 60's TV special effects, I heard something vaguely familiar. A little piece of incidental music – a short violin and cello flourish, which sounded exactly like music from the Death Star™ scenes in *Star Wars*.

This got me thinking -- if John Williams, multiple Oscar™-winning composer, can recycle material, why can't we?

Now, I'm not talking about recycling plotlines or scenes, but rather, coming up with a list of 'go to' phrases and terms you can use from screenplay to screenplay – a writer's equivalent to those little flourishes John Williams pulled from one work and placed in another. Sort of a <u>personal dictionary of clever turns of phrase</u>.

Certain actions recur in screenplay after screenplay. Characters turn to face others, cross rooms, walk down halls, threaten, laugh, eat, are saddened, etc. Character descriptions often duplicate. Locations, as well. If these occur repeatedly, so too can the ways to describe them – not necessarily within the same screenplay, but certainly from one script to the next. Might be nice to have a repository of go-to phrases already created, so you can focus your creative energy on the unique aspects of the screenplay. To help with this, let's start your own, personal dictionary. This will consist of the clever ways you describe things, places and characters. As your dictionary grows, you'll find a veritable bank of catchy stock phrases that are entirely your own.

If all this seems like anathema to artists, please see: Williams, John on the previous page. The idea isn't to recycle aspects of your story that are unique, but rather, to apply your creativity to creating clever ways of expressing recurring aspects of a screenplay. Dialogue should be character-specific to the point where it's not reusable by other characters (with the *possible* exception of secondary roles) and shouldn't be included in this process.

<u>SET 1: Personal Dictionary</u>   **CREATIVITY**   **<u>Total Reps</u>: 4**

Certain actions happen all the time in screenplays, so let's find some clever ways to express them to kick off your dictionary. Take the following words and come up with more precise synonyms – ones that have **connotative** meanings to augment the **denotative** definitions.

For simplicity, we'll break connotative meanings into positive and negative. A positive connotation means the action is meant to be seen as something good. Negative should evoke a bad or less positive feeling. Neutral should evoke mostly the denotative meaning. I'll do the first row to demonstrate.

How many ways can you say...

LOOKS
(as in: to look)

In a positive way	In a neutral way	In a negative way
studies	gazes	leers

MOVES
(ways of moving)

In a positive way	In a neutral way	In a negative way
glides	walks	trudges

These last two are a bit trickier, so there are fewer alternatives to create. But, see what you can do. Oh, and feel free to use phrases rather than single words.

ENTERS

In a positive way	In a neutral way	In a negative way
bursts in	walks	storms in

EXITS

In a positive way	In a neutral way	In a negative way
escapes	leaves	slinks out

If you had difficulty with those last two, in ways, that's the point. By creating more evocative ways of saying commonly recurring actions ahead of time, you can avoid getting stuck coming up with just the right word when actually writing your script. This enables you to stay in the flow of the scene and keep moving forward.

Notice that the more neutral ways of expressing these thoughts almost always require adverbs to clarify and describe. By choosing stronger, more connotative ways of expressing these actions, you pack more description in less space.

This technique isn't just for actions; we can use other go-to phrases to create more evocative ways of expressing any aspect of the script. Two ways to create feeling, and at the same time, employ a little movie math (letting the audience add 2 +2), are simile and metaphor. Novelists and poets use these tools all the time, yet for some reason, screenplays tend to take their writing cues from the inventors of appliance manuals. Fine for that blueprint model of screenwriting, but that's the production aspect of the script. It may not get to production without evocative writing, painting pictures, creating feelings, and so forth.

SET 2: Like Simile and Metaphor   **CREATIVITY**   **Total Reps: 4**

Use simile and metaphor to describe the following generic descriptions.
Oh, and just in case you may have drifted off during 6th-grade English…
A **simile** compares two unlike things using 'like' or 'as'. Ex: rock you like a hurricane.
A **metaphor** also compares unlike things but without 'like' or 'as'. Ex: She's a rollercoaster of emotions.

A room that is neat:

simile: _____

metaphor: _____

A room that is messy:

simile: _____

metaphor: _____

A crowded subway station:

simile: _____

metaphor: _____

A massive party:

simile: _____

metaphor:_____

Note that simile and metaphor don't necessarily save space, but the tradeoff is increased impact, which helps details stick in the mind of the reader. This in turn helps create a more memorable experience, which increases the odds of the script moving to the next level. Hard to recommend a script if you can't remember it. Using unique, evocative prose is just another way to help your script make a lasting impression – one that helps it stand out in a pile of instruction manuals.

SET 3: Making Memories　　　　　**CREATIVITY**　　　　　*Total Reps: 4*

Think of quick, clever ways to describe the following:

A hot, sunny day:

A glance between two lovers:

Someone hurrying to a job interview:

A very old man:

By using a combination of evocative imagery and precise language, you communicate more effectively with your audience, helping your script stand out, while at the same time, helping you stand out as the writer who was able to paint pictures in the minds of your readers. Hmm... I wonder if there's a word for that? Oh yeah – successful. :)

WORKOUT PROGRESS – CREATIVITY

Compile your totals!

EXERCISE	SKILL GROUP		TOTAL REPS	
	SET #	TYPE	ACTION	AVAILABLE	COMPLETED
Personal Dictionary	1	Creativity	Application	4	
Like Simile and Metaphor	2	Creativity	Application	4	
Making Memories	3	Creativity	Application	4	
			TOTAL REPS		

CREATIVITY — TOTAL REPS + BONUS — 12

Indirect Characterization Toolset
Building the Bond Between Audience and Character

Of all the tasks a movie must accomplish, building the bond between audience and character is among the most critical. The early parts of most films are dominated by the filmmaker's attempts to get you to latch on to a character, to care, admire, or at the very least, empathize with a character.

But, just how is this done?

As with all things film, the ways to bond audience and character are as different as the characters themselves. Yet, the process remains fairly consistent.

One way to bond your audience to a character is through **Indirect Characterization.**

> **Indirect Characterization** – a cinematic technique that reveals character through indirect means helping to bond the audience to a character.

Basically, indirect characterization is just that – an indirect way of revealing character. The power of the technique lies in its ability to **guide the audience** into drawing conclusions about characters without directly stating these elements.

Let's face it, being told something is boring – kinda like being lectured to. It's quick, perhaps the fastest way to reveal information, which is why we see it so often, but it's less impactful. Figuring something out on your own is far more interesting – and powerful. This is our movie math deal from earlier. You remember that, right?

Indirect characterization works the same way by hinting at certain character traits and allowing the audience to piece them together. Of course, as filmmakers we usually want to make sure the audience adds it up correctly to draw accurate conclusions, and that's where indirect characterization comes in.

The Indirect Characterization Toolset

Simplicity itself. There are five basic elements:

1. Appearance:
   What a character wears within the world of the story reveals tons of information.

2. Actions…
   Speak way louder than words. Choices reveal character.

3. Private Thoughts:
   These are difficult to get to cinematically, but still a useful tool. Private thoughts motivate the external aspects we can see.

4. Speech:
   Not just what a character says, but how it's said reveals loads of character. Also, what's not said.

5. Reactions of Others:
   How other characters react to a character cues audience reactions to the character – if others like the character, chances are we will too (unless the others who like the character are unlikeable themselves).

And, that's it!

Working with this toolset is easy, but don't be suckered by the simplicity. You can achieve very complex combinations to build deeply nuanced characters using these tools. You can also create surprise, reveals, twists and irony through characters who appear one way, but are actually something else entirely. For example, a character dressed like a bumpkin who says incredibly intelligent things and so forth. As with any tool, overuse leads to cliché, so it's up to you to find fresh, new ways to use these tools in conjunction with each other.

The power of this technique comes from the fact that it hints at something more about the character, which implies there actually is something more. This creates the illusion that characters are more complex than they appear – almost like they're actual, living, breathing, real human beings.

SET 1: Indirect Characterization **CRAFT** **Total Reps: 5**

Pick a movie <u>you haven't seen (yet)</u> and analyze the main character using our Indirect Characterization Toolset. For this analysis **concentrate on when the main character is introduced**. You can then compare these results to later in the film.

Character: _____   Movie: _____

1. Appearance
   Describe:

   What message does the character's appearance send?

   After watching more of the film, was this message accurate?

2. Actions
   How does the character behave?   What actions do they take?

   What message does this behavior send?

   After watching more of the film, was this message accurate?

3. Private Thoughts
   Unless a VO is involved, directly communicating thoughts, the audience pieces this together using appearance, speech, actions and choices. We'll focus on choice since it's not already covered by the toolset.

   What are some choices made by the main character (if any)?

   What does the character appear to be thinking based on these choices?

   After watching more of the film, were these assumptions about character thoughts correct?

4. <u>Speech</u>
   What messages about the character are sent by <u>how</u> this person speaks?

   What messages are sent by <u>what</u> the character says?

   What messages are sent by what the character does <u>not</u> say? (if applicable)

   If there's a beat where the character says nothing, what's the character appear to be thinking in this moment?

   Was this an accurate assumption? (once again, if applicable)

5. <u>Reactions of Others</u>
   How do other characters react to the main character?

   What message(s) does this send about the character to the audience?

Now, using your findings, let's see if we can get at the main character's design.

SET 2: *Design Indirectly*   **CRAFT**   **Total Reps: 4**

Based on the indirect characterization of the character you just chose, what do you think are the character's...

Defining Characteristic: _____ Flaw: _____

Humanity: _____ Paradox: _____

Based on the film as a whole, do these assumptions seem accurate?

BONUS SET: Apply It!   **CRAFT**   **Total Reps: 5**

Analyze one of your own characters to see what indirect messages you're sending about this character's personality.

Character: _____

1. <u>Appearance</u>
   Describe:

   What message does the character's appearance send?

   Is this message intended to be accurate or do you plan to reverse it on the audience?

2. <u>Actions</u>
   How does the character behave?   What actions do they take?

   What message do these behaviors send?

   Is this message intended to be accurate or do you plan to reverse it on the audience?

3. <u>Private Thoughts</u>
   What are some choices your character makes?

   What does your character appear to be thinking based on these choices?

   Are these assumptions about character thoughts correct?

4. <u>Speech</u>
What messages about your character are sent by <u>how</u> this person speaks?

What messages are sent by <u>what</u> the character says?

What messages are sent by what the character does <u>not</u> say? (if applicable)

If there's a beat where the character says nothing, what's your character thinking in this moment?

Do your character's actions, speech and appearance reflect these thoughts?

5. <u>Reactions of Others</u>
How do other characters react to this character?

What message does this send about the character to the audience?

How (or if) you use this tool is entirely up to you. You can choose to have the indirect details mislead the audience, creating reversals and surprise. Doing that, we could have a janitor who turns out to be a math genius. Conversely, you can use them to accurately hint at who a character is. Notice that by hinting at the character traits using indirect characterization, you're giving the audience something to predict and the means to test these predictions. This engages the audience because now they're interacting with your movie.

As with many of our tools for analysis, this one can also be used to create.

SET 3: Indirect Creations   **CRAFT**   **Total Reps: 5**

Given the following design, how would you reveal this character indirectly?

Defining Characteristic: motorcycle gang leader   **Flaw:** quick temper
Humanity: adores his eight-year-old daughter   **Paradox:** writes poetry

Character Name: _____

1. **Appearance**
   Describe:

   What message does the character's appearance send?

   Is this message intended to be accurate or do you plan to reverse it on the audience?

2. **Actions**
   For this one, let's drill down into a specific scene.
   Pretend a Jerky Teacher is giving the daughter a hard time at school and our main character has been brought in for a parent-teacher conference.

   How does the main character behave in this situation?

   What messages do these behaviors send?

   Is the message intended to be accurate or do you plan to reverse it on the audience?

3. Private Thoughts
   Same scene as before. It's a long conference…

   What are some choices your character makes?

   What does your character appear to be thinking based on these choices?

   Are these assumptions about character thoughts correct?

4. Speech
   Feel free to use the conference scene, or you can consider the movie as a whole.

   What messages are sent by how this character speaks?

   What messages are sent by what the character says?

   What messages are sent by what the character does not say? (if applicable)

   If there's a beat where the character says nothing, what's your character thinking in this moment?

   Do your character's actions, speech and appearance accurately reflect these thoughts?

5. Reactions of Others
   How do other characters react to this character?

   What message does this send about the character to the audience?

Using this tool, you can consciously make decisions about how you wish to portray a character, whether or not you wish to mislead the audience to create reversals, and you turn more abstract notions, such as our Biker Dad, into concrete details that can be communicated to your audience.

SET 4: Build it!   **CRAFT**   **Total Reps: 10**

Just for fun, let's build a story out of ol' Biker Dad.

Some points to consider:
Given the character design and how you portrayed the characteristics, how might a story with these characters play out?

Just to refresh, here are our characters so far:

Biker Dad   **8-year-old Daughter**   **Jerky Teacher**

Hmm... we can do more with that teacher.

Given our main character's Paradox, what would be a good subject for our jerky teacher to teach? _____

Now, obviously given the daughter's age, she's probably in elementary school, so the teacher may not teach a specific subject, but if you said English, I'm with you on that. This ties back into the main character's paradox, creating a binary opposition pairing.
Or, we can change the teacher into something else to create more interesting conflicts.

What if Jerky Teacher was a principal instead?
Might be interesting -- both the main character and this character are now leaders. Could create an intriguing dynamic.

Or, perhaps Jerky Teacher is the school counselor.
How might this relate back to our main character? Perhaps Biker Dad had a run in with a school counselor when he was in school. All sorts of possibilities.
And decisions to make...

Create a basic structural outline for a movie featuring these characters.
Feel free to change the teacher to something more interesting if you wish. You can also add characters if necessary, but do keep the conference scene. Did you catch how this scene brings all the main character's design traits into play? The defining characteristic creates a fish out of water dynamic, with our Biker Dad in a formal school setting. He may get mad at the teacher, being a jerk and all, which plays on Dad's flaw. The daughter serves as a unifying device, and depending on how you play her, might be a source for conflict if dad embarrasses her at school. And, depending on how you play the teacher, the paradox could come into play as well. Good stuff. Oh, and give the film a title. Each structural beat counts as a rep.

Title: _____

1-5 Hook:

10 Inciting Incident:

17 Central Question:

30 Reaction to Central Question:

45 First Big Hurdle:

60 Apex:

75 False Happy Ending:

90 Low Point:

Ending:

As you worked through the story, did you modify the characters at all? Just curious...

At the design level, feel free to change characters if necessary to create the most dynamic combinations. That's one advantage to creating story through design – it's an efficient way to work through the plot and characters while ensuring that the elements you've picked all work together. Better to discover that here than on page 77 of your first draft.

With indirect characterization, you provide the audience with concrete details that allude to the design informing them, allowing your audience to create subconscious predictions about the character that you can then reverse or confirm, adding extra layers of resonance to your scenes you characters, and ultimately, your movie.

WORKOUT PROGRESS – CRAFT
Compile your totals for this unit.

EXERCISE	SKILL GROUP			TOTAL REPS	
	SET #	TYPE	ACTION	AVAILABLE	COMPLETED
Indirect Characterization	1	Craft	Analysis	5	
Design Indirectly	2	Craft	Analysis	4	
Apply It!	Bonus	Craft	Analysis	5	
Indirect Creations	3	Craft	Analysis	5	
Build It!	4	Craft	Application	10	
				TOTAL REPS	

CRAFT — TOTAL REPS + BONUS — 29

Setting:
The Other Main Character

Location, location, location. It's the first rule in real estate and in business. Obviously, this refers to the idea that a business or home needs to be in the right place geographically (or in search engine results) to succeed or increase in value. In screenplays the same idea applies, but in a very different way.

In real estate and in business a great location is one that's desirable. Good foot traffic, a great view, you know the deal.

In scripts it's just the opposite.

We want locations that make the lives of our characters more difficult, more challenging. They can be beautiful to look at -- there's a reason James Bond movies aren't set in Anytown, USA, but what we want are **locations that create complications.** This is our prime real estate. Complications lead to conflict, and conflict is the heart of drama.

As you consider the different settings in your script, think of them as characters, full of personality. And, if you want to create an additional layer of conflict for your other characters, think of setting as an antagonist, making your characters' lives more difficult, more challenging, and more interesting to follow on screen.

Setting can also serve as contrast to the content of your scenes. It's much more interesting to see two characters falling in love on the side of the road changing a tire, than it is watching them tumbling through the grass by some waterfalls complaining about sand getting everywhere. In this way, by choosing a setting that makes your characters work harder to achieve their goals, you're highlighting the efforts and motivations for your characters. It's easy to fall in love by a waterfall on a gorgeous day. But, stuck on the side of the road with a bunch of rusty lug nuts in your hand? Far more telling because this subtly informs your audience – this is something special between the characters -- nothing else can explain it.

With this in mind, consider the following scenarios and ask yourself -- what is the absolute worst location I can set each scene? One that makes the character goals the hardest to achieve and makes the lives of the characters the most difficult. Entire films can be generated from just this moment, so make them good!

SET 1: *Location, Location*　　　　*CREATIVITY*　　　　**Total Reps: 8**

Examine the following basic scenarios/situations and list the setting(s) that can create the most intriguing conflicts. Then, describe the possible conflicts and complications that could result from this pairing. Really let your imagination run wild! Who knows? One of these might inspire your next screenplay.

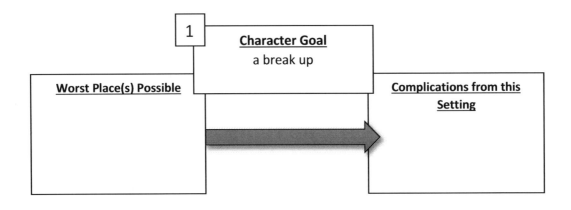

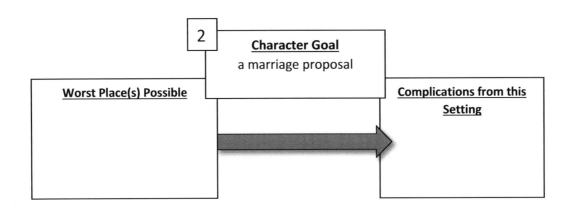

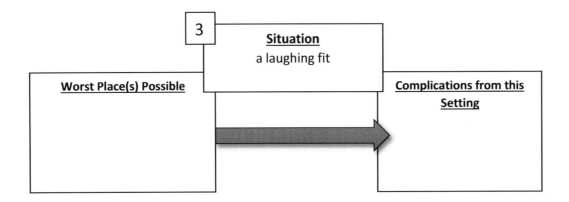

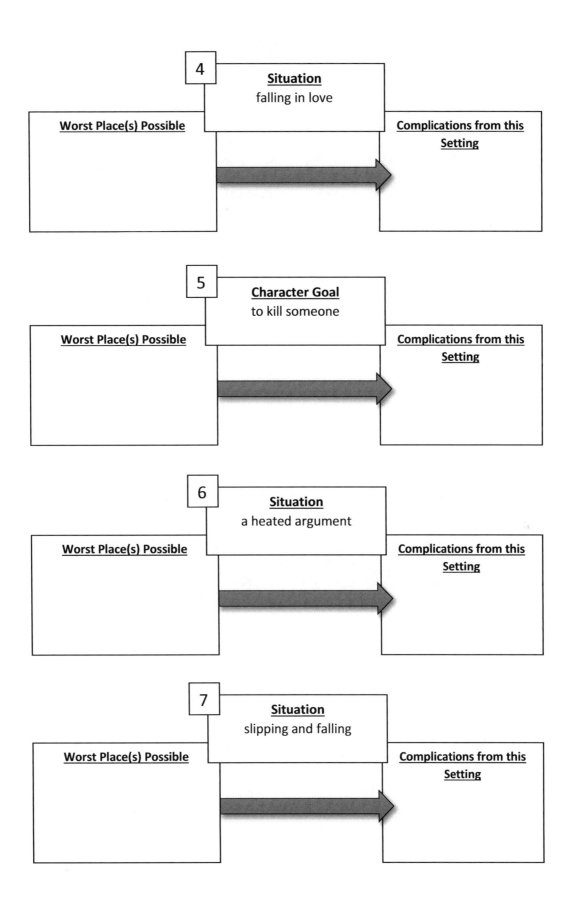

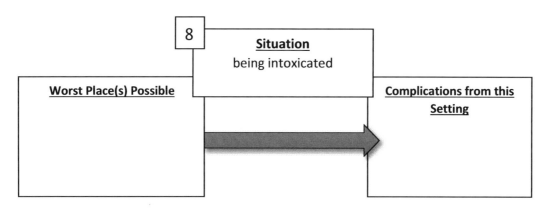

Note:
The worst place may vary depending on the characters involved. So, slipping and falling at a prom may be emotionally devastating for a vain homecoming queen, but no big deal to the school janitor. And, for a tightrope walker, it could be life or death.

***BONUS SET*: Up Setting**   **CREATIVITY**   ***Total Reps*: 1**
Examine one of your screenplays to see if you're getting the most out of your settings and revise if necessary.

WORKOUT PROGRESS – CREATIVITY
Compile your totals!

EXERCISE	SKILL GROUP		TOTAL REPS	
	SET #	TYPE	ACTION	AVAILABLE	COMPLETED
Location, Location	1	Creativity	Application	8	
Up Setting	Bonus	Creativity	Analysis	1	
			TOTAL REPS		

Mixed Relations
The Art and Science of Revealing Character

We've all seen them – characters who come alive on the screen. Characters we feel we know. Rich and vibrant. Full of personality. Movie characters can be open books. Or, they can be mysterious and unknown. But however you cut it, aloof or gregarious, charming or sinister, the tools for revealing these personality traits remain the same – the only differences are the traits you choose for your characters.

Seems simple enough. And yet the trick is…

How do you reveal a character's personality so that he or she seems real?

Hmm… Not much of a trick. Like juggling a single ball. Let's make it a bit harder.

Because not only do you have to reveal personality, but you can't make it too obvious that this is exactly what you're doing. Otherwise it comes off as hammy and contrived, and nobody wants that. So we'll throw in a little **conflict** to disguise the fact that we're revealing character.

Still too easy. We're only juggling a couple balls. Let's muck it up some more.

For you see, revealing character is further complicated by the fact that you have a story to tell, and the primary means to tell it is through character.

So, how do you reveal personality, do it with at least some degree of subtlety, and still have characters who serve the plot and story functions thrust upon them?

Okay. Now we're getting somewhere! We've got three balls in the air – and believe it or not, that's the part that turns this from a trick into an art.

Because it's not enough to do these things separately. That's like juggling one ball, putting it down, then grabbing another.

No.

To pull this off you need to reveal character, through subtle cinematic means (think conflict), and move the story forward – **all at the same time**.

And, to do this requires an examination of the tools specific to creating movie characters and revealing their personalities. Because, before we can create a person, we need to create a personality.

Problem is… how do you do that?

Perhaps we should start at the beginning…

SET 1: Getting to Know You! **CRAFT** **Total Reps: 3**

Read and answer.

A Question for You:
In real life, how do you figure out someone's personality? Jot some responses here:

```
┌─────────────────────────────────────────────────────────────┐
│                                                             │
│                                                             │
│                                                             │
│                                                             │
└─────────────────────────────────────────────────────────────┘
```

Basically, we observe people's behaviors in given situations and gauge their reactions to form a perception of their personality – their character if you will.

We also observe their interactions with us. How they make us feel when we're with them. We observe how they interact with others. How others perceive them, etc.

But, we truly don't know all the facets of a person until we've spent some time with them.

<u>And **time**, as it turns out, is the main determining factor in revealing character and personality</u>.

The more time we have, the more accurately we can assess someone's personality.

It's the same with movie characters.

Correction.

It *can* be the same with movie characters.

Because there's a problem with our observations.

People act differently depending on:
   1. Who they're with.
   2. What they want.
   3. And the situation they're in.

Let's face it – most people behave differently depending on the circumstances. Someone in a courtroom probably acts differently than when alone with a significant other. Then, again... these are interesting times in which we live. But, for the most part, an average person is likely to change behavior based on setting.

So what does this mean for you?

You must place characters in different situations to accurately portray character.

Seems obvious, but so is a rock in the path after you trip on it.

There's also an implication here.

You need scenes. Lots of 'em. So you can quickly establish a character's personality by showing us a variety of situations and how that character responds in each. The more complex the personality, the more moments we need to portray it – and test it.

But, let's start with something simple...

Rebel Without Applause: A Test Scenario

Let's establish a basic character trait in a movie -- a character who's rebellious. To do this you put them in a situation they'll rebel against. Seems easy enough.

But, here's the catch.

If a situation is something *anyone* would rebel against – for example, being asked to kill loved one, then you've not necessarily revealed character. Because if the situation is such that practically anyone would react to it in the same way, you've haven't shown us this character's specific personality, but rather the typical personality of a generic person – an anyone. Make sense?

To get around this, let's alter the scene a bit...

If the character agrees to kill a loved one, without a second thought, this reaction is unexpected, character-specific and reveals loads of character. However, it doesn't reveal the personality trait we set out to establish – rebelliousness. It reveals a different personality.

Unless...

You add another scene, in which the character reveals they will not go through with it. They rebel against the decision.

Of course, that could be misinterpreted as remorse, or regret.

So, you may need yet another scene in which they rebel against something else.

Or, perhaps a whole series of scenes in which the character rebels against everything they're asked to do.

Sheesh! This script is getting long, and we're only trying to convey one, simple character trait. There must be a better way.

As it turns out, there is.

Let's return to our switched up scene. The one where the character agrees to off their loved one. The issue isn't with the character's decision, the issue is what they're being asked to decide. For you see:

Unexpected character reactions reveal personality.

The trick is simple.

<u>Given a situation in which most people will react one way, have your character react the opposite way, or at least differently than expected.</u>

Bringing us back to revealing rebelliousness, here's how it works.

Create a scenario in which a typical person would not rebel, then have your character rebel against it.

This will mean changing the scene. In this case, perhaps the character is being presented with a suitcase full of cash. And, they refuse it -- just because.

Have we established rebelliousness?

Not exactly.
We need to know the context in which the cash is being given. Perhaps the character is concerned they'll owe a favor if the cash is accepted. Perhaps the character's not materialistic. Perhaps the character doesn't need the money.

We also need to know something about who is giving the cash.
Is it blood money? Counterfeit? Is it this person's life savings, thus our character would feel guilty about accepting it?

As you can see, it's difficult to establish even the simplest of personality traits with any degree of clarity in a single scene. We either need multiple scenes or dialogue to help clarify things.

Sticking with our single scene, let's add some dialogue to get at this character's rebellious nature.

While dialogue serves many story functions, the one we're zeroing in on is removing the other possible motivations for this character to refuse the money, so we can get at expressing the notion of rebelliousness.

So, the money is offered. The character refuses it. The person wants to know why. And, the character says – just because you want to give it to me.

Notice that the dialogue helps. But, we still can't be sure it's outright rebelliousness. The character may simply dislike the person with the cash.

So, perhaps we add another line. Maybe the character says he/she likes the person.

But then, how would the other person react to that?

That would call for yet another line of dialogue to explain.

Keep this up, and soon you have three pages of talk, and not much happening.

Further compounding this notion is that if you have a back and forth Q&A between these characters, a truly rebellious character might not answer the other person's questions. She/he would rebel against that.

Now, we can continue piling on dialogue until we've clarified this character is a rebel.

Or… We can simply embrace a fundamental aspect of cinematic storytelling:

> One of the joys of watching a film is the ongoing process of getting to know your characters.

283

Does this mean you abandon the idea of trying to reveal character in a single scene? Not at all!

What this means is <u>revealing character is a continuous process</u> that may require many scenes to establish, many different situations to refine, and even more situations to test before an audience can be sure they've got it right.

It also means <u>characters should possess very consistent personalities during the early part of this process.</u>

Characters can, and do, have multi-faceted personalities, but to establish these, you must first establish a character's **baseline personality** (think Defining Characteristic from our Hollywood Character Design.)

Once the baseline is established, an audience has a personality trait to bounce a character's actions and dialogue off of to get a fuller picture of the other aspects character's personality – a truly three-dimensional character.

So, with rebelliousness…

<u>Once we establish our character is a rebel</u>, we can then explore many facets of his or her personality by placing the character in situations in which rebelliousness is tested.

Back to our suitcase full of cash…

If eventually our rebel accepts the money, we may demonstrate that the character's greed outweighs his or her rebellious nature. Or, perhaps our rebel accepts the money to help a loved one, which shows the audience that this loved one means so much, our character is willing to sell out his or her values for this person.

Lots of different possibilities to reveal character open up once this baseline personality trait is established. However, it's important to note:

Audiences gravitate toward characters with strong personalities.

And, while rebelliousness is a strong personality trait, let's not have our rebel give in to that suitcase of cash so easily. After all, how would a truly rebellious character handle this situation?

To explore this, let's go back to our earlier observation and break it down further. Here's the observation:

People act differently depending on:
   1. Who they're with.
   2. What they want.
   3. The situation they're in.

Revealing Character

1. The Who

In many ways we're defined by the company we keep. It's much the same with character.

Looking at revealing character through this lens, we see that a character can be defined by those around him/her.

You can use the characters around your character to:

- Act as Contrast
  Given a situation, secondary characters can serve to highlight a personality trait in your main character as well as help define our relationship with this character as well.

- Act as Reinforcement
  You can reinforce character traits by having secondary characters confirm our ideas about a character. Having your secondary character say – "Dude! You're crazy!" can help reinforce the notion that a character is out there.

- Provide Perspective
  With their inside knowledge of the story world, secondary characters can provide much-needed perspective on events occurring within the story. By doing this, secondaries help reveal the main character's traits by providing differing points of view. How a main character reacts to this alternate way of doing things reveals loads of character.

- Bring Out Different Sides
  We act differently around friends, colleagues, family, strangers, authority figures. Using secondary characters to fill these roles, then thrusting your main character into interactions with these characters can reveal many different sides to a character's personality.

These character mixes are vital to establishing personality.

While other functions are served by looking at character through this means, one thing should become clear – notice how efficient this approach can be. Because…

As you define one character, you're also defining the other characters in the mix.

The key to this approach is to develop a host of situations and characters -- all designed to allow an audience the ability to discern character. In other words, you're providing proof of who a character truly is by showing various perspectives.

2. The What

What a character wants says a lot about that character's personality. <u>What they're willing to do to get it says even more</u>. The pursuit of what a character wants drives the character (and thus your story), but it's also a tremendous opportunity to reveal the inner workings of a character's personality.

In story design, think of the want as an <u>outer representation of a character's personality</u>. In other words, what a character wants is directly related to who that character is.

So, our rebellious character might rebel to get what he or she wants and may seek out opportunities and/or things to rebel against.

Or, the want may be a symbol of rebellion. Maybe the character wants to get a Harley because it stands for rebelling against the establishment.

Conversely, the character may realize that rebelling may not get them what they want, and thus, may try a different approach. If this strategy runs counter to the character's personality, it creates inner conflict for the character, as well as anticipation in the audience as they wait for the character's true colors to show.

When a character adopts a different personality trait to obtain something he or she wants, you have the opportunity to show the audience different sides of a character's personality – secondary traits that can provide depth and complexity to a character.

3. The Situation

As mentioned earlier, we tend to act differently depending on the situation. Movie characters can do the same, but as an overarching tendency, they do not. Typically a character's personality is so strong they maintain the same one no matter what the situation. They simply can't help themselves. It's this very consistency that helps you create characters that feel real.

Think about a person you know who acts the same no matter where he or she is. They are who they are. Even if the person's a jerk, the inclination to be true to oneself tends to be a highly endearing trait. At least you know what to expect. And, by knowing that, audiences are much more likely to accept it.

The audience's relationship to a movie character is similar. Characters who are who they are despite the situation not only allow the audience to understand personality, but this same aspect endears the audience to these characters.

Later, once a personality trait is defined, you can change how characters behave, depending on the situation. This clues the audience in that the situation is important enough to the character for him or her to try to change (or at least try to be someone else.) Because the personality trait has been established, we know the character's actions aren't truly who they are, and this 'inside' knowledge can bond the audience even further to a character.

Putting It All Together
What we get with this approach is a system of communication so that an audience understands a character's personality. This understanding leads to familiarity, which leads to an audience believing they know a character. Which in turns leads to perhaps even caring about a character. Which in turn leads to…

A Question for You.
In real life, how do you know that you truly know someone? Respond in the space below.

| |
| |

You may have responded in a number of ways, but if you think about a close friend, or someone you've known for a long time, I bet you could say that you have a pretty good idea of how that person would react in a given situation. In other words, when you think you know someone, they become almost…

Predictable.

There, I said it. It bears repeating.

Predictable. So, how can predictability be a good thing? Isn't it anathema to cinematic storytelling? Yes. Sometimes. But perhaps more rarely than it may seem.

For you see, the ability to predict what a person will do is a hallmark of friendship. When you know someone, really know them, you probably have good idea of what they'll do, how they'll respond in any number of situations. You just know. Whether it's a friend, buddy, significant other, doesn't matter. You almost always know what response you'll get. Indeed, a part of friendship is being able to go to this person to get the reaction you expect. As filmmakers, this real-life phenomenon can become a powerful tool at your disposal because:

> Giving the audience the opportunity to predict how your characters will respond gives them the illusion that they know a character.

Here's something else:

The greater the degree of accuracy in these predictions, the more the audience feels bonded to a character because it's as if they're known this character all their lives.

This implies that characters should be consistent and relatively predictable when we first meet them so that the audience feels like they know who these people are.

However...If you've been paying close attention, you should notice an inherent contradiction in that bolded statement.

Did you catch it?

I'll save you the effort of flipping a few pages back and just restate something we mentioned earlier: Unexpected character reactions reveal personality.

Okay. Wait just a second.

If unexpected reactions reveal personality, how can a character be both unexpected and predictable?

Simple.

And as you should know by now -- whenever the word simple shows up in regards to movies, the answer is anything but. However, this time it truly is the essence of simplicity.

The Intersection of Plot and Character

To reveal multiple character personalities, we need situations within the framework of your story, in other words, the plot.

Just so we're on the same page, I'm going to throw something at you. An idea. Just to see if it sticks.

<u>Plot exists solely to advance our understanding of character.</u>

This may seem backward to those who enjoy a good tale, so I'll repeat:

<u>Plot exists solely to create events to allow for the exploration of character.</u>

Hey! Now we're getting somewhere! For you see…

Plot events serve as character-defining moments within the overarching story. The choices characters make based on the plot they find themselves in provide the audience with not only character, but also the means to enter the narrative.

In other words, audiences experience the story through the characters – either by observation or by relating directly to the characters. Either way, when we watch a movie we're watching a marriage, a merging, of plot and character.

Like two dancers moving as one.

Now, to reveal character personalities in plot events, the trick is simple…

<u>Create a situation and have multiple characters react and interact toward it.</u>

Hmm… underlined and bolded. Must be an important idea.

In essence, a movie can be defined as a series of situations or events that enable characters to have opportunities to react. Likewise, for the sake of efficient storytelling, having multiple characters reacting to the same event in different ways enables you to define more characters without having to create all-new events.

Taking this notion further, once the characters react, they hopefully affect story events moving forward, and so you achieve a synergistic relationship between plot and character. Or putting it another way – the story feels alive rather than contrived, because the characters, characters that we can see, appear to drive the story forward rather than some unseen filmmaker standing just off screen.
To achieve this effect, remember:

CHARACTER CHOICES MUST AFFECT PLOT!

Okay, underlined, centered, bolded, and all caps? This must REALLY be important. And, indeed it is.

In order to pack the sufficient complexity within both character and plot to create a compelling film, you as filmmaker must be extremely efficient. Time is always working against you. And, as we explored earlier, the indirect nature of cinematic storytelling works against you – even while trying to establish something as simple as a character trait.

One of the most efficient ways to achieve complexity within characters and create a sense of unexpectedness within plot is to have the narrative driven by the choices your characters make. Look at what it accomplishes:

Character Choices...

1. Define Characters
Both through the choices and other characters reactions to these choices.

2. Create Conflict
If characters have strong convictions and make choices that bring them into opposition – the possibility for conflict invariably ensues. And because choice causes the conflict, this opens up characters to inner conflict as well.

3. Make the Plot Less Predictable
People make surprising decisions all the time. We're used to it in real life. Characters can do the same in your movie. Their unexpected choices keep the plot fresh, while giving the illusion that the story is not a contrivance.

4. Make the Narrative Come Alive
Characters reacting to story events and in turn shaping the story through their active decisions and choices gives the illusion that what we're experiencing is actually happening, as opposed to being the brainchild of some caffeine-fueled filmmakers.

5. Create Stakes
Choices carry consequences for the characters making them. Once again, this creates the illusion we are watching events unfold as we watch a film, rather than something that is predetermined. It has the added benefit of investing characters in their world, which in turn, invests an audience in the world of the film.

Your Turn!

Think of another benefit to using character choice to drive plot and add it to the list on the blanks below. Be sure to explain the benefit.

6. _____

_____

_____

Now, here's where it gets interesting – because just when it seems we've gone off on a tangent...

Character choices are the outer manifestation of a character's personality.

Choices reveal who a character is as a person. The harder the choice, the more character-revealing it can be.

They can also be used to track changes in personality – the character's arc. Simply repeat similar situations throughout the film so audiences can see for themselves whether a character has changed. Remember, for this to work – that baseline personality has to be established first. Otherwise, we have no way of knowing whether the personality changed. The character will simply come across as unpredictable, and therefore undefined.

Notice when we were trying to establish the personality trait of rebelliousness earlier, each example involved some kind of choice the character had to make. It really is that simple.

What this also means is that you have to create situations that test this very trait. In other words, you have to design story events to fit the personality traits you wish to reveal.

If the situations are inappropriate to reveal a particular character trait, the story may seem to lack focus and clarity. Likewise, if you create characters whose personalities aren't tested by the situations they face, once again the result tends to underwhelm.

To sum, the choices characters make should be rooted in a character's <u>deep-seated beliefs</u> and <u>personality</u>. The events in the movie are then created to challenge a character's beliefs and complicated by a character's personality. Beliefs are fairly easy to change. Personality is not. Therefore, a convincing character arc often involves a process of disproving beliefs before tackling (or as a step toward) the more difficult process of making a real personality change.

From a narrative design standpoint the process looks something like this:

1. Establish a character's <u>baseline personality trait</u>. The one that will undergo change as the movie progresses. It can be a flaw, or defining characteristic.

2. Re-establish this trait so that the audience understands it.

3. Reinforce this trait by establishing a <u>belief</u> the character has based on it.

4. Test the belief and personality trait through a series of plot events designed to explore these things.

5. Use <u>character choices</u> throughout the process to refine, test, and reveal beliefs and personality traits.

6. Rinse and repeat. Escalating events until a <u>major event</u> forces a huge character choice.

7. Re-test the belief and trait after the <u>major event</u> that should have changed the character.

8. Have the character use the change to succeed. Often this may be the final test to see if the change is permanent.

It's this process that makes a character's personality seem real.

It's also the process used to communicate a character's arc.

Let's apply it to our rebellious character.

1. **Establish a character's <u>baseline personality trait</u>.**
   The one that will undergo change. It can be a flaw or defining characteristic. *Done: Rebellious. Let's intro the character in a scene showcasing this trait.*

2. **Re-establish this trait so the audience understands it's a pattern.**
   We'll need another scene in which our character interacts with different characters and in different situations to confirm our character is indeed rebellious.

3. **Reinforce this trait by establishing a <u>belief</u> the character has based on it.**
   Our character believes no one can be trusted – especially authority figures. Our character only relies on himself. Seems to be an easy fit for our rebel.

4. **Test the belief and personality trait through a series of plot events designed to explore these elements.**
   So we need a plot that will involve our character learning to have to trust and rely on someone other than himself -- perhaps an authority figure.

5. **Use <u>character choices</u> throughout the process to refine, test and reveal beliefs and personality traits.**
   As the story progresses the character continually makes rebellious choices that get him into deeper trouble. Nothing seems to change the character's belief that he can only rely on himself.

6. **Rinse and repeat. Escalate until a <u>major event</u> forces a huge character choice.**
   After a series of rebellious choices, our character makes a choice that causes his best friend to die. Now the only person he even remotely trusted is gone, AND, even worse, the character can no longer even trust himself.

7. **Re-test the belief/trait after the <u>major event</u> to see if it changed the character.**
   The character, after undergoing this traumatic event gets an insight that perhaps his beliefs are wrong. This may be a point to bring in that authority figure mentioned earlier. Looks like the character may have changed.

8. **Have the character use the change to succeed.** Often this may be the final test to see if the change is permanent.
   The character undergoes a final test in which rebelliousness and lack of trust are on the line. The character no longer rebels and now trusts others (and thus no longer relies on just himself.)

                                                         FADE OUT.

And, just for fun, let's call this character Maverick and title the movie *Top Gun*.

Okay, now it's your turn!

SET 2: Arcing Traits   CRAFT   Total Reps: 16

Pick a personality trait and use this system to create plot events/scenes that will explore it. <u>Be more specific with your scenes than the provided example.</u>

Character Name: _____

Personality Trait: _____

1. Establish character's <u>baseline personality trait.</u>
Make this the character's introduction and describe this scene here:

2. Re-establish this trait.
List scenes/beats and new character mixes to reveal and highlight this trait below:

3. Reinforce personality trait by establishing a <u>belief</u> based on it.
So, based on this trait, what logical belief would stem from it? Write the belief here:

4. Test belief and personality trait through plot events.
List a few plot events that could be used to explore the character's belief and trait.

5. Use character choices throughout
Given the plot events you just listed, what choice does the character make as a result of each event and how do these reveal the character's belief and personality trait?

Choice	How this reveals character's belief and personality

6. Rinse and repeat.
Essentially the same as above, only this time, take these events and describe how they build the plot, culminating in a major event – what's the big choice here?.

Describe how your scenes also advance the plot:

Building to the Major Plot Event:
Describe this scene, how it's driven by the character's belief and personality, and what *choice* the character makes (or is presented with) that also reveals character:

7. Re-test the belief and trait after the major event.
If the character has changed, the behavior you've established earlier will also change. If the character has not changed, this behavior remains the same. If the character is on the fence, they might not know how to react and this is a period of indecision.

What's this scene?

How does the character act differently?

What BIG CHOICE must the character make here?

8. The final test.

Typically this is the final showdown with the antagonist. It's designed to play on the character's belief and trait. Perhaps a last temptation to go back to the character's old ways. Usually, this scene mirrors an earlier one to give the audience the ability to directly compare results, thus enabling them to isolate the variable (in this case, the character's arcing trait), which enables the audience to know that the character has truly changed.

Describe this scene:

How does the change help the character pass this test?

What choice does your character make now that's different as a result of the change?

Once the character changes for good, this usually marks the end, but that's not nearly challenging enough, now is it?

Now, take the same plot elements you listed in **Steps 4, 6, 7 and 8** and add a NEW CHARACTER with a DIFFERENT PERSONALITY to the mix. Ideally, this personality trait contrasts that of the previous character.

You'll then ask how someone with this personality would react to the same events.

New Character Name: _____

New Character's Personality: _____

Now pick ONE situation/event from steps 4, 6, 7, 8. List them below, and briefly describe how this new character would react. BE SPECIFIC! Don't choose generic reactions. They should come directly from the character's personality trait.

4. Event: _____

   Reaction:

6. Event: _____

   Reaction:

7. Event: _____

   Reaction:

8. Event: _____

   Reaction:

Now, if you want to make this thing even tighter, you can have the choices a character makes directly affect another character.

<u>Take a look at steps 5 and 6.</u> How will the choices here affect our new character?

Let's find out.

<u>List some of the choices in steps 5 and 6</u>. Then describe how our new character is affected. Please note: this may require a little tweaking of character and/or choice. Also note: how would our new character react to these choices?

Choice: _____

Effect it has on new character:

New Character's reaction to this choice:

Choice: _____

Effect it has on new character:

New Character's reaction to this choice:

Choice: _____

Effect it has on new character:

New Character's reaction to this choice:

The BIG CHOICE from Step 6:
_____

Effect it has on new character:

New Character's reaction to this choice:

Okay, good. You should have the basics of a story or a plot designed from the ground up to reveal character.

Fun, huh?

Now let's go back. Way back. To juggling those balls.

Remember, we started this with trying to establish a single personality trait. Just one. Something simple.

And yet, as you can see – what comes out of this is anything but simple.

This is why we start with simplicity. Just that one baseline personality trait. That one characteristic you establish early in your film and stick with throughout the course of the story. Will you add things to it? Of course. Expand upon it? You bet. But from this one element you achieve great complexity that is still understandable.

Not only that, but this one predictable trait that we, the audience, understand about your character, enables us to believe we know who your character is. And, once we think that, we assign complexity to the character that may or may not be there. We also bond with this character, invest in them, worry about them as though they're a friend in peril.

Look at how many balls you can juggle with this one, simple tool.

Now, how do you avoid predictability from becoming boring?
This leads us back to those unexpected reactions and the idea that even **a predictable reaction can (and should) lead to unexpected results and consequences.**

The process an audience goes through when getting to know your character is one that moves from unfamiliarity to familiarity to predictability. But, once we feel we know the character, that's where his or her personality can truly shine.

Even the best of friends can surprise us. But, to achieve surprise, you have to know their tendencies first. In other words, to get an unexpected reaction, you must first have a set of expectations. And these expectations are the very predictability we've been discussing.

Put another way -- characters must be predictable for them to be unpredictable.

The idea here is that you as filmmaker must teach the audience what this one, predictable personality trait is -- a trait that's unique yet identifiable. In this way, you can bond an audience to almost any character, quickly and efficiently, while at the same time maintaining interest in the character.

Would you put this much time and effort into any old character trait?

No. This method is more for those aspects of character you wish to define with precision, to ensure the audience understands them. Other character traits can be more interpretative, more loosely defined – as long as the audience is in the ballpark with these, that's fine – better even in ways because the audience is personally defining these.

Specifically, this process is reserved for a vital aspect of character – the <u>Arcing Trait</u>. We discussed this facet of character back when we were hanging out with Indiana Jones collecting rare and unusual artifacts, but as a reminder – the arcing trait is the character behavior you've picked to demonstrate growth or change in a character.

However, even for characters who do not arc or grow as a result of the journey through the plot, this process is used to convince an audience they know someone they just met as well as they might know a good friend – the perfect travelling companion for the journey through your story.

See?

Told you it was simple!

WORKOUT PROGRESS – CRAFT

Compile your totals!

EXERCISE	SKILL GROUP		TOTAL REPS	
	SET #	TYPE	ACTION	AVAILABLE	COMPLETED
Getting to Know You!	1	Craft	Analysis	3	
Arcing Traits	2	Craft	Application	16	
			TOTAL REPS		

CRAFT — TOTAL REPS + BONUS — 19

Something Like an Outline

Most outlines are ways to organize your story content. A place to work through the plot and characters. A plan to tell a story. And, that's great. Outlining is a terrific way to catch story problems before you write.

But, another way to outline is by ow you want to affect an audience. It's like a beat sheet of sorts, but rather than describing the contents of the scenes, you describe how you intend each of your scenes to impact your audience.

The trick with this technique is to be bold, to challenge yourself and to see if you meet your own challenges. Here's how it works.

For each scene in your script, make a <u>declarative statement</u>. This is your pact with the audience for that scene. It's what you intend to do to the audience, to show the audience; how you want the audience to feel. To do this, simply say the following:

In this scene, I will _____...

Then, fill in the blank with a strong, impactful statement.

So, for example:

>In this scene I will <u>dazzle the audience with something they've never seen!</u>

>In this scene, I will <u>make the audience laugh so hard it hurts.</u>

>In this scene, I will <u>make the audience cry.</u>

And so forth...

The idea is to create goals for how your scenes will affect an audience, and then, live up to them. You can be as detailed as you like, or focus on the broad ways you want the audience to feel or react. The choice is yours.

<u>PLEASE NOTE</u>: Each scene should have multiple goals. Yes, you can make us laugh, but you also must move the story forward, provide exposition, create suspense, etc. **at the same time.**

If you find your goals for impacting the audience or conveying your story aren't being met, creating an intention-based outline gives you a plan to address this, something to shoot for in rewrites. If many scenes have similar goals (or similar effects), you can use this method of outlining to identify redundant beats in your story, your pacing, and whether you're creating contrast between scenes to keep the audience engaged.

You may find that in the process of telling the story, you're not *selling* the story, if that makes sense. In other words, using this approach as an analytic, you may discover that the script conveys the story, but the audience experience needs work. Or, you may discover your script is on point, and you rock as a writer.

You can retrofit this outlining method to an existing script or use it as a prewriting guide. But, however you use this technique, the key is to make <u>bold, strong, declarative statements for each scene</u>.

And, why?

Because each of your scenes should make bold, declarative statements in your movie.

It's a simple as that.

For outlining, this approach adds an additional layer to a story-based outline. It doesn't replace traditional outlines, but rather, this approach charts the effects of scenes on an audience, giving you a map of the audience experience, which you can then modify to achieve the impact you want.

Ultimately, this technique is a way of assessing how a screenplay or movie functions at the scenic level. In other words, it measures what a scene does, not what it is. By measuring the functionality of your scenes, what you're really doing is outlining the audience experience of your story. This approach also gives you a way to compare your intent versus your content, giving you an indicator of whether what you intended for your scenes matches your content, what you actually wrote.

To give this approach to outlining a try, we'll start by using this tool to outline the first ten scenes of a screenplay. We'll then use the exact same tool to analyze the first ten scenes of an existing screenplay or movie.

SET 1: Something Like an Outline   CRAFT   Total Reps: 10

For this exercise, use the form below to outline the <u>first ten scenes</u> of a script to be written later. Feel free to use any of the ideas you've developed in this book, or you can apply it to a different script you intend to write.

The tool breaks each scene down like this:

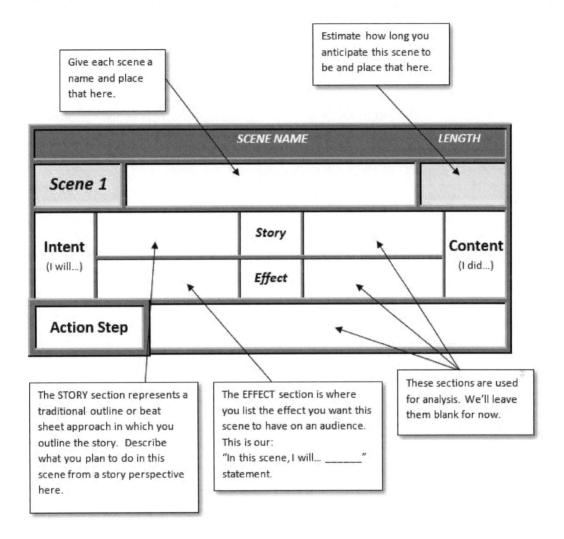

For the scene's length, you can estimate this by page count or estimated runtime. Page counts in scripts are measured in eighths of a page. So, for a scene that runs 1 ½ pages you'd list this as 1 4/8ths (not 12/8ths.) A scene that's a quarter of a page is 2/8ths, and so forth. If you want to convert this to runtime, a script page with an average mix of dialogue and action runs about a minute. Dialogue scenes typically go faster, action scenes a bit slower. It's not unusual for a two page dialogue scene to only take up a minute of actual screentime.

Okay, time for outlining adventure! Or romance. Or drama. Or…

Outline the first ten scenes of a screenplay below.
The content and action plan sections should be left blank for now. You'd use these AFTER the screenplay is written to check effectiveness.

Define what constitutes a scene as you see fit.
You can go slugline to slugline, or you can define a scene more in narrative terms. For example, let's pretend we have a scene with a couple arguing. It starts in the kitchen, one slugline; continues into the driveway, another slugline; and while driving in the car, yet another slugline; finally concluding on the side of a freeway, which would call for, you guessed it, another slugline. In writing terms, this could be defined as a single scene. In production management terms, this sequence is four separate scenes.

Something Like an Outline:
A Pact With my Audience for…

Title of Work: _____

Genre: _____ **Writer:** _____
(can be a blend)   (name)

	SCENE NAME	LENGTH
Scene 1		
Intent (I will…)	**Story** / **Effect**	**Content** (I did…)
Action Step		

	SCENE NAME			LENGTH
Scene 2				

Intent (I will...)		*Story*		**Content** (I did...)
		Effect		

Action Step	

	SCENE NAME			LENGTH
Scene 3				

Intent (I will...)		*Story*		**Content** (I did...)
		Effect		

Action Step	

	SCENE NAME			LENGTH
Scene 4				

Intent (I will...)		*Story*		**Content** (I did...)
		Effect		

Action Step	

	SCENE NAME	LENGTH
Scene 5		

Intent (I will...)	**Story**		**Content** (I did...)
	Effect		

Action Step	

	SCENE NAME	LENGTH
Scene 6		

Intent (I will...)	**Story**		**Content** (I did...)
	Effect		

Action Step	

	SCENE NAME	LENGTH
Scene 7		

Intent (I will...)	**Story**		**Content** (I did...)
	Effect		

Action Step	

	SCENE NAME	LENGTH
Scene 8		

Intent (I will...)		Story		**Content** (I did...)
		Effect		

Action Step	

	SCENE NAME	LENGTH
Scene 9		

Intent (I will...)		Story		**Content** (I did...)
		Effect		

Action Step	

	SCENE NAME	LENGTH
Scene 10		

Intent (I will...)		Story		**Content** (I did...)
		Effect		

Action Step	

If you write a screenplay based on this outline, you could then analyze the CONTENT you've written using this outline to see if the execution matches the intent. To explore using this tool for analysis, turn the page.

SET 2: *Something Like Analysis*   **CRAFT**   **Total Reps: 10**

Let's analyze the first ten scenes of an existing work -- either a feature film or a screenplay (yours or a different one.)

This time, you'll fill in the content sections for their story and audience effects. If you're using your own screenplay, the intent sections should be known. If you're analyzing the work of another, you'll have to give the intent sections your best guess. To do this, watch or read each scene carefully and ask what you think the filmmaker is going for in the scene. You can then compare this intent to what the content is doing to measure the filmmaker's effectiveness.

The same definitions you used for outlining you'll use here for defining scenes and determining scene lengths.

Special Note: If analyzing your own work, you can fill in the ACTION STEP portion. Essentially, if you encounter a scene where your intent doesn't match your content, you'd note how to address this in the Action Step section.

Something Like an Analysis

Work Analyzed: _____
(title)

Type of work: _____   **Writer:** _____
(screenplay, movie, etc...)   (name)

Genre: _____   **Release Year:** _____
(can be a blend)   (or year written)

	SCENE NAME	LENGTH
Scene 1		
Intent (I will...)	Story / Effect	**Content** (I did...)
Action Step		

SCENE NAME		LENGTH
Scene 2		

Intent (I will...)	Story		Content (I did...)
		Effect	

Action Step	

SCENE NAME		LENGTH
Scene 3		

Intent (I will...)	Story		Content (I did...)
		Effect	

Action Step	

SCENE NAME		LENGTH
Scene 4		

Intent (I will...)	Story		Content (I did...)
		Effect	

Action Step	

SCENE NAME		LENGTH
Scene 5		

Intent (I will...)		Story		Content (I did...)
		Effect		

Action Step	

SCENE NAME		LENGTH
Scene 6		

Intent (I will...)		Story		Content (I did...)
		Effect		

Action Step	

SCENE NAME		LENGTH
Scene 7		

Intent (I will...)		Story		Content (I did...)
		Effect		

Action Step	

	SCENE NAME	LENGTH
Scene 8		

Intent (I will...)		*Story*		**Content** (I did...)
		Effect		

Action Step	

	SCENE NAME	LENGTH
Scene 9		

Intent (I will...)		*Story*		**Content** (I did...)
		Effect		

Action Step	

	SCENE NAME	LENGTH
Scene 10		

Intent (I will...)		*Story*		**Content** (I did...)
		Effect		

Action Step	

When analyzing intent versus content, in ways you're examining the writer's effectiveness. So, if you analyzed your own work, did your scenes do what you intended?

When you write a script, in actuality, you're writing three scripts:

1. The script you think you wrote.
2. The script you actually wrote.
3. And, the script we read.

And, the kicker? All of them are completely different.
Think about it. A reader's perception of the script can be drastically different from what you intended. Likewise, there can be a disconnect between our own perceptions of what we've written and what we actually wrote.

What this tool is designed to do is help align what we want to do as writers and what we're actually doing. When these two are the same, you have a much greater chance of achieving the impact you wanted when you began the script. One way to do that is to analyze, find the misalignments, and rewrite. Or, you can get a jump on this process and use this tool to outline *before* you write. Either way, by honing the experience of your story, you give yourself a far greater chance of getting your intentions across to an audience, increasing your chances of success. Who doesn't want that?

WORKOUT PROGRESS – CRAFT
Compile your totals for this unit.

EXERCISE	SKILL GROUP		TOTAL REPS	
	SET #	TYPE	ACTION	AVAILABLE	COMPLETED
Something Like an Outline	1	Craft	Application	10	
Something Like Analysis	2	Craft	Analysis	10	
			TOTAL REPS		

CRAFT — TOTAL REPS + BONUS — 20

Any Way You Say It

Dialogue. Some consider it the death of cinema, harkening back to the days of the silent picture. Others (think Aaron Sorkin) owe their careers to it. That snappy verbal banter, the clever turn of phrase, just the right thing said at just the right time – there's nothing like it. Such dialogue can be the cherry on top, or it can be the main course. Perhaps my favorite quote about dialogue goes something like this: "When the script is written, and the dialogue is added; we're ready to shoot." Good quote that one. For to me it represents dialogue's place in our craft – if you can't show it, I mean REALLY can't show it, say it. There are obvious exceptions – verbal comedy, parlor dramas, courtroom dramas, the list goes on. But, whatever your relationship is with the spoken word, one thing's for certain – dialogue can be a bear to get right. Some use it as a blunt tool for telling the story directly to the audience, feeding us the entire story through the spoken word. Others use it to simply convey information that can't be easily told through more cinematic means. But, whether it's advancing the plot or just getting a laugh, the key to vibrant, crisp dialogue lies in a simple premise – dialogue is a manifestation of character.
Or, at least it should be...

With that in mind, check out the following activity.

SET 1: Bottom Lines　　　　　　　　　　**CRAFT**　　　　　　　　　　**Total Reps: 24**
For this exercise, you'll take generic statements and make them character specific.

You'll find a list of statements below an average person might say. This is the problem -- if anyone can say it, it's not coming from character, it's coming from a generic anyone. This results in inefficient dialogue that's less entertaining. Yes, you could make a case that generic dialogue often gets to the point quicker and with greater clarity, speeding up the delivery of narrative information. And yes, there are times for that. However, that sort of dialogue is also inefficient because it's wasting prime opportunities to reveal character, and actually make the audience *care* about getting to the point and advancing the story.

You'll be given limited information to work with – just each character's Defining Characteristic, but even with such limitations, I hope you discover that lines with even just a touch of character are more interesting than their generic counterparts. Okay, enough with the intro – let's work up a sweat!

Anyone can say: <u>I want to go out with you.</u>
How would the following characters say that? Be creative!

Forrest Gump's Twin Sister:

A successful 50-year-old CEO:

A 35-year-old teamster from Detroit:

A tough biker:

A tenured literary professor:

A self-confessed soccer mom:

A trained assassin:

A 13-year-old girl:

Now, try this statement: <u>I want to break up.</u>

Forrest Gump's Twin Sister:

A successful 50-year-old CEO:

A 35-year-old teamster from Detroit:

A tough biker:

A tenured literary professor:

A self-confessed soccer mom

A trained assassin:

A 13-year-old girl:

Same drill, only now with this: <u>You are the best friend I ever had</u>.

Forrest Gump's Twin Sister:

A successful 50-year-old CEO:

A 35-year-old teamster from Detroit:

A tough biker:

A tenured literary professor:

A self-confessed soccer mom

A trained assassin:

A 13-year-old girl:

Hopefully by now, you've noticed a few things -- that also influencing dialogue are:

1. Who the dialogue is being spoken to
2. The relationship between these characters
3. The setting

Also notice that our generic phrases don't require this background information because anyone can say them – and, remember – that's the problem!

Because generic dialogue has a plug-and-play quality about it, fitting any character in any setting, it's much easier to write, which is perhaps why we see it so often. But, to paraphrase Mark Twain – easy writing makes for hard reading. It also makes for unmemorable reading, which typically doesn't bode well for what's being read. So, to prevent this from happening to you, let's keep working that dialogue skillset.

<u>SET 2: Dialogue and Setting   CRAFT   Total Reps: 24</u>
This time, you'll take the same generic lines from before and now, in addition to making them character specific, you'll also need to account for the SETTING in which the line is spoken. The generic lines will be provided so you don't have to flip back.

Generic Statements

I want to go out with you.   I want to break up.   You are the best friend I ever had.

Statement (choose one):   **Setting: a funeral**
_____

Forrest Gump's Twin Sister:

A successful 50-year-old CEO:

A 35-year-old teamster from Detroit:

A tough biker:

A tenured literary professor:

A self-confessed soccer mom

A trained assassin:

A 13-year-old girl:

Statement: **Setting: a wedding**
_____

Forrest Gump's Twin Sister:

A successful 50-year-old CEO:

A 35-year-old teamster from Detroit:

A tough biker:

A tenured literary professor:

A self-confessed soccer mom

A trained assassin:

A 13-year-old girl:

Statement: _____   **Setting: a crowded diner**
_____

Forrest Gump's Twin Sister:

A successful 50-year-old CEO:

A 35-year-old teamster from Detroit:

A tough biker:

A tenured literary professor:

A self-confessed soccer mom

A trained assassin:

A 13-year-old girl:

You may have noticed that some of your lines carried over from the first set. If so, let's address that before we move on.

BONUS SET: Dialogue and Setting Redux   CRAFT   Total Reps: 1

If you have lines that the setting didn't influence, pick ONE and change the setting for each so that it does change the line. Or, if the line would still be the same, ask yourself how the setting would change the delivery of the words, rather than the words themselves, and choose a setting that would achieve this.

Character: _____   Generic Line: _____

Character Line: _____

Old Setting: _____   New Setting: _____

New Character Line: _____

Just for curiosity – did your new setting make things more difficult for the character to say the line? If so, you just discovered how setting can add to conflict, and how that can be reflected subtextually through dialogue. If not? You may have just discovered something else…

When establishing a character trait, an early part of the process is keeping characters remarkably consistent. This is to establish a pattern of behavior that the audience can then piece together into the character's personality. So, if your character is a loud-mouthed jerk, they'll be a loud-mouthed jerk whether they're in a busy airport or at a funeral. So, if some of your characters didn't change their lines depending on the setting, examine the personality types. Would they be considered among the stronger personalities?

In cases where the dialogue doesn't change because of setting, examine the setting to see if it creates the greatest amount of conflict for the character and the character's goal within the scene. While we're only examining dialogue in this exercise, because it's a manifestation of character, changes in what characters typically would say in a situation provide you with a means of externalizing a character's inner mindset. In this way, dialogue can reveal changes in personality, which can reinforce a character's arc or the relative importance of the situation and setting to the character. All of these factors influence your approach to dialogue.

So far we've been examining dialogue from a character perspective, but what about its effect on an audience? Suppose we shouldn't leave them out; after all, they're the ones listening to all those words. And when we listen, often we're trying to figure out what's being said, what's *really* being said, why it's being said, and what's not being said. Who a line is being delivered to also influences what a character says. With all these factors to consider, it's little wonder why dialogue is such an underutilized aspect of our craft. Well, for everyone but you now, right?

Okay, let's blend all of these together into a short dialogue scene.

SET 3: *Getting in Lines*   **CRAFT**   **Total Reps: *9***

For this exercise, let's blend all of these techniques together to create a short dialogue scene. For easy reference, here are the factors to consider:

    1. Character (well, duh!)
    2. Character's goal (did you catch how our sample lines implied goals?)
    3. Setting (chosen to create conflict and complications for the goal)
    4. Who the dialogue is being delivered to and relation to speaker
    5. Is this scene indicating a character change reflected through dialogue?
    6. What's really being said (subtext), usually as a result of a character not being able to say something directly because of goal, setting and/or who's being spoken to.

Character 1: _____
(name)

Pick a Defining Characteristic for this character (can be one we've been using or one of your own):

_____

Character 2: _____
(name)

Pick this character's Defining Characteristic (can also be one we've been using or one of your own):

_____

Goal:

What goals do these characters have? Once again, these can be ones we've been using or original ones.

Character 1 Goal: _____

Character 2 Goal: _____

Setting

Pick a setting that will make it difficult for the characters to clearly communicate their goals through dialogue:

_____

Write your dialogue scene in the space provided on the following pages.

Be sure to include subtext if appropriate. You can also include other characters as needed.

Write your scene in screenplay format.

Oh, and yes, please give your scene a name. <u>The scene counts as five reps.</u>

Scene Name: _____

Your Scene (cont'd)

Conclusion

Dialogue that reveals character and reflects a character goal helps you create lines that sound different for each character, eliminating a common ailment in scripts – all the characters sounding the same. Ironically, differentiation in character voice doesn't necessarily come from differing word choice and cadence, but rather, it comes from the audience understanding the character and the character's goal.

BONUS SET: *Let's Open a Dialogue*   **CRAFT**   **Total Reps: 1**

Analyze one or more of your dialogue scenes and revise lines if necessary to reflect character.

WORKOUT PROGRESS – CRAFT

Compile your workout totals for this unit.

EXERCISE	SKILL GROUP			TOTAL REPS	
	SET #	TYPE	ACTION	AVAILABLE	COMPLETED
Bottom Lines	1	Craft	Analysis	24	
Dialogue and Setting	2	Craft	Analysis	24	
Dialogue and Setting Redux	Bonus	Craft	Analysis	1	
Getting in Lines	3	Craft	Analysis	9	
Let's Open a Dialogue	Bonus	Craft	Application	1	
			TOTAL REPS		

CRAFT   TOTAL REPS + BONUS   59

The Twisting Cliché

Cliché. Let the word just kind of waft over you for a bit. Those old familiar scenes. Those moments you've seen a thousand times. The same old solutions to the same old situations. They're like old friends – predictable, reliable, but therein lies the problem. So, how do we turn a problem into an opportunity?

I suppose it may be helpful to define what that problem actually is.

Clichés are tricky in a sense. Two people falling in love might seem like the oldest cliché in the book; after all, we've seen it a thousand times – the very essence of cliché. And yet, it's not a really a cliché. By that definition, two characters meeting each other is cliché – we see it in nearly every film, but chances are your movie won't get very far without this occurring.

Cliché doesn't necessarily lie in the event, it lies in the execution of the event. So, two people falling in love isn't cliché, but if you depict this in ways we've seen in countless other movies, the depiction is cliché. To turn these tired, old clichés into something new, we'll need a few clichés – preferably some really stale ones.

SET 1: Top Five Clichés   **CREATIVITY**   **Total Reps: 5**

Create a list of your Top Five Movie Clichés and write them below. These should be ones you're *really* sick of seeing.

1.

2.

3.

4.

5.

The problem with cliché is that it was once original. But, like making a copy of a copy of a copy, it degrades over time. Loses that originality that once made it innovative. The other problem is that they're so darn easy. They're easy to write (after all someone else already did that.) They're easy shortcuts (the audience already knows what's coming, so you can skip all that boring set up stuff.) And, they go great with procrastinating until 3:00 A.M. the night before a deadline.

Despite the negatives, clichés do offer an advantage. Audiences know them, too. And, often expect them. Once expected, if we change them around just a bit, we get the best of both worlds – unpredictable predictability. In other words, taking the familiar and putting a twist on it, still leaves us with the comfort of something familiar, but with the freshness of a new spin, a new take. It's like built-in contrast. Our expectations are reversed. To eliminate clichés, try creating new and unique ways to execute these familiar story devices. With that in mind…

SET 2: *Let's Do the Twist*   *CREATIVITY*   Total Reps: 5

Take the clichés you just listed on the previous page and put a fresh spin on them. Find ways to take those worn, tired ideas and turn them into something we wouldn't expect. You can do a complete reversal of a cliché or simply create variations. So, for example, if you picked the action movie cliché of the hero walking away from an explosion looking all cool, your new version may feature the explosion engulfing the hero instead.

Write your creative twists below:

1.

2.

3.

4.

5.

You may have found a few things occurring when you twisted a cliché.

You may have discovered that your new version added complications. Cliché's tend to be easy solutions, which is yet another reason why they're used so often. However, by creating an unexpected outcome to complicate things, you now have the opportunity to dazzle the audience with a creative solution. Depending on the cliché you chose, you may find the entire story shifting just by changing the expected outcome.

If you chose to twist a dialogue cliché, these may be less impactful on the story, but usually yield a nice reversal of expectations, depending on the line of course. Because the reversal differs from the expected response, it can be more memorable than the line we've heard before.

You may find that these twisted clichés, particularly the complete reversal ones, often yield comedic results. So, our hero walking away from the explosion looking all cool who's suddenly engulfed in the flames can be moment of levity and humor if handled that way.

By twisting clichés, you can often reverse expectations on the audience, while still delivering the familiarity of the cliché – our coveted <u>unique, yet familiar</u> combination.

Now that we've explored clichés in other films – how about yours?

BONUS SET: *Cliché Finder*   **CREATIVITY**   ***Total Reps*: 5**

Examine one of your scripts for clichéd bits of dialogue, actions, scenes and characters. Identify any clichés you find, then create alternative ways of executing the same story beats. While we're at it, please give each scene a name.

If your script doesn't contain clichés, feel free to try this exercise with any tropes, stock characters, smaller character interactions, etc., the script may contain.

Page Number	Scene Name
Cliché:	
Replace With:	

Just for fun… How would this change affect your story?

Briefly describe and explore the ramifications of this change here:

Page Number	Scene Name
Cliché:	
Replace With:	

How does this change affect your story?

Briefly describe and explore the ramifications of this change here:

Page Number	Scene Name
Cliché:	
Replace With:	

How does this change affect your story?

Briefly describe and explore the ramifications of this change here:

Page Number	Scene Name
Cliché:	
Replace With:	

How does this change affect your story?

Briefly describe and explore the ramifications of this change here:

Page Number	Scene Name
Cliché:	
Replace With:	

How does this change affect your story?
Briefly describe and explore the ramifications of this change here:

Like any of the changes? If so, incorporate them into your script!
It can be a fun way to inject originality faster than an action hero can say – We've got company! Unless, of course, you're getting too old for this... :)

WORKOUT PROGRESS – CREATIVITY

Compile your totals! Hmm – we've done this before. Wonder if it's cliché?

EXERCISE	SKILL GROUP		TOTAL REPS	
	SET #	TYPE	ACTION	AVAILABLE	COMPLETED
Top Five Clichés	1	Creativity	Analysis	5	
Let's Do the Twist	2	Creativity	Application	5	
Cliché Finder	Bonus	Creativity	Analysis	25	
			TOTAL REPS		

CREATIVITY — TOTAL REPS + BONUS: **35**

Build-a-Tale 2:
Product Placement Edition

Next up on Build-a-Tale, you'll write a 30-second narrative commercial in regular screenplay format. As a narrative spot, your commercial should tell a short story while plugging the product.

As with all the Build-a-Tale Exercises, you'll randomly select the characters and other story parameters by choosing four numbers from one to ten. Let's do that now. And remember, no peeking!

Choose your Adventure!
Pick a number from <u>one to ten</u> for each category, and write it in the space provided. Choose wisely...

Special Notes on this Build-a-Tale:
The products have blank spaces in front of them for you to insert a specific brand if you wish.

While you can have a spokesperson to shill the product, the main task is to tell a short story using all the elements you just selected. <u>This exercise counts as ten reps.</u>

And now, a word from our sponsor...

SET 1: Product Placements   **CREATIVITY**   **Total Reps: 10**

Create a story using the parameters you picked. The numbers you chose on the previous page correspond to the numbers in each category below. You may add another character, but your commercial must include every selected element.

Circle the numbers you chose in each category to begin.

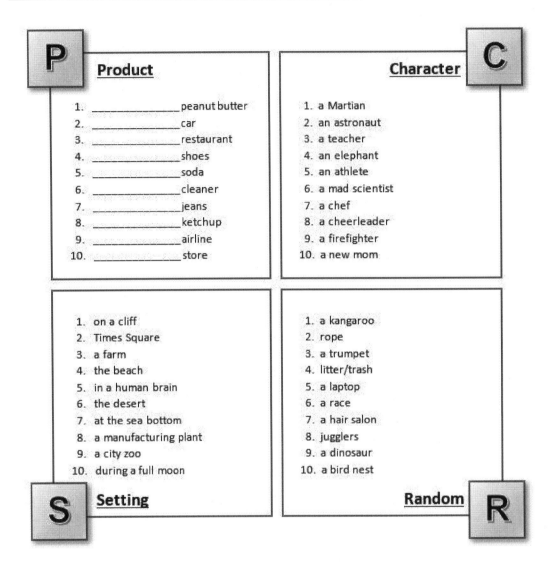

Product	Character
1. _____ peanut butter	1. a Martian
2. _____ car	2. an astronaut
3. _____ restaurant	3. a teacher
4. _____ shoes	4. an elephant
5. _____ soda	5. an athlete
6. _____ cleaner	6. a mad scientist
7. _____ jeans	7. a chef
8. _____ ketchup	8. a cheerleader
9. _____ airline	9. a firefighter
10. _____ store	10. a new mom

Setting	Random
1. on a cliff	1. a kangaroo
2. Times Square	2. rope
3. a farm	3. a trumpet
4. the beach	4. litter/trash
5. in a human brain	5. a laptop
6. the desert	6. a race
7. at the sea bottom	7. a hair salon
8. a manufacturing plant	8. jugglers
9. a city zoo	9. a dinosaur
10. during a full moon	10. a bird nest

Using this combination, complete the following to create your story:

Title: _____

Basic Concept:

Write your story in screenplay format on the next two pages, or you can type it.

FADE OUT.

Obviously, you may not wish to write commercials, but the idea here was to give the script a goal – in this case to sell a product, and to do so within a compact space. On a bigger scale, this goal could be considered a theme. So, the theme for the commercial you just wrote may be something like – this product is good, or buy this product it will make your life better. Notice that by giving the story a purpose, this serves as a unifying device to bring all the elements together.

As you write your screenplay, consider the theme or artistic statement you wish to make as the main unifying device for the story, serving to give each scene a function beyond moving the plot. You may just find this approach can alleviate writer's block while simultaneously giving each scene momentum and drive. Pretty good selling points. Maybe we should advertise them. ;)

WORKOUT PROGRESS – CREATIVITY
Compile your workout totals for this unit.

EXERCISE	SKILL GROUP		TOTAL REPS	
	SET #	TYPE	ACTION	AVAILABLE	COMPLETED
Product Placements	1	Creativity	Application	10	
			TOTAL REPS		

CREATIVITY — TOTAL REPS + BONUS — 10

Driving Through Kansas
Image Systems and Narrative

If a picture's worth a thousand words, imagine all the typing you'd save with a few, choice pictures, or better yet, a system of images to help you tell your story.

As with every detail in your script, choose your imagery with precision. We may not understand what we're seeing, or why, but a strong, vivid image can thrust the reader into your world. This in turn can get people to 'see' the movie and not just a bunch of words strung together on a page.

Imagine all the mental tricks we have to play to convince ourselves to care about your characters and the world they inhabit. We have to believe in people we've never met; people we cannot see, cannot hear. Think about it. Not only must your characters convince us they're real, they must also convince us to be concerned for their welfare, be concerned about their problems, be fearful of their failures. And that's just the characters. Same thing goes for the world they occupy. Not an easy task. We have to get readers to see your characters, to see their world. And the way to this is not to barrage us with thick paragraphs like this one. The way to do it is through a few, select details.

> Like red fingernails.

Meaningful details create the world of your story. And, the way to create imagery with meaning is to give it significance. This can be done metaphorically, so that we come to understand the meaning, adding an extra layer of depth. It can be done descriptively, painting pictures in our minds so we engage the world of your story.

Or, it can do both. Which brings us to Kansas. If you've ever driven through Kansas, the thing that grabs you is the enormity of virtual nothingness. As far as the eye can see, to the horizon in every direction, a sea of fields. In this emptiness even the mundane stands out. An occasional tree. A cow. A telephone pole. A wind turbine. Things you'd otherwise overlook, suddenly pop.

It's similar to screenwriting. Strong details stand out in a sea of prose. Vivid images that contain our desire to find meaning in what we read help us enter your world. And once we do that, your script stands out in that vast sea of other scripts.

But, you don't have to take my word for it…

SET 1: *Driving Kansas* **CREATIVITY** **Total Reps: 3**

Riddle me my questions three. Answer the following (without going back!)
Didn't know there would be a quiz, now did you?

1. What are the two ways imagery can engage an audience?

2. What four things stood out on my drive through Kansas?

3. What color are the fingernails on the previous page?

So, how'd you do? If you missed the fingernails one, we *really* need to work on those reading skills… :)

Hopefully, your eye was drawn to those red fingernails, that little sentence fragment in the middle of the page. While that image may not have conjured up any earth-shattering insights, it wasn't intended to do that. It was simply meant to stick, to draw attention to itself. To pique interest. And, to do so with an economy of words. After all, as the saying goes – books are written for people who love to read; scripts are written for people who hate to read. While that's a bit of an overstatement, it's something to bear in mind as you approach your screenplay.

We tend to seek meaning in every aspect of your script, particularly the details you're choosing to evoke images and convey less obvious aspects of the story, such as theme. To accomplish this, your task is to provide **only those details with meaning**. Too many details, and we get lost. Too few, and we can't picture enough to engage the story. It's a balancing act.

Which leads us to your image system.

An image system is like a motif in literature. It recurs throughout the script, or at minimum, near the beginning and end, to subtly convey story elements.

Choosing precise images that convey story and character gives your imagery meaning. It's not the complete story -- it needs us to fill in the picture, but at the bare minimum, it helps us to picture your world -- which will hopefully make your script a bit more exciting than driving through cornfields.

SET 2: *Image Systems*   **CREATIVITY**   **Total Reps: 4**

Create image systems for the following scenarios. Pick strong, vivid images that convey a simple story progression. Make them stick!

For each scenario you'll need to create at least three specific images:

    1. An opening image

    2. A character introduction image

    3. A closing image

Once again, you can do more, but those three are our minimum.

Your opening and closing images should contrast each other to tell the story in a nutshell by depicting the **change** that's occurred as a result of the hero's journey. Hmm… hero's journey. That suggests…

An Example:
In *Star Wars* (1977), the movie opens on the vastness of space. Cold. Lifeless. Then, a massive starship glides above, attacking a smaller ship, suggesting the Empire's size, power and aggressiveness.

The contrasting closing image shows the hero surrounded by friends (and family as it awkwardly turns out.)

This is not a story about freeing the galaxy by destroying battle stations the size of small moons. That's the plot. The story is about a young man finding his family – or at least, that's what's conveyed in the contrast between opening and closing images.

Okay, got it? I hope so because we're going to turn up the heat.

In addition to conveying story, each detail should also be designed to:
    1. Evoke or portray character.
    2. Suggest a theme.
    3. Illustrate progression.
    4. And, still paint that vivid, memorable picture.

Easy peasy.

All right, enough talk. Let's get our Bob Ross on.

Scenario 1:

A contemporary story about an old-fashioned introvert who goes from being alone to having a significant other.

Opening Image:

Character Intro:

Closing Image:

Scenario 2:

A busy socialite who needs to slow down and appreciate the little things in life.

Opening Image:

Character Intro:

Closing Image:

Scenario 3:

A high school student must learn to stand up to a bully.

Opening Image:

Character Intro:

Closing Image:

Scenario 4:

An aging model faces growing old.

Opening Image:

Character Intro:

Closing Image:

As you were creating your stunning images, did you notice you needed to think through the differing ways each scenario could play out? If so, these are hopefully the same connections you'll be making in your audience to help your script stand out among the cows and cornfields.

BONUS SET: Not in Kansas Anymore   **CREATIVITY**   **Total Reps: 1**

Try this out on one of your screenplays. Specifically, look at your opening and closing images. Are they evocative? Memorable? Tell the story? All three?

Then, check the first time we meet your main character. Do you have a specific image that gives us a clue as to who this character is by conveying Defining Characteristic or Flaw? Is this imagery related thematically or otherwise to the rest of the story?

If not, you know what to do.

Go for a drive. :)

WORKOUT PROGRESS – CREATIVITY

Compile your workout totals for this unit.

EXERCISE	SKILL GROUP			TOTAL REPS	
	SET #	TYPE	ACTION	AVAILABLE	COMPLETED
Driving through Kansas	1	Creativity	Analysis	3	
Image Systems	2	Creativity	Application	4	
Not in Kansas Anymore	Bonus	Creativity	Application	1	
			TOTAL REPS		

CREATIVITY   TOTAL REPS + BONUS   8

The Obstacle of Course

Whenever I watch a war movie, one of my favorite sequences is boot camp. You know the deal...

The in-your-face drill instructor barking out a collection of middle school insults. The recruits standing there, scared witless – all except the cocky misfit we're supposed to like. The buzz cuts, the chow line slop, the "I don't know, but I've been told..." marching songs, the push-ups in the mud 'til you die.
And, of course, the inevitable, obstacle course.

Here recruits face all the standard challenges: swinging over mud pits, the balance beam thing, crawling under ropes, and almost always the wall obstacle some hopeless recruit can't climb until the cocky misfit we're supposed to like sacrifices their shot at the course record to help. Ah, good stuff, flying by at virtually 24 clichés per second. BOO-YAH!

But, there's one thing you never see in these movies – they never let the recruits pick the obstacles. Makes sense. If I'm picking out obstacles, you better believe I'm not shimmying under barbed wire. My obstacles are more like – the battery on my remote needs changing. I can't find the keys to the Ferrari. You know, real challenges. Let me pick out obstacles and you know what you get? Easy obstacles. And why? Because real obstacles hurt. And, who wants that?

Turns out quite a few people want that – most of them, members of your audience. In boot camp, the obstacle course helps turn raw recruits into soldiers. It trains them to withstand the rigors of war. It makes them strong; it forms bonds, helps them grow. It tests them mentally, physically, emotionally.

It's the same with your characters. The obstacles they face make them strong, help them grow. They test characters mentally, emotionally, physically. Breaking them down until they are worthy enough to receive the big prize.

But, here's where we get in trouble. Many writers love their main characters. It's natural. After all, we created them; we gave birth to them, and like any good parent, we don't want to see bad things happen to our babies.

And, that's the problem.

Because as much as we may not want to see bad things happen to our characters, the audience does. So, to address this...

341

WELCOME TO CHARACTER BOOT CAMP!

ALL RIGHT! LISTEN UP! TODAY WE'RE GONNA CHALLENGE YOUR CHARACTERS! WE ARE NOT GONNA THROW WIMPY OBSTACLES AT YOUR BELOVED PROTAGONISTS! WE ARE GONNA BACK THEM INTO A CORNER AND THROW ROCKS AT 'EM TIL THEY DIE! WE'RE GONNA MAKE THEM FACE THEIR FEARS, THEIR FLAWS! STRIP THEM OF EVERYTHING THEY LOVE! DO YOU GET ME?!

This is the part where you're supposed to say: SIR, YES, SIR!
So, I can reply – "I can't hear youuuu!"
Hmm... tough to do that in a book. Guess if we wanna do this right, you can go here:
https://discord.gg/qDQ5gUnCuA
This is an invite to my Discord server. Not much there, but if you really wanna do the 'sir-yes-sir' thing, or reach out to me, feel free to join. You'll have to manually enter the link in your web browser, but that's not much of an obstacle, is it? :)
OKAY, LET'S GET TO CAMP!

SET 1: Character Boot Camp   CREATIVITY   Total Reps: 7
For this exercise your task is to <u>write as though you are an antagonist</u>, one who will stop at nothing to keep the main character from succeeding. And, to do this we need a character.

Create your character using <u>three of the four parameters</u> we have for creating Hollywood characters. The ones you'll use are:

      Defining characteristic   Humanity   Flaw (strength/flaw)

We'll hold off on paradox for now. Because, as I hope you'll discover, the paradox can be your secret weapon.

You'll need to give your character a goal. Something they want or need to achieve. This can be anything. Please write the goal as an infinitive phrase – examples:
to pass the class, to get the treasure, to win the battle of the bands, etc.

Once you have a character with a goal, you'll throw obstacles in the way to keep this person from achieving the goal.

To pick really strong obstacles, be an antagonist. Throw everything you have at the character. Once an obstacle has been chosen, you'll need to figure out how the character will overcome it. Be creative -- really back yourself (and the character) into a corner. If this doesn't stop the character, you'll then pick another, even more nefarious obstacle, one that's sure to stop the character. You then figure a way around this, and so forth.

These obstacles form the basic plot of the story until we reach the final obstacle. Here is where we will choose the paradox. Because in a tightly-constructed screenplay, it's often the paradox that will allow the character to overcome the big obstacle, well, that and learning the lesson of the movie as a result of confronting the flaw. But for now, let's stick to the paradox.

Let's get started!

Character Name: _____

Defining Characteristic: _____

Humanity: _____

For this one, keep it simple and make it something the character <u>loves</u>.

Flaw (or Strength-Flaw): _____

The flaw often creates some deep-seated fear in a character. Briefly describe this fear here:

Goal: _____

Once you have these, you'll pick out a tough obstacle to stand in the way of the character achieving the goal. Don't go easy on yourself. Challenge your creativity.

To get started, the first obstacle will be <u>the setting</u>.

Pick a setting that will make it difficult for this character to achieve his/her goal and describe in the space provided.

<u>Setting Obstacle:</u>

Once you have a challenging setting, figure out a way to overcome it. Be creative!

My character will overcome this obstacle by….

Once your character has passed this obstacle, you'll conceive another obstacle. For this one, let's pick another character to oppose our hero – an antagonist.

Character Obstacle – Antagonist:
Describe how the antagonist will keep our main character from achieving the goal here:

My character will overcome this obstacle by….

Once your character has overcome this obstacle, time for another one.

Let's turn up the heat.

Look back at the character design on the previous page. See this character's flaw? Let's attack it. Create an obstacle that will force the character to face their flaw. Make this one particularly nasty.

Flaw-Based Obstacle:

My character will overcome this obstacle by….

Um... in case you've forgotten -- your job is to stop this character from getting the goal! Crank it up a notch! Create an obstacle that involves the character's fear. Make the character confront it! Let's see what this character is really made of!

Fear-Based Obstacle:

My character will overcome this obstacle by....

We're not being tough enough! This character keeps wriggling out of these situations. Fine. Dandy. Let's see how they like this:

Keeping within the parameters of the story...

Create an IMPOSSIBLE SITUATION for this character to overcome.

Take away this character's strength.
Eliminate the goal.
Eliminate the character.

Use that defining characteristic and humanity. Force the character to choose between the goal and something else they love dearly.

Bring that fear.

Matter of fact, let's combine all these things into one obstacle to take out this character once and for all.

I don't care how you do it, but get mad, get vicious and STOP THIS CHARACTER!

The Impossible Obstacle:

Okay. Hopefully you're sitting there looking at a really tough obstacle to overcome. Now let's bring out your secret weapon -- the paradox.

Please Note: in the course of a regular story, the paradox may have been planted early on. Simmering. Waiting. Quietly forgotten until needed.

Pick a paradox that will help your character overcome this specific obstacle.

Paradox: _____

Incorporate the paradox to overcome this final obstacle and finally achieve the goal.

My character will overcome this obstacle by….

Just for fun, what possible themes or lessons could this solution communicate? Jot some possibilities below:

And, that's the end of your movie.

                                                        FADE OUT.

As an exercise, this can yield some nonsensical solutions and goals, but imagine if you were to plan this approach from the beginning -- writing as an antagonist whose sole goal is to stop the hero. What a ride that could be, with tough challenges escalating to even tougher ones, culminating in a seemingly impossible one. Don't know about you, but I'd watch that movie.

Of course, this approach does have a side effect – it can make the writing more difficult. In this way, writing as antagonist runs counter to the typical goal of any screenwriter – finishing the script. After all, as writers, we do have a story to tell, and impossible obstacles don't exactly make that process any easier. But, it does make the experience of the story more exciting, more entertaining, as we watch your characters struggle to overcome increasingly difficult challenges. We may even feel sorry for the hero and begin to root for the character. And, once the pattern of ever-increasing difficulty is set, the audience may even begin to look forward with anticipation to the next obstacle, which is sure to be even more difficult. We may even begin to admire the hero's creative solutions to these tough obstacles.

While creating incredibly difficult obstacles may make telling the story more challenging, it also creates a far more entertaining experience for the audience. Paint yourself into a corner, really push the bounds and challenge yourself. It may take a while to figure out a solution, and it should, assuming you've chosen strong obstacles. The audience won't know it took six weeks to figure your way out of that corner -- all they'll see is a challenging problem to overcome, one they're not quite sure how they would solve. And, they'll marvel at your character's clever solution without ever realizing the effort and work it took to create it.

But then, that's the obstacle course we face as writers, now isn't it?
Feel free to do the 'sir, yes, sir' thing from earlier if you like… :)

WORKOUT PROGRESS – CREATIVITY
Compile your workout totals for this unit.

EXERCISE	SKILL GROUP		TOTAL REPS	
	SET #	TYPE	ACTION	AVAILABLE	COMPLETED
Character Boot Camp	1	Creativity	Application	7	
			TOTAL REPS		

The Curious Question of Conflict

What is it about conflict that makes it so compelling? Ever wondered?

We tend to avoid conflict in real life, and yet, when it comes to film, we're back in high school crowding around a couple sophomores duking it out in the hall.

Why?

Seriously. If you think about it, what's the appeal?

A case can be made that it's interesting to watch. It's different. A break from the ordinary world of polite conflict resolution. Cathartic as Aristotle might say. Something to be said for that. But, in movies, conflict's the norm. We see it all the time, so it's not like it's anything particularly new, different, or even cathartic.

And, for a screenwriter, slapping words on the blank canvas of your script, we don't even get the cool visuals that can make conflict intriguing to see. It's just more 12-point Courier for us. No, there's something else afoot with conflict. Some other aspect of it that makes it interesting.

But what?

Perhaps it may help to examine just what exactly conflict is.

The traditional definition of conflict holds that it is two forces in opposition to each other; an antagonist and a protagonist; a goal, opposition to the goal, and an unwillingness to compromise in achieving the goal. We can even break conflict down into convenient categories that make excellent multiple choice fodder for teachers – person versus nature, person versus self, person versus person, person versus fate, person versus society, and so on.

Yet none of those things actually define conflict. Not really. Oh sure, they quantify it, categorize it, describe it – but none of them define what conflict truly is. And none even come close to explaining why you need it. To do that, we need to change our notion of what conflict is.

Introducing our new and improved definition of conflict...

> **Conflict is any combination of elements that throws the outcome of a particular moment into uncertainty.**

The moment may be a beat or a scene, a dialogue exchange or a sword fight -- even an entire movie. Elements can be actions or events, characters or situations – any two (or more) things you can put together to create unpredictability within the story.

That's it. That's all there is to conflict - <u>creating unpredictability within the narrative</u>. Well, okay. Maybe that's not entirely it…

If creating unpredictability is the key to conflict, then conflict should be easy to create.

SET 1: Conflicting Results   CRAFT   Total Reps: 3

Check out the following and answer the questions.

An example:

> *Let's say we're watching a typical RomCom.*
> *It's near the end. Our lovers are reunited.*
> *And, just as they lean in for that BIG KISS…*
> *BOOM!*
> *A nuclear strike takes them out. Poof. Vaporized. All they are is dust in the wind.*
> *Roll credits.*

Talk about unpredictable! A nuke? In a romantic comedy? Sweet. And, to make it even more unpredictable, let's assume the filmmaker didn't set this up at all.
Just outta nowhere – DEFCON 1.

Even sweeter, right?

Well… not exactly. Because while it's unpredictable, it would also be unsatisfying. The question for you is why?

<u>Why would such a moment probably be unsatisfying?</u> (Jot your response in the space below.)

Turns out, the answer is simple -- there's no conflict in that scenario.

Sure, there's violence, irony, surprise. There's a goal and megatons of opposition to it. There's the whole person vs. society, person vs. fate, maybe even person vs. person thing going.

But, no conflict.

None at all. Not even a hint of it.

The question for you, once again, is why.

<u>Why is there no conflict in the scenario above?</u>

This answer is not quite as simple. For, you see, by our definition, conflict creates unpredictability, and unpredictability carries an intriguing side effect – predictability. In other words, once an outcome is uncertain (and therefore less predictable), it opens up the possibility for an audience to predict what will happen.

Notice the key word – outcome. The outcome is unpredictable, not necessarily the event itself. Put another way, **conflict creates a set of outcomes for the audience to predict.**

In this instance, think of the word 'set' as a range – a range of possible outcomes in a given situation. This range is defined by you, the filmmaker, with the help of the audience. Chances are, if you liked our romantic comedy ending, it's because the possibility of a nuclear attack existed within your range of possible outcomes. This only works because we know nothing of the story leading up to the attack. In other words, if that ending worked, it's because the reader filled in the necessary set ups to make it work.

To put it yet another way, because the example was so short, a nuke exists within the range of possible outcomes because that range has not yet been defined. And, because we have nothing invested in the characters, the shock value alone becomes a point of intrigue. But, for an audience invested in your characters and their story, this becomes a huge issue.

A Situation:
Let's say you want to throw something <u>utterly unpredictable</u> at the audience. **What does the previous paragraph imply about where in the story you'd place such an event?**

[ ]

If you said early, kudos. <u>For as your film unfolds, the audience begins to subconsciously predict what will happen based on what you show them.</u> And, what's hopefully shown is a range of possible outcomes given the characters and their situations. The audience doesn't mind being wrong in their predictions – so long as what actually happens is with the range of possibility. However, at the beginning of the movie nearly anything can happen because the range has not yet been established. Bit of a side note, to be sure, but an important one – and one that ultimately will lead us back to conflict. But, before we tie this back to conflict, what are some of the factors determining range?

Home, Home on the Range
Range of possible outcomes is influenced by:

- <u>Genre and Tone</u> – realistic genres like drama call for more logical outcome possibilities. Comedy can push the bounds considerably more. Animation, even more.

- <u>Character</u> – obsessed and extreme characters expand the range. Mundane, passive characters shrink it.

- <u>The Filmmaker</u> – yes, you. Set it up and chances are the audience will accept it. Establish a world in which anything can happen, and suddenly the range becomes huge. For example, establish violence and violent solutions are possible.

- <u>The Audience</u> – in the absence of all other criteria, your viewers will react with their own sense of logic to predict possible outcomes. Oh, what fun!

- <u>Plot and Story</u> -- narrative events and where we are in the film's timeline alter range. If the story calls for a character to get revenge, you better believe that's in the range – we're expecting it. If we're early in the film, just about anything can happen.

Great! So what does all this mean? And how does conflict fit in? Perhaps another example is in order…

SET 2: Checks and Balances **CRAFT** **Total Reps: 7**

Complete the following:

Check Please! A Scenario:

Let's put some of these principles into action within a simple scene:

```
INT. DINER - DAY

A CUSTOMER takes his bill to the counter and pays the
WAITRESS.  He leaves a tip and exits.
```

Given this scenario, what's LIKELY TO HAPPEN NEXT and what's UNLIKELY TO HAPPEN NEXT?

List some SPECIFIC ACTIONS (and REACTIONS) on either side of the line below:

Likely to Happen NextUnlikely to Happen Next

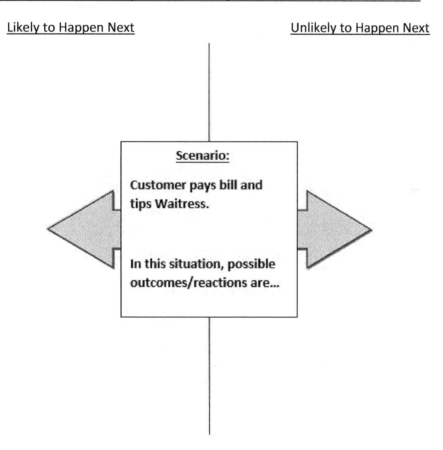

Scenario:

Customer pays bill and tips Waitress.

In this situation, possible outcomes/reactions are…

These are the possible outcomes given this scenario. This gives us the range of predictable outcomes given the events we just witnessed.

Now that we have the range, here's a simple question:

Which of these do you actually expect to happen next and why?

[ ]

Did you struggle at all to predict what would actually happen next? Did you care what happened next?

If you answered yes to either of these questions – want to know why?

Hopefully you noticed that the previous scene contained no conflict.

The lack of conflict makes predicting outcomes nearly impossible. This leads to yet another question:

When a scene lacks conflict, why do you think it's difficult to predict what will happen next?

[ ]

The answer is deceptively simple.

<u>Without conflict, there's basically nothing to predict.</u> There are no outcomes (at least no interesting ones); therefore, there is no range of possible outcomes from which to base predictions.

Here's where it gets intriguing.

<u>If there's nothing to predict, you can't get unpredictability.</u>

The way it works is this: yes, you could have a zombie apocalypse suddenly descend on the diner, but that has no relation to what we just saw. It comes out of nowhere (which, as you recall can work early in the film), but this isn't unpredictable – it's simply random. As such, chances are it's not within the range of outcomes. Therefore, it can feel forced and out of place – or just simply wrong.

Ever read those scripts where the ending just doesn't seem right? Or it just comes out of nowhere? How does that feel?

The reason many of those moments don't quite work is that those events are not in your range of predictable outcomes. As such, you can feel cheated. And typically you'll reject them and thus the movie as a whole.

What conflict does for you is open up the range of possible outcomes.
It actually creates the range by giving the audience a list of focused, manageable outcomes from which they can make predictions. May not seem like it, but it's oh, so simple.

Let's see how it works by changing our diner scene:

```
INT. DINER - DAY

A BURLY CUSTOMER stiffs his LOUD-MOUTHED WAITRESS.
He's about to skip out on the bill when...
```

Okay, now that we've added some conflict, let's see if any possibilities open up…

Once again, list some SPECIFIC ACTIONS (and REACTIONS) on either side of the line . For these, list what you expect to happen next and what you don't expect to happen next.

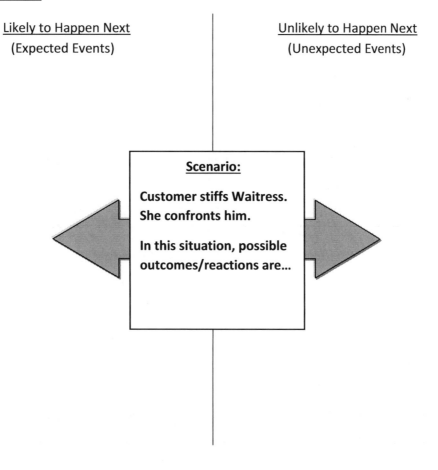

Hopefully, you discovered this list was not only easier to create but also contained more interesting outcomes and reactions.

This is what conflict does. It opens up the range of possible outcomes within a scene – and ultimately the story itself. The effect conflict has on narrative is seismic, extending into character as well.

The Relationship Between Conflict and Character

Ever wonder why most successful films feature strong, active characters obsessed with their goals? Let's explore it by altering our previous scene. Only this time, we'll change just a single characteristic.

```
INT. DINER - DAY

A BURLY CUSTOMER stiffs his ~~LOUD-MOUTHED~~ MEEK WAITRESS...
```

Activity:
Okay, now that we've changed our waitress, re-examine the previous list and cross out any actions (and reactions) that would no longer happen. If you feel a particular action would still happen but is now less likely (or vice versa), indicate this by drawing an arrow from the action to the other side of the line.

What did you discover once the waitress changed from loud-mouthed to meek?

Typically a couple things happen...
One, we begin eliminating possible outcomes.
And two, we start making some outcomes less likely to occur – which are therefore less plausible in the eyes of the audience, requiring a bit more time (and work) to set up.

Notice when the conflict stops (one side gives in or emerges victorious), the scene stops. You run out of actions and reactions. There's simply no place for the scene to go...

Except into another scene.
This is the essence of set up and payoff, as well as the idea of scene chaining (linking scenes through cause and effect.)
But I digress... After all, we're talking about character.

Eliminating possible outcomes makes the narrative more predictable, so characters are typically designed to maximize conflict possibilities to keep the range of possible outcomes high.

What does that mean?

Basically, you should design your characters so that they open up the maximum range of possible outcomes, actions and reactions.

Even traits such as gender can factor in to the range of possible outcomes. How would our scene have changed if the characters had been two males? Two females? A female customer and a male waiter, a non-binary server?

You should have also noticed something else:

> Changing character traits shifts possible outcomes from likely to less likely and vice versa.

Typically (but not always), you want outcomes and actions to fall in the 'Likely to Happen' category. The less likely an action, the greater risk an audience will say – "Oh, please. That would NEVER happen."

So, if we want the maximum number of possible outcomes to be likely within the mind of the audience, how do we achieve this?

Simple.

We create characters to do it for us.

However, to fully explore this notion we need to play with our categories a bit.

Instead of what's likely and not likely to happen next, let's further subdivide those categories.

Defining the Range of Outcomes

Remember, our range of outcomes is simply the possible reactions and outcomes presented by what's happening on the screen. It gives the audience a list of possibilities to mull over. The audience then watches to see which of these possibilities plays out.

Likely to Happen Next
Actions we expect may happen. They're logical within the framework of the story and characters. Actions in this realm make sense and tend to be the more predictable.

We'll have two sub-categories – Typical and Believable.

- Typical – normal 'real world' reaction or outcome
    - Dull but realistic, typically doesn't require set up because it's what average people would do in a given situation.

- Believable – Given the world of the story, a distinct possibility of what might happen
    - More unexpected than a typical reaction and requires more set up.
    - More exciting and intriguing than a typical reaction yet still logical.

Less Likely to Happen Next
Actions we're not expecting. If set up, these can work. However, if they're set up, they tend to shift into the Believable Category given our understanding of the characters and the world they inhabit. These are less predictable and can be interesting but also carry the risk of alienating the audience.

Two more categories – Atypical and Unbelievable.

- Atypical – Our Sweet Spot!
  Stretches logic so it may alienate many, but with some effort you could sell it.
    - Often character-specific. As such, it requires considerable set up to work.

- Unbelievable – way out there, pushing the bounds of reality and utterly illogical or unexpected.
    - Risky but definitely unexpected. Requires the greatest amount of set up to pull off, and even then will probably be rejected by an audience.

Given these categories, let's go back to our romcom with a nuclear twist story.
Which category would the nuclear attack fall under?

Chances are, most people would pick either atypical or unbelievable.

Now, let's change the story…

What if one of the romantic leads is an employee at a government nuclear defense agency?

What category would the nuclear attack *now* fall under?

```
┌─────────────────────────────────────────────────┐
│                                                 │
│                                                 │
└─────────────────────────────────────────────────┘
```

<u>Notice, by changing a character, suddenly we've altered the range of possible outcomes, making things that normally would be unbelievable, believable.</u>

To explore this notion further, let's head back to that diner. Hope the food's good.

SET 3: **Second Helpings**   **CRAFT**   *Total Reps:* **1**

For this exercise, YOU pick the personalities of the characters. The basic situation's the same.

Fill in the blanks with your new character traits and outcome. <u>Choose at least one adjective and one noun for each character.</u>

```
INT. DINER - DAY

A _____ STIFFS A _____.
      (our customer)                    (our server)

The _____ is about to skip out when...
```

Now, let's examine the range of possible outcomes based on the scenario you created using our new list of categories.

Play out possible reactions and outcomes to <u>your</u> diner scene on the next page:

Your Diner Scene

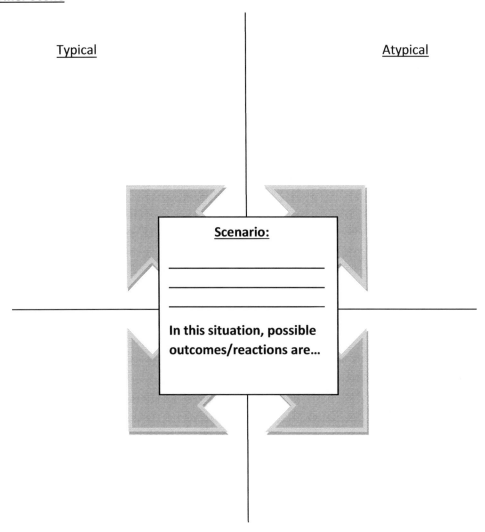

If you picked an interesting combination of characters, the range of possible outcomes could be virtually endless.

Let's say you chose a male suicide bomber eating his last meal -- perhaps when confronted he opens his jacket to reveal dynamite strapped to his chest.

If you chose a female undercover cop as a server, perhaps she pulls her badge and demands payment.

If you chose two disguised international assassins as the leads…

You get the idea.

Who knows? Maybe you could chose a bible-verse quoting hitman who recently witnessed what he believes to be a miracle and who simply wants his wallet back.

But, whatever you choose...

The more interesting the character, the more interesting the conflict can be.

Hmm... that hitman sounds familiar. Let's play with him a bit. The expected reaction from a hitman would be to respond with violence. The unexpected reaction is to respond calmly. In this way, <u>you can create conflict out of non-action, or a subdued response, because the conflict is internal to the character and thus, less predictable.</u>

In other words, what we're seeing is the fusion of character and conflict to create unpredictable responses. Indeed, these elements are intractably interrelated. Without conflict, it's nearly impossible to reveal character. Without character we have very little on which to hang conflict. Except...

If conflict is indeed a combination of elements that throws the outcome of a particular moment into uncertainty, it's entirely possible to have conflict without character. The issue with this is simple: **will we care enough about the outcome from such conflict to even want to predict what will happen next**?

This same question can be applied to characters we don't care about. In other words, if we don't care about characters, we don't care enough to want to make predictions about outcomes. This is the interrelationship between character and conflict – the dance they do, if you will.

Conflict reveals character,
which in turn can create empathy for a character,
which in turn can give stakes and meaning to the conflict,
which makes us want to predict what will happen next for a character,
which then leads to creating hope and fear in the audience for one set of outcomes to happen,
which in turn creates suspense,
which then engages the audience,
which then makes them invest in the characters and the choices these characters make,
which invariable leads to...
more conflict,
which in turn leads to...
Another chart.

Putting it All Together

If conflict is all about creating unpredictability for the audience within the framework of the story, then it may be useful to frame conflict in terms of audience reactions. In other words, we can factor in audience expectations.

On our chart, Expected Outcomes are on the left. These are reactions likely to happen.

Unexpected Outcomes are on the right. These are outcomes that are possible yet surprise an audience.

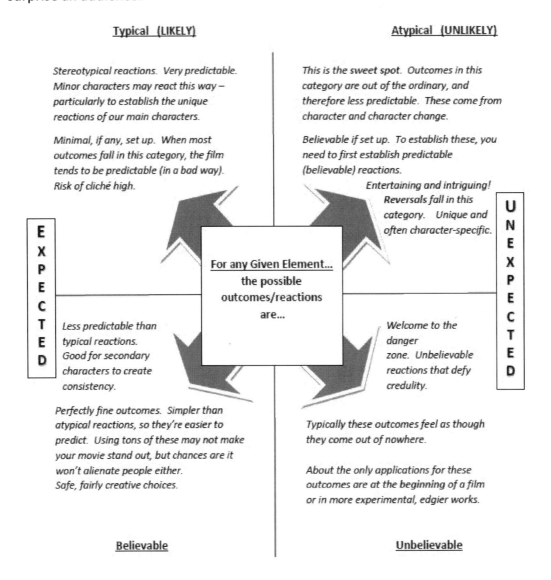

Examining the audience's relationship to your characters, remember that the audience feels they know a character when they can predict what that character will do. This creates the illusion of familiarity with the character.

Atypical responses from a character are evidence of change and are what the audience uses to measure character arc. We'll explore this notion further in our character design sections, but for now, let's stay focused specifically on conflict because while we've talked about what it does, we still haven't quite defined what it is...

The Curious Question of Conflict
Because conflict creates uncertain outcomes, it yields one of the most powerful narrative aspects of conflict, and one of its simplest...

Conflict asks a question. And, to paraphrase Elie Wiesel -- every question possesses a power not found in the answer.

The effect is profound on cinematic narrative, for not only does conflict ask a question...

CONFLICT *IS* A QUESTION.

Obviously there's more to it than that, but at its core, that's all it is.

Conflict's not violence, although it can be violent. It's not a fight, although it can involve fighting. It's not yelling or screaming or disagreeing or arguing or any kneejerk definition we may give to it.

Simply put, conflict is a cinematic event that raises a question and demands a response from the characters as well as the audience (and consequently the filmmaker.) These two elements – question and response, are the secrets of conflict when it comes to cinematic narrative.

But notice, it's an <u>indirect question</u>. You, the filmmaker aren't the one asking it. <u>Through conflict you raise a question that the audience then asks.</u> That's the key to understanding conflict. It's indirect.

Think of your film as a long Q & A session, with conflict raising questions that characters must answer, that the story addresses, that the audience ponders, and that the filmmaker uses to hook the audience throughout a film.

<u>Some answers you withhold.</u> This is how you build a moments in scenes and hooks for your film. You give the audience a moment to ask its question before you answer it – that's the essence of a moment, giving the audience time to allow them to make predictions.

<u>Some questions you answer immediately</u>, but through answering them, more questions should arise.

As with most things film, there's a trick to this approach. <u>You, the filmmaker, must understand what questions you are raising.</u> Answer a question the audience did not ask, and they may disengage from your movie. The scene, or moment will feel pointless or underwhelming. But, as long as the answer lies within the range of possible outcomes, typically you're on solid ground.

All of this may sound like a lot of work, but it's worth it.

Any way you slice it, conflict remains the single, most efficient means of creating questions in the narrative that the audience doesn't realize are questions. In this way, conflict is a form of subtext.

It's the efficiency of conflict that makes it so effective in cinematic narrative. In one fell swoop look at what conflict does:

- Conflict raises questions to serve as hooks and to keep the story moving forward.
- Conflict creates unpredictability in the narrative.
- Conflict reveals character and can create empathy for characters.
- Conflict creates tension.
- Conflict creates surprise (through unpredictability)
- Conflict expands the range of possible outcomes.
- Conflict creates suspense
- Conflict can generate subtext.
- Conflict demands responses (creating self-contained character motivation)
- Conflict can create visual interest

The list goes on and on.
That's the reason you need it. Look at the brutal efficiency.

And yet, so many writers avoid conflict. Ever wonder why?

It's ironic. For all the benefits, it's that one main function of conflict that many writers wish to avoid – unpredictability.

Let's face it, when you don't know the outcome of a scene or a moment, the story becomes more difficult to write. For you see, conflict gets in the way of something precious – telling the story.

Let it.

That's my advice to you.

Let conflict get in the way of your story. Let it muck it up. Make it more difficult. Paint yourself into a corner. It may take you days, weeks, months, to figure your way out of it. If so, that's okay. The benefits far outweigh the effort. So much so, that we better make this official:

A Conflict Resolution
Think of this as a New Year's resolution – hopefully the one you won't break.

Repeat after me:

I, _____, promise to include some form of conflict in every scene of every screenplay I write.

Signed: _____   Date: _____

Okay, so that's not LEGALLY binding, but you get the drift.

Examining conflict through the lens of creating unpredictability and raising questions, let's explore some revised forms of conflict.

Forms of Conflict
The differing types of conflict can be defined in several ways, but for now we'll focus on several broad categories you can combine to create your own, personalized definitions of conflict. To do this we'll examine conflict through three different lenses:

1. The elements picked to create conflict.
2. The types of questions these elements raise through conflict
3. When these questions are answered or addressed.

Let's address the simplest one first...

<u>1. Elements:</u>
These can be almost anything in your script – from inanimate objects to characters. An element may also be an idea, an action or a plot event. But, almost every form of cinematic conflict requires at least one character to function.

2. Types of Questions

These are the questions posed when elements are brought together. So, how do you bring elements together?

Simple. Give them an <u>oppositional goal</u>. This is the old 'two dogs fighting over a bone' definition of conflict, and it still holds true. But, in our system, the bone has little significance. In terms of function it's simply a unifying device to bring conflicting elements together. Can you assign meaning to it? Sure. Absolutely. And, you should. But, in terms of functionality, a bone is a bone is a bone.

Remember: you're not the one asking the question – the audience is. You simply pose the question by showing the audience conflict between story elements.

<u>Some Typical Questions Resulting From Conflict:</u>

How will this turn out?
What is the character thinking?
How does this character feel?
Why is this happening?
How will a character act/react?
What will happen next?
What does this character want?
Why does a character act this way?

And so forth…

3. When Is a Question Answered

We'll use two basic timeframes for this one – Immediate and Hanging.

- <u>Immediate Conflict</u> results when answers are given upon asking. These are immediate reactions.

- <u>Hanging Conflict</u> results when you withhold answers to the questions raised by conflict. This can be when you hold the answer for a beat during conflict. You may withhold the answer for an entire scene, an act, or the entire movie. Hanging conflict creates suspense and anticipation.

Using this system, here are some ways to combine all three to define differing forms of conflict:

1. **Intercharacter**

    Elements: character interactions with other characters. Can be immediate or hanging conflict. So, for example: in a fight, every punch has an undetermined outcome, but the response usually comes quickly. In dialogue, every line has the potential to change the outcome of what's to come, and is usually addressed fast, but can have moments of hanging conflict throughout.

    Some typical questions raised include:
    - How will this turn out?
    - How will a character act/react?
    - How will the other character respond?

2. **Intracharacter**

    Internal conflict for a character. Usually provided by the audience.
    Elements may include: character + backstory or plot event or previous plot event
    Conflict in these moments usually requires background knowledge of a character and previous moments within the film. Often this is hanging conflict – with nothing else to react to in a scene, we'll have to wait for answers to the questions raised. For example: a quiet character moment after a traumatic event.

    Some typical questions raised include:
    - What is the character thinking?
    - What will the character do next?
    - How does this character feel?

3. **Interfilmic**

    Representative conflict. Think of it as manifestations of the thematic elements being explored. Elements: ideas and characters. Plot events and previous plot events (scenes/previous scenes)
    Some examples: rich vs. poor, fate vs. chaos, etc. basically the philosophical underpinnings of the conflict we're watching, which raise moral questions extending beyond the film into society. Another form of hanging conflict.

    Some typical questions raised include:
    - What does this mean?
    - What will the character do next?

4. **Interaudience**

    Sense of conflict within the audience itself. In other words, audience members may feel conflict toward the film, its characters, and so forth because of their interactions with the material.

    Some typical questions raised include:
    - Why do I like this?
    - What do others think of this?

Those are just some of the possible combinations, but you can create your own.

SET 4: *The Fifth Element*   CRAFT   Total Reps: 1

Create a **fifth form of conflict** and explore it using elements, question types and when they're answered

5. _____
       (name your type of conflict)

Describe it here:

Elements needed:

Typical questions asked:

When are these questions often answered for this form of conflict? (immediate/hanging/both?)

Intensity of Conflict

Obviously not all conflict is created equal. An arena fight to the death is typically far more intense than a spat between lovers, so some examination of conflict intensity is warranted.

Intensity serves several functions. It can heighten the stakes, creating an even greater need in the audience to know the answer to the question. The degree of this need shifts your timeframe to answer the question. With enough intensity, the shift occurs from hanging to more immediate. Intensity also creates a greater desire to know the outcome.

Ultimately, the intensity of the conflict serves to expand the range of possible outcomes, which is the main reason why conflict can be so darn entertaining. It also moves those unlikely outcomes to more likely as the stakes and intensity increase, thus creating a world in which almost anything is possible.

On the surface, conflict may appear to make writing more difficult. But, in reality, it's your best friend when it comes to creating an immersive, interactive cinematic experience for your audience. Indeed, conflict is perhaps the single most powerful tool in your writing arsenal.

Don't believe me? Suppose we could fight about it. :)

Hmm... I wonder what the possible outcomes of that would be...

WORKOUT PROGRESS – CRAFT

Compile your totals for this unit.

EXERCISE	SKILL GROUP		TOTAL REPS	
	SET #	TYPE	ACTION	AVAILABLE	COMPLETED
Conflicting Results	1	Craft	Analysis	3	
Checks and Balances	2	Craft	Application	7	
Second Helpings	3	Craft	Application	1	
The Fifth Element	4	Craft	Application	1	
			TOTAL REPS		

CRAFT — TOTAL REPS + BONUS — 12

Delivery Drivers

Ever listened to someone tableread your script and just butcher your dialogue?

Those lines, those meticulous lines you hear so perfectly in your head sometimes don't quite come out right when read by another. The inflection's wrong. The tone is off. The passion, the subtlety, all gone. What happened?

Chances are, it wasn't on the page to begin with.

Line delivery starts with the writing. Sure, it can be directed. Sure, a good actor can nail it. But before the script gets to a director or an actor it has to be read first. And, that line delivery, that voice of the character, has to shine through from the page.

> **Training Tip:** One of the best ways to make your script stand out is to write dialogue your readers can hear in their minds.

To help your reader 'hear' the dialogue, it must be written in such a way that the intonation, the voice of the character, can be heard as though the page were speaking directly to the reader. But, how do we do this?

Line delivery can be forced. You can underline words for emphasis, load up the script with parentheticals, cap words, stick in ellipses for effect, and so forth.

Or...

You can take into account a very simple formula:

$$\text{Line Delivery} = \frac{\underline{\text{Context} + \text{Subtext}}}{\text{Character}}$$

Great. That clears it up.
Just for fun, let's delve into what this formula actually means.

The way a line is delivered or intended to be said is determined by the context in which the line is spoken, and the subtextual meaning of the line, which is a function of character.

In other words, to understand how a line should sound, we have to understand:

- the <u>situation</u> in which the line is said (context)
- the <u>personality</u> of the character speaking it (character)
- what this character <u>wants</u>
- what this character actually <u>means</u> by those words (subtext)
- and <u>who</u> the line is being delivered to

May sound complicated but it's actually quite straightforward once you see it in operation.
To do this, let's explore an example...

Consider the line, <u>"How did you get in here?"</u>

Without context and character you have no way of knowing intention or the character's mindset. Should it be delivered in a hostile fashion? A nervous squeak? A seductive tease? Incredulous amazement? Unabashed delight? Is the party to whom this line is being delivered an intruder, an axe murderer, a spouse, a best friend?

All of these things have an impact on the line delivery.

Let's give it a context.

```
INT. BEDROOM - DAY

Carrie wipes sleep from her eyes and looks down at the
adorable puppy snuggled next to her. She smiles.
                    CARRIE
          How did you get in here?
```

How'd she say that line?   Were you able to hear the line delivery?
Hope so.

Notice some of the cues – the snuggle, the smile. All of it geared to clue you in on how she feels, so you'll understand how she'd deliver the line.

Let's play with the same line in a different context.

```
INT. BEDROOM - DAY

Carrie wipes sleep from her eyes and looks at a MAN,
standing impassive in the doorway. Staring at her.
                    CARRIE
          How did you get in here?
```

How'd she feel this time? How'd she deliver THAT line? See what I did there? ;)

Hopefully, that second one was a little trickier. To me, it needs a bit more context to clarify how the line should sound. Does she know the man? Is he a stranger? A former lover? Does she recognize him from the news? How would these differing contexts affect delivery?

Obviously, these are fairly simple scenarios. Given more time we could establish character and add that to the mix so that the situations can be more complex, but line delivery should still shine through, even with the limited information we have.

Okay, I've had my turn.
Now it's yours…

SET 1: Delivery Drivers   CRAFT   Total Reps: 9

For this exercise, choose THREE of the lines below and create THREE different deliveries for each. To do this, you'll need to:

1. Create a basic situation or scene
2. Think of the line's subtext (what's said versus what's really being said)
3. Who the characters are and the relationship, if any, between them
4. How the character saying the line feels in this situation

<u>Here are the lines:</u>

1. I don't have the money.
2. We have to do something.
3. It can't be true.
4. The train has left the station.

5. What can I do for you?
6. I don't want this.
7. Is this what I think it is?
8. Can I trust you?

<u>On the following pages, write your scenes as they'd appear in a screenplay</u> – three scenes for each line you picked to explore the differing deliveries. Keep them short, including just the details necessary for a reader to hear the lines.

Scenario 1:
Line (from previous page):
_____

Scene for First Line Delivery:

Scene for Second Line Delivery:

Scene for Third Line Delivery:

Scenario 2:
Line (from list): _____

Scene for First Line Delivery:

Scene for Second Line Delivery:

Scene for Third Line Delivery:

Scenario 3:
Line (from list): _____

Scene for First Line Delivery:

Scene for Second Line Delivery:

Scene for Third Line Delivery:

How'd it go? Were you able to alter line deliveries without resorting to parentheticals? Or underlining, bolding or all-capping? To find out, try the following:

BONUS SET: What's My Line   ***CRAFT***   ***Total Reps: 3***

Have someone read your scenarios then deliver the lines. Listen to where your reader places emphasis in each line. Does it shift? Does it match how you heard the delivery? If not, play around with them until they do.

BONUS SET: Apply Within   ***CRAFT***   ***Total Reps: 1***

Try these techniques on one of your screenplays. Pay particular attention to spots where you may have relied on parentheticals or other means to force the delivery.

The power of this technique lies in the very subtle effect it has on your readers. It makes them feel they know your characters because they can 'hear' them speak. Not the literal meaning or words, but the tone and attitude informing the words. How a line is said often carries greater impact than what is said. It also carries another subtle but equally powerful effect: when we can hear the intended delivery, we feel as though we're inside a character's mind. In short, we 'get' them, which reinforces our bond with the character. Ever doubt the power of tone? Ask a parent of a back-talking teenager. I'm sure they'll clarify it for you. :)

WORKOUT PROGRESS – CRAFT
Compile your workout totals for this unit.

EXERCISE	SKILL GROUP			TOTAL REPS	
	SET #	TYPE	ACTION	AVAILABLE	COMPLETED
Delivery Drivers	1	Craft	Application	9	
What's My Line	Bonus	Craft	Analysis	3	
Apply Within	Bonus	Craft	Analysis	1	
			TOTAL REPS		

CRAFT   TOTAL REPS + BONUS   **13**

Making Connections

Perhaps it's the indirect way movies convey story.
Perhaps it's human nature to enjoy putting things together.
Or, maybe it's just plain fun.

Whatever the reason, making connections between the story elements you're presenting is the chief way we interact with a film. The process is straightforward. You, the filmmaker, present us, your audience, with beats, scenes, a look here, a line there, and allow us the freedom to connect these statements to other such beats, looks and lines to help form a complete picture out of incomplete parts.

With this exercise let's stretch creativity and associate some things that wouldn't normally go together.

SET 1: *Character Connections*   **CREATIVITY**   **Total Reps: 10**

Pick a character from one of your screenplays (or one you've created in this book) and ask the following questions. Respond as the character in the spaces provided.

If you were a car, what kind of car would you be? _____
Why this one?

If you were a restaurant, what would you be? _____
Why this one?

If you were a soup, what would you be? _____
Why this one?

If you were a city, what would you be? _____
Why this one?

If you were an animal, what would you be? _____
Why?

Hey, maybe we just discovered what this character drives, where they eat out, what they had for dinner and the city where they live. Maybe that animal becomes their pet. Lots of possibilities.

Of course, those details may not be appropriate for the character, but the ability to connect the essence of one thing and relate it to another helps provide the conditions necessary for the audience to do the same – to relate to the material. Just for fun, let's do the same exercise again. Only this time, let's pick a character closer to home – you.

SET 2: Personal Connections   **_CREATIVITY_**   **_Total Reps: 10_**

Same drill, only this time YOU'RE the star.

If you were a car, what kind of car would you be? _____
Why this one?

If you were a restaurant, what would you be? _____
Why this one?

If you were a soup, what would you be? _____
Why this one?

If you were a city, what would you be? _____
Why this one?

If you were an animal, what would you be? _____
Why this one?

Just for curiosity, were your responses similar to those for the character you picked? Like I said, just curious. Sometimes writers show up in the funniest places…

One way to think of this approach is like reverse engineering, where you take apart a finished product to see how it's constructed. Only of course, our product isn't a product at all, it's a person, but a similar principle applies: breaking apart a complex personality into its parts allows you to show us the parts and lets us, the audience, put them together into the character were watching on the screen.

Now, let's stretch those connective tissues a bit more.

SET 3: Connecting Flights   *CREATIVITY*   **Total Reps: 10**

Same questions, only this time with an <u>idea</u> rather than something tangible. For this round, use the following idea:

courage

If courage was a car, what would it be? _____
Why did you pick this?

If courage was a restaurant, what would it be? _____
Why this one?

If courage was a soup, what would it be? _____
Why this one?

If courage was a city, what would it be? _____
Why this one?

And, if courage was an animal, what would it be? _____
Why this one?

By finding the essence of something as ethereal as an idea and connecting it to the essence of something tangible, you can communicate abstract ideas with subtlety and nuance, making the choices in the script somehow just feel 'right'. And, because the audience makes the connection, they in turn can connect to your movie. These are the movies that soar. Okay, that last part was a bit melodramatic, but I just *had* to connect it back to the title of this exercise. :)

WORKOUT PROGRESS – CREATIVITY

Compile your workout totals for this unit.

EXERCISE	SKILL GROUP		TOTAL REPS	
	SET #	TYPE	ACTION	AVAILABLE	COMPLETED
Character Connections	1	Creativity	Analysis	10	
Personal Connections	2	Creativity	Analysis	10	
Connecting Flights	3	Creativity	Application	10	
			TOTAL REPS		

CREATIVITY — TOTAL REPS + BONUS — 30

Build-a-Tale 3:
Heroes and Villains Edition

For this rendition of Build-a-Tale, you'll explore the relationship between a hero's strength and flaw, character design, and how to integrate heroes and villains to create interesting conflicts.

As with all the Build-a-Tale Exercises, you'll randomly select the characters and other story parameters by choosing four numbers from one to ten. Let's do that now. And remember, no peeking!

Choose your Adventure!
Pick a number from <u>one to ten</u> for each category, and write it in the space provided. Choose wisely…

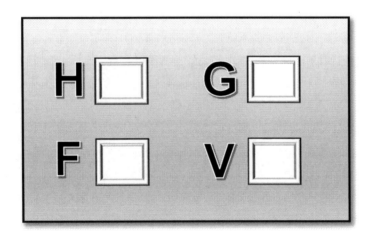

Special Notes on this Build-a-Tale:
Heroes and villains have blank spaces in front of them. Once you discover which hero and villain you've chosen, fill in a descriptor. This forms the DEFINING CHARACTERISTIC for each. These should be chosen to maximize conflict between the two characters.

SET 1: *Heroes, Villains and Story*   CRAFT   *Total Reps:* 2
Create a story using the parameters you've picked. Remember, the numbers you chose on this page correspond to the numbers in each category. You may add characters, but you must include the ones picked at random.

Circle the numbers you chose in each category to begin.

H — Hero

1. a(n) _____ boy
2. a(n) _____ mother
3. a(n) _____ actor
4. a(n) _____ athlete
5. a(n) _____ man
6. a(n) _____ woman
7. a(n) _____ biker
8. a(n) _____ stoner
9. a(n) _____ girl
10. a(n) _____ cop

G — Goal

1. to get married
2. to become famous
3. to be respected
4. to find a lost object
5. to help a loved one
6. to buy a home
7. to receive a promotion
8. to finish school
9. to win a game
10. to create a masterpiece

F — Strength-Flaw

1. super-intelligent
2. articulate
3. dedicated to family
4. attractive
5. driven
6. generous/giving
7. good with numbers
8. truthful
9. fashionable
10. curious

V — Villain

1. a(n) _____ drug lord
2. a(n) _____ mother
3. a(n) _____ father
4. a(n) _____ teacher
5. a(n) _____ politician
6. a(n) _____ creature
7. a(n) _____ hairdresser
8. a(n) _____ bully
9. a(n) _____ store clerk
10. a(n) _____ dog

Using this combination, complete the following to create your story:

Title: _____

Concept/Logline: (do this <u>after</u> you've figured out your story on the following pages)

Hero	**Villain**
Name: _____	Name: _____

Complete the rest of your character design

Defining Characteristic	Flaw/Strength-Flaw		Defining Characteristic	Flaw/Strength-Flaw
Paradox	Humanity		Paradox	Humanity

Given this combination, what are the characters'...

Want (this is often the goal):   **Want** (this is often the goal):

Need (this is related to the flaw):   **Need** (this is related to the flaw):

Brainstorm Space

How are the characteristics you've chosen for these characters designed to fit together AND oppose? Describe:

What are some interesting conflicts that could arise from bringing this hero and villain together? Jot some thoughts here:

How are the goal and villain designed to explore the hero's flaw? Remember: flaws often bring the hero into conflict with the villain. Describe:

How can the pursuit of the goal expose the hero's flaw? Describe:

To create the story, combine the best of the elements from the previous page. Remember, the hero's pursuit of the goal is opposed by the villain. Ideally, this pursuit exposes the hero's flaw – makes the hero aware of it. Then, the hero must overcome both the villain AND the flaw to achieve the goal. Now that you have these basic parameters in place – let's outline your story!

SET 2: *Structural Outline*   **CRAFT**   ***Total Reps*: 9**

Outline your story and describe how you will creatively show these beats.

1. Hook (1-5)
Can be the birth of the flaw, power of the antagonist, creatively introduce the hero's world or all.

2. Inciting Incident (10)
Overturns the hero's world; introduces a subplot, etc.

3. Central Question (17)
The main story question that will be explored throughout the rest of the movie.

4. Reaction to the Central Question (30)
This is the hero's first attempt to answer the Central Question.

5. First Big Hurdle (45)
Stakes raise. Add a new character to the mix.

6. Apex (60)
Passive to active in relation to the FLAW.

7. False Happy Ending (75)
Looks like we've answered the Central Question in the hero's favor, without addressing the flaw.

8. Low Point (90)
Furthest from answering the Central Question. Must confront GREATEST FEAR to overcome/fix/address FLAW.

Ending:

Now that you've worked through the story, return to the concept/logline section and write a compelling logline/concept for a screenplay with this combination of elements.

If the logline seems bland, revisit your elements to see if you have the most intriguing combinations and revise if necessary. This should affect the outline as well, but no need to revise that, unless, of course, you intend to write this script!

WORKOUT PROGRESS – CRAFT

Compile your workout totals for this unit.

EXERCISE	SKILL GROUP			TOTAL REPS	
	SET #	TYPE	ACTION	AVAILABLE	COMPLETED
Heroes, Villains and Story	1	Craft	Application	2	
Structural Outline	2	Craft	Application	9	
				TOTAL REPS	

CRAFT — TOTAL REPS + BONUS — 11

Positively Negative:
Connotative and Denotative Language

In some ways, the art of screenwriting lies in how much meaning you can pack into a limited amount of space. One way to use language to this effect is to choose loaded words – ones with additional layers of meaning beyond their surface definitions. Whenever possible, use words with connotative meanings as opposed to their denotative counterparts. Just as a reminder – connotative definitions are the feelings surrounding the meaning of a particular word. Connotations tend to be positive or negative, depending on the feeling associated with the word. Denotative language is more neutral – typically just the actual definition. So, while denotative words are useful when conveying something nondescript, connotative words convey tone and attitude in addition to meaning. With this in mind, consider the following:

SET 1: Choice Words **CREATIVITY** **Total Reps: 27**

Examine the list of words below and decide whether they have positive or negative connotations. Use a + to mark positive connotations, a – for negative, and an N if the word is neutral and therefore more denotative in nature.

Connotation	Connotation	Connotation
corrupt	ensnare	invade
destroy	infect	enter
empower	take	save
enslave	steal	flirt
guide	inspire	tempt
help	argue	transform
break	mangle	borrow
crave	use	procure
exit	depart	leave

Notice how connotations vary in strength and can change depending on the context. So, a word like 'use' may be neutral when using a computer or negative when using another person. What about its *use* in the next sentence?

Using strongly connotative language enables you to generate reactions and create feelings about certain actions in virtually the same amount of space as using less descriptive denotative words. So, next time you're searching for just the right word, take into account connotative and denotative interpretations to help create a more visceral experience for your reader.

BONUS SET: Checked Language   CREATIVITY   Total Reps: 1+
Check your script for language choice and replace denotative words with connotative ones where appropriate. One rep for each, so feel the burn!

WORKOUT PROGRESS – CREATIVITY
Compile your workout totals for this unit.

EXERCISE	SKILL GROUP			TOTAL REPS	
	SET #	TYPE	ACTION	AVAILABLE	COMPLETED
Choice Words	1	Creativity	Analysis	27	
Checked Language	Bonus	Creativity	Application	1+	
			TOTAL REPS		

CREATIVITY   TOTAL REPS + BONUS   27+

DANCING WITH DEVILS

It's been said the devil is in the details. If true, then meet your new dance partner, for choosing the right details is vital to your success. So, what makes a detail 'right'? Let's hit the dance floor and find out.

In ways, a film is taking specific details and combining these to create an implied whole. This collection of precise details creates a reality that exists beyond the screen. This reality forms the world of your story and can also represent the abstract concepts and ideas you're exploring. The art of this approach lies in choosing the right objects, the right details to give the GUIDED ILLUSION OF REALITY. Simply put, the guided illusion of reality is just that: it's guided because you select which details to share, and it's an illusion because the audience takes these fragments and combines them to create a reality that extends beyond the screen.

Critical vs Non-Critical Story Details
As you write your script, sometimes you'll want to be vague in certain descriptions. Non-critical story details are just that; a reader can miss them and still follow the story. These details can be a bit more vague. That's to help draw attention to those details vital to our understanding of the story – story-critical details. Sometimes a screenwriter will ALL CAP story-critical details to make them pop.

Sometimes they'll be placed on their own, stand-alone lines – like this one.

While those are effective techniques for drawing a reader's eye to these details, they may not stick unless they're specific and vivid. But, if EVERYTHING is described to this degree, the script may be tedious, overwhelming to read. Too vague and readers can't picture what's happening, potentially pulling them out of the story. So, the trick here to choose your spots with care, balancing specificity with broadness.

The art of this technique is finding just the right balance between broad and specific details – a tricky proposition, especially considering we, as writers, don't have a way of knowing what that balance is for an individual reader, which is yet another reason to get eyes on your work: to see if you've struck the right balance and to measure the effectiveness of your specific details. Even trickier is when you wish to describe something abstract, an idea or theme you're exploring that you wish to reinforce through the specific imagery you're describing.

Abstract Detailing

The application of a few, choice, thematically relevant details will enable you to communicate the abstract ideas your script is exploring by turning them into concrete details that a camera can be pointed at and a reader can picture. Notice this is an indirect technique, requiring the reader to make connections between details and theme, but that's also the power of this approach because it provides opportunities for your reader and the audience to make personal connections to the material and to fill in the world of the story without you resorting to excess description, making the script faster, more efficient and more vivid.

To explore using specific details to evoke strong imagery and abstract themes, check out the exercise below:

SET 1: Abstracting Details   ***CREATIVITY***   ***Total Reps: 4***

Think of specific objects that would <u>exemplify the abstract ideas</u> below. Then, think of ways you can integrate these objects into a script. BE CREATIVE!

<u>Abstract idea: HOPE</u>

Three specific objects you could include in a script that would represent this idea:

1. _____

2. _____

3. _____

Choose **one** of these images and describe why you picked it. In other words, how does this object exemplify the abstract idea?

Describe how you would integrate this object into a screenplay by writing a brief script passage below:

Abstract idea: WEAKNESS

Three specific objects you could include in a script that would represent this idea:

1. _____

2. _____

3. _____

Choose **one** of these images and describe why you picked it. In other words, how does this object exemplify the abstract idea?

Describe how you would integrate this object into a screenplay by writing a brief script passage below:

Abstract idea: STRENGTH

Three objects that you could include in your script that would represent this idea:

1.
_____

2.
_____

3.
_____

Choose **one** of these images and describe why you picked it. In other words, how does this object exemplify the abstract idea?

Describe how you would integrate this object into a screenplay by writing a brief script passage below:

Abstract idea: LOVE

Three specific objects you could include in a script that would represent this idea:

1.
_____

2.
_____

3.
_____

Choose **one** of these images and describe why you picked it. In other words, how does this object exemplify the abstract idea?

Describe how you would integrate this object into a screenplay by writing the script passage below:

Got the hang of it? If so, great! Now, let's try this same activity using one of your screenplays.

BONUS SET: Detailing Your Script   **_CREATIVITY_**   **_Bonus Reps: 1_**

Using one of your screenplays, choose concrete details that symbolically or subtextually convey the themes or ideas you're exploring.

Theme/Abstract idea: _____

Three objects that you could (or did) include in your script that would represent this idea and evoke a dramatic image:

1.
_____

2.
_____

3.
_____

No need to write how you'd integrate this into the screenplay here as you did previously. If you like what you picked, just write it into your script! Oh, and look for other opportunities for this technique while you're at it.

Then, do a pass for all the concrete details you've chosen throughout your script to see if you're getting the most out of your action-description.

BONUS SET: Sharing is Caring   **_CREATIVITY_**   **_Bonus Reps: 1_**

To check your effectiveness, share your descriptions with someone else to see if your abstract ideas are being understood and if your details are evoking visuals for your readers.

If you like, compile your results in the space provided below:

So, while the devil may be in the details, so too are opportunities for you to use their power to evoke imagery and allow opportunities for readers to make connections between these images and the abstract themes and ideas informing your screenplay. When readers can 'see' your screenplay, it helps it stand out from the others, increasing your odds of success.

WORKOUT PROGRESS – CREATIVITY

Compile your workout totals for this unit.

EXERCISE	SKILL GROUP			TOTAL REPS	
	SET #	TYPE	ACTION	AVAILABLE	COMPLETED
Abstracting Details	1	Creativity	Application	4	
Detailing Your Script	Bonus	Creativity	Application	1	
Sharing is Caring	Bonus	Creativity	Analysis	1	
			TOTAL REPS		

CREATIVITY — TOTAL REPS + BONUS — 27+

Guessed Speakers

Okay, let's stretch that imagination!

SET 1: **As You Were**   **CREATIVITY**   **Total Reps: 7**

Answer the following:

1. If you were a tree, what would you say to people carving names in your trunk?

2. If you were a cloud, what would you say to the people down below?

3. If you were a pebble, what would you say to a kid throwing you into a pond?

4. If you were sand, what would you say to people on your beach?

5. If you were a car, what would you say to the person driving you?

6. If you were a house, what would you say to the people living in you?

7. If you were a toy, what would you say to the children playing with you?

   What toy would you be?

   Why this toy?

Examine your answers as though you were a stranger meeting this person for the first time. What conclusions can you draw about the personality of the person writing these answers? Did you find any patterns to the responses?

What we're exploring is the idea that external choices, actions and dialogue indirectly inform others about the internal makeup or characteristics of a person. It's the same for movie characters.

SET 2: As They Are *CREATIVITY* **Total Reps: 9**

Ask the same questions of a major character in one of your screenplays. Or, if you don't have a screenplay, use any of the characters you've created in this book.

Character Name: _____

1. If you were a tree, what would you say to people carving names in your trunk?

2. If you were a cloud, what would you say to the people down below?

3. If you were a pebble, what would you say to a kid throwing you into a pond?

4. If you were sand, what would you say to people on your beach?

5. If you were a car, what would you say to the person driving you?

6. If you were a house, what would you say to the people living in you?

7. If you were a toy, what would you say to the children playing with you?

   What toy would you be?

   Why this toy?

Based on the responses, what conclusions about this character's personality could you make?

Audiences use context clues to piece together a character's personality, and in so doing, personalize the character to work for them. In other words, if your character injects personality into every action, choice or line of dialogue, the audience creates a personality based on these indirect clues, and they do it in a way that makes sense to each individual. It's a guess to be sure, but an informed one. And, of course that guess creates a prediction that can engage the audience as they watch to see if their prediction is correct.

These guesses lead an audience member to create a character that works for them, which increases the chances of bonding with the character and actually caring about this person. Characters we care about make for movies we care about. And, movies audiences care about make long careers for those who write them. This leads to a final question just for fun:

If you were a screenplay, what would you say to the person writing you?

_____

Funny, but depending on how seriously you answered that last question, that response may prove to be the best screenwriting advice you'll ever encounter. Of course, that's just a guess…

WORKOUT PROGRESS – CREATIVITY

Compile your workout totals for this unit.

EXERCISE	SKILL GROUP			TOTAL REPS	
	SET #	TYPE	ACTION	AVAILABLE	COMPLETED
As You Were	1	Creativity	Application	7	
As They Are	2	Creativity	Application	9	
			TOTAL REPS		

CREATIVITY — TOTAL REPS + BONUS — 16

Act 3

The Cooldown

Interactive Screenwriting for Fun and Profit

So, the other day I'm hanging out with some people, and I found myself cornered in a one-way conversation with a guy who just wouldn't stop talking. Frustration city.

If you've ever talked with a talker, you know the drill. You try to wait for a pause, for them to actually take a breath, something, anything, so you can get a word in. Then there's that awkward, trying not to be rude and just interrupt them phase while you wait,

and wait,

and wait

for a natural opening in the conversation. Problem is, an opening never comes. They keep going on with their story, whether you want to hear it or not. And, even when you can squeeze in a comment – BANG, they ignore it and continue. Of course, just because they're talking doesn't mean I have to listen. :)

So, standing there, with nothing to do, I tuned out, did the token nod and pretend like I'm listening deal, and started thinking about film narrative. This led to a conclusion:

In many ways, a movie is like the ultimate one-way conversation.

And believe it or not – that's a problem.

Because as I stood there, stuck in this one-way conversation, I realized I wanted to be anyplace other than there, listening to this fool drone on. And, this is a bad thing. So let's clarify our earlier statement...

In many ways, a bad movie is the ultimate one-way conversation.

Don't believe it? Then ask yourself this. You ever watch a bad movie and start talking to it? Busting on it? Making fun of it? Like your own personal Mystery Science Theater 3000? Now, if you haven't done that, chances are you know someone who has. If you don't know anyone like that, go to a theater and listen to the audience. They'll talk to the movie – tell the characters not to do something or gripe when they do something stupid.

And, when people do this, you're witnessing a fundamental aspect of film:

> **People want to converse with a movie so they can interact with it.**

Interestingly, it's often a bad movie that gets an audience commenting out loud. The reason? Because no one is speaking for the audience. The audience has been left out of the film, so they are forcibly inserting themselves into it, into the conversation. This is not how we want to interact with a movie. But, it raises an interesting question:

How do you have a two-way conversation with an audience through film?

After all, the film is set. Picture is locked. It wrapped photography long ago. It was written before that. The actors have moved on. You can't be there at every screening to talk to the audience, to listen to the audience and respond.
So if you can't do that personally, who can?

As it turns out, you can – but not directly.

Because film is set, you have to <u>plan ahead</u> and <u>anticipate your conversation with the audience</u> and provide them with what's lacking in a one-sided conversation -- **points of insertion** -- those moments where we, the audience, <u>your</u> audience, can insert our thoughts, our feelings. Places where audiences can put themselves into characters, and as a result, into the movie.

<u>**Insertion Points**</u>**: opportunities provided for an audience to allow them to enter a film. You can invite the audience into a character, into the world of that character, and thus, into the story itself.**

Looking at it another way, insertion points are invitations to join the party. They're our cues to enter the conversation, add our contributions and interact with the film.

We can categorize points of insertion into two groups, **Character Insertion Points** and **Story Insertion Points**. Although these may appear to be separate categories, I think you'll find a great deal of overlap between character and story – even more so when you consider the following:

Audience is a character in your story.

Think about it.

You ever watch home movies? They're almost always horrible. The sound often stinks. The picture, even worse -- blown out, shaky-cam, zoom in, zoom out. And that's just production value. Never mind performance. All those uncomfortable parts where people struggle to say or do something remotely entertaining, then can't think of anything, so they wind up sticking out their tongues or making goofy faces. Why does anybody watch those things?

Simple.

We like to see ourselves on the screen.

Matter of fact -- people <u>love</u> to see themselves on the screen. And, we'll sit through all the wind noise, all the lousy camerawork, just to experience that. So what does this mean for you?

It means you write roles for the audience.

The idea here is that you write parts for the audience to play in the unfolding of your narrative. Sometimes we're piecing information together. Sometimes we're enjoying the thrill of the ride. Sometimes we're vicarious observers, and sometimes we become the characters. But any way you cut it...

The audience must see themselves on your screen.

If we can't find ourselves somewhere in the characters or the events of the story, you're leaving us out of the conversation. You're doing all the talking, telling your story, never letting us in.

And, this is deadly.

A key point to consider:
Movies that remove an audience's roles from the story often play flat because the filmmakers have taken the audience out of the story.

And, this is a big problem because not only is audience a character in the story, but...

Audience is where character and story meet and become one.

This leads us back to <u>points of insertion</u> and those two broad categories because:

Insertion points serve as <u>invitations</u> for an audience to enter the characters and the story.

Characters should be designed to provide us with the roles we would want to play in the film. And, the story should be structured to give us opportunities to experience what these characters are experiencing, which then leads us to enter the world of the story. It's as simple as that.

So what does all this have to do with our two-way conversation?

You must anticipate what questions the audience will have. It's like a well-rehearsed Q&A session in which you anticipate the questions and plan your answers ahead of time. <u>You then enact the conversation</u> by having characters address the audience's point of view by acting for the audience.

> **Film narrative is a conversation by proxy, in which characters speak on behalf of the audience.**

Simply put, characters ask questions and respond to the story for the audience, which is why character identification is so crucial -- <u>if we don't have a character representing us, we are left out of the conversation, and ultimately out of the film</u>.

Seems easy enough. But here's the trick.

Not only do you have to provide places for us to enter, we have to <u>want</u> to enter.

That is what's missing from a one-sided conversation. We aren't being given chances to join in. And then, even if we're given those opportunities, it has to be a conversation we want to join. Otherwise, once again, we are not engaged. Of course, we never quite know how someone will react, so...

The more points of insertion you provide, the more opportunities you give us to engage the film.

Everyone responds differently to film. So savvy filmmakers provide multiple opportunities and ways for us to enter. You never know exactly what individuals will latch on to, so you try to cover as many ways as possible. You also have to implant the desire in an audience to want to enter.

Although it seems like a lot to consider, it's just looking at movies through a different set of eyes – the eyes of your audience. And, doing that starts with our two main points of insertion – character and story.

Character Insertion Points: opportunities you create that are designed to allow us to enter your characters. Remember – just because we have the chance to enter, doesn't mean we will. You also must implant the desire. But once the desire is planted, we still need these opportunities.

We'll get to desire in a moment (it's a function of story), we need to examine the players first.
Central to understanding this approach is one critical concept:

Characters serve as <u>proxies</u> for the audience.

Just so we're clear…

A proxy is someone with the authority to act on our behalf. A substitute for us.

One thing should jump out at you in this definition – a proxy is someone <u>we</u> authorize. In other words, we, the audience, decide who will be our proxy, our substitute. We must give these characters that power of our own free will – which provides you with some intriguing possibilities…

The decision to pick who will represent us in the story forms the key way you, the filmmaker, interact with us, the audience. You shape our decisions, manipulate them, by shifting us from character to character.

If you want us to react objectively to a scene, you provide us a character reacting objectively.

If you want us to react emotionally, you give us an emotional character in the scene.

If you want us to react with horror, with passion, with outrage, with love – you give us characters who react within a scene with these exact same emotions.

But, as always, there's a bit of trick.

<u>If none of the reactions to events on the screen represent ours – then we won't necessarily bond with any of the characters we are watching.</u> This means that we are left out, and the scene may collapse. Enough of these scenes and the entire movie will collapse.

<u>The other trick is knowing how we are reacting and what we're wanting to know at any given moment.</u> Most of the time, you can't quite be sure of that, so you cover your bases by having numerous characters for the audience to latch on to early in the story, then strip these away by the end.

Or, you provide one clear character that can serve as a proxy for virtually anyone – our hero.

The key is understanding what an audience wants and when they want it.

Also, be aware that the needs of the audience shift over time and from moment to moment.

The early part of a film, any film, is dominated by the audience's desire to know what is going on – the rules of the story, and who they should pick as their proxy.

In the opening moments of a film, the audience is objective. Studying. Testing the rules of the world. Evaluating whether or not this is worth their time.

Looking at these audience desires, you'll need characters to match them – a character who wants to know what's going on, a character exploring the rules of the story, and ultimately, you'll need to present a character worthy enough, mysterious enough, entertaining enough, neutral enough to be a proxy.

This leads us to our first major character insertion point.

Any character, in any scene, who wants to know what we want to know provides an opportunity for character identification by inviting us to insert ourselves into that character.

It also leads us to our second insertion point:

Characters who entertain us provide strong <u>early</u> insertion points.

The thought here is simple. We like characters who entertain us. And, in the absence of any other information about a character, we'll bond with those who amuse us. It's not a particularly strong bond, but it's a starting point.

Putting these tools into practice…

Let's say you want to withhold information from the audience – things we want to know. Then you simply withhold that information from a character who wants to know it.

Now, this can be frustrating. We really want to know this information. So, the key is to have the character get frustrated. Have the character's reactions mirror our own.

Something to think about:
Ever wonder why it's hard to get an emotional reaction out of audiences in a short film? It's because we watch films objectively at first. To get at an emotion requires an intimate bond between character and audience, which takes time to develop. It's doable in a short, but it requires a firm understanding of character insertion points.

<u>In the opening of Pixar's *Up* we see a prime example of these tools at work.</u>
Notice in that opening, the characters are essentially silent. Anything they may say, may not be what we would say, and this would break the bond. Furthermore, by having the characters be silent the filmmakers are using one of our major character insertion points:

<u>**The Silent Scene**</u>
Characters who react silently provide us with a huge opportunity to go inside them. These moments must be set up. We must understand what the character might be thinking. We may be wrong, and that's okay, because we are transferring our thoughts to the character. The character is neutral at this point. Standing there. Waiting for us to enter. These moments serve as invitations to go inside a character and make him or her our own.

Notice that if a character speaks in that moment, the spell is broken. Chances are anything the character says is wrong because, chances are, what you have that character say won't be what we would say. In addition, as soon as that character talks, we're listening to them, we are no longer them.

Let's go back to our opening example – that one-sided conversation that prompted all of this. The talker never gave me a silent moment to enter. It's the same with story.

Many filmmakers become so occupied with telling their stories they forget to give us moments to enter them. If you do this, you deny us the ability to enter the story and experience it for ourselves.

Back to *Up* and that silent sequence of two people getting married, growing old and never realizing their dreams. <u>It doesn't work as a silent; it works *because* it is silent.</u> That silence forces us to go inside the characters, and when we do this, we become the characters, and the characters become us. This is essential to achieving the emotional reaction the filmmakers want at the end of the sequence.

Also understand that within the sequence itself are smaller, silent moments, teaching us how to interact with the film. In other words, we are being trained to think like these characters, and we're being shown that our thoughts are correct.

If this sequence in *Up* did not work for you, chances are the training did not stick, or something else happened that influences this technique. We have to want to insert ourselves into a character.

Creating Character Insertion Points

Remember – character insertion points are invitations for us to enter the characters, to identify with them and to pick them as our proxies. Of course invitations can be refused. So sometimes, we have to make the audience a few offers they can't refuse.

Because audiences want to interact with a film, the simplest way to create character insertion points is to have characters function as the audience's proxy for interacting with the story itself.

Functional Tools for Bonding Audience to Character:

1. Have your characters say things we wish we could say. We'll admire them for it – especially if they're saying what we want them to say.

2. Have characters do things we wish we could do. We'll admire them for that, too, and for the same reasons as above.

3. Have characters feel how we would feel in a scene. We'll identify with them.

4. Have characters think what we are thinking and express it. This enables us to converse with the movie. Very identifiable. It turns the one-way conversation into a two-way one by proxy.

5. Have characters react the way we would react. Secondary characters are great for this. Ever wonder why the hero has so many of these floating around? It's to give us a voice in scenes when we are not the hero. Once we complete the bond with the hero, we may no longer need these characters.

Character Insertion Points Summary

Basically character insertion is all about <u>providing the audience an interface to interact with the story</u> through characters. All the tools of character identification work together to get us to care for characters and invest in their lives. Some techniques for inserting the audience into your movie include:

1. Silent Scenes

In the writing class we do an exercise in this. Now you know why. To recap: it's an invitation to invest our thoughts into a character's thoughts. Remember, the more a character says, the less identifiable that character may become. This leads us to…

2. A Silenced Character

A scene in which a character can't speak up for themselves -- often as the result of an injustice. This technique works on the consideration that the audience also cannot speak.

3. Proxy Characters

Any characters substituting for audience reactions in a given scene. These are often manifestations of our narrative point of view character functions.

4. Birth of the Flaw

When you take a person who could be any one of us (the audience) and hit them with an event on screen that causes an inner wound or flaw, we wonder how we would react in that situation.

5. TMI Characters

Characters who reveal everything about themselves early on in the film often turn us away. Can be used for villains, but dangerous for heroes. If we know everything about a character, we get no…

6. Secrets and Lies

Characters who hold secrets are intriguing. We want to know more. And we feel special when we share that character's secret. Characters who lie, and regret it, also hold the promise of drama to unfold.

7. Admirable Traits

Things we admire in people make for welcoming invitations to join with a character. Just don't make them too perfect. And don't make it too obvious that you're trying to get us to admire a character.

8. Actions

Speak louder than words. They work silently to forge bonds when they mirror audience reactions.

9. Choices
Speak even louder than actions, forcing us to ask ourselves what choice we would make given the circumstances – and given the limited amount of information we know about a character.

10. Start Small. Go Broad. End Small.
Our first point of insertion is small and broad – usually a single character. It's simple, easily understood. We then begin to insert in several characters, getting different points of view and using characters to gauge the information we are being presented. We then end small, bonded with one character (typically the hero) whose complexity only we have come to understand through the events in the story.

Some General Notes on Character Insertion Points

- Silence and mystery pull us into a character.
- We tend to admire characters who do things we wish we could do.
- Insertion opportunities for characters must be presented quickly. Start simple. A line or an action to get us intrigued by the character. Then stick them in an easily relatable situation so we can form our initial impression, and gradually increase the levels of complexity as we get to know the character.
- Remember, we experience the story through your characters and their reactions, and early on, their reactions must mirror our own. Characters can assert their individuality later in the story, once we've bonded with them.
- Remember where the audience is at any given point in your story and insert the audience into your story through characters.

Character Insertion and In-Group, Out-Group Dynamics
A more advanced way of looking at character insertion points takes into consideration an audience's relationship with a character and the story. In-group, out-group dynamics means that we often define ourselves by our relationships. In-groups are groups to which you belong: families, co-workers, teams, classes, etc. Out-groups are others – outsiders.

As an audience, we start in the out-group. We're outsiders to the story, the world of the story, the characters, etc. Observers looking in.

Over the course of a movie, we are invited to join the in-group. You show us why we'd want to be part of the in-group, how cool it would be to be part of the in-group. How much fun it is to be on the inside. How exclusive. Just to clarify, in-group isn't a clique per se; it's most often the hero's team.

For example: in *Twister* we start in the out-group. We use Melissa as our point of identification. She doesn't know storm chasing. We don't know storm chasing. She's an outsider. We're outsiders. Then, over the course of the movie, we are taught to be storm chasers. Melissa is moved out of the story -- discarded because we no longer need her as a point of identification. We are now part of the in-group: Jo and Bill. And, we feel special because of it. And that's the key.

Ever wonder why heroes typically go into the final battle alone? Either stripped of their allies or with just a sense of singularity?

It's to make us feel special.

This is the ultimate in-group dynamic. Now it's just us (the audience) and the hero. We've spent the whole movie getting to know the hero, forming our bond, so that in this moment we only need to identify with the hero. In other words, early on we may have many different character insertion points. But now, we typically only have the hero -- which means if the hero loses, we lose. This dynamic helps to personalize the stakes. And, when we win, it puts us in exclusive company.

Some Notes About In-Groups and Out-Groups:
In-groups are characterized by their own specialized language. Think of the slang you and others your age use. It's the same in movies. The audience is taught slang and jargon exclusive to the movie's in-group to help us identify with, and be part of, the hero's group.

Remember, we were outsiders when this movie started, now we've been taught some jargon, some slang, what certain things symbolize, etc., this makes us feel a group identification with the characters responsible for getting us in. We are now part of the group. Initiated into the group.

We should have to work to get into the in-group. If we instantly go there, we feel less special because it means anyone can get in.

A side note: this dynamic also works outside the film. An audience, seeing a movie, is now part of a group of moviegoers who have seen the film. They can then define themselves by this experience.

In-Group, Out-Group Dynamics create a number of creative opportunities for audience interaction with story and within individual scenes. One function of secondary characters is reliability. They tend to offer consistent, predictable reactions. Once we know these reactions, we can then use In-Group, Out-Group dynamics in later scenes by introducing Out-Groups to these characters. For example: let's say we have a blunt, wise-cracking secondary character we've come to know. This character is part of our In-Group. Now we bring in a stranger later in the film. Someone foreign to both us and the character. This Out-Group character doesn't know how our blunt friend will act, but we do. So as a scene unfolds, we're waiting for our friend to do what they do, say something smart-alecky, put that stranger in his or her place. We anticipate it, and feel special because we know what's going to happen, and this poor outsider doesn't. Small moments like these reinforce our position within the In-Group, provide proof that we're correctly interpreting the story by giving us opportunities to confirm our predictions.

<u>We can also use In-Group, Out-Group to force the audience to make choices and pick sides.</u>

Out-Group character scenes are easy. We tend to not pick them because they aren't 'one of us.' More complex choices can be offered to the audience if you present two In-Group characters we've come to know, but who are strangers to each other. You can put them together in a scene to let us see how that dynamic will play. This scene may result in the audience having to pick a side, and the tougher this choice, the greater the bond and the deeper the story will seem.

You can also use this technique to bring new members into the fold, for use later in the story. A character trying to join our In-Group offers an opportunity for the audience to realize how special they are for being in the In-Group, and can offer a chance to create empathy for the character trying to enter.

Once you get your audience picking sides, we are making active choices in the film, and it is now a two-way conversation, rather than a one-sided story.

The trick for the audience is that we know we can't influence the outcome; we know we're watching a movie, but we can choose how we interact with the film because we are being given choices and opportunities to interact with the characters in the story.

The ramifications are profound.

<u>As a filmmaker utilizing this approach, you will have to prove to an audience that you will let them into the characters.</u> You'll have to prove that it will be worth the audience's time and effort to do so. And, you will have to prove that once in, we will feel special for having made this effort.

Final Point on Character Insertion Points

While these opportunities must be presented to an audience, the audience will only choose them if they feel the adventure will be worth it.

After all, entering a character is rather personal. We're not going to do this if we feel there is not a reward for doing so. The reward is your story. It's living the events of your story, and that can only be done through its characters.

Although the story may be considered a reward, part of the story's real function is to do something else entirely...

Story Insertion Points: opportunities you create for the audience to enter the story. These are moments that invite the audience to put themselves directly into the narrative.

Remember, your story is something very external to us. It's unknown, and, at the risk of sounding melodramatic, it's something rather scary. When we approach the unknown most people tend to be a bit reluctant, cautious. We want to study it before jumping in. We want to see if it's worth our time.

Now, because it's a movie, there's no real danger, so we make the leap far more quickly than in real life. But, this time of reluctance is still a very real phase we go through in deciding whether or not to enter your story. And, just as with a character, we need points, places, to enter and interact with this external world. But first, you will need to convince us that the story is something worth entering.

Story Insertion Overview
Early story insertion points are all about creating <u>desire</u> in an audience to enter the narrative. They are invitations to the audience that the story will be worth their time, so if they really want to experience it, they best get to know these characters because that's how they're going to experience the ride.

Remember, movies are experiential. Characters experience story events at the same time we do. This is a primary source of bonding between audience and character. In other words...

> **Story is the common element to unite audience with character.**

Or to put it even more simply – we're in this together facing a common enemy (the external events of the plot.)

<u>Inserting an audience into a story is actually character insertion</u>. This means, in order to examine story insertion points we have to look at a character-based structure – because this structure is where character intersects with story. Myth structure and act structures are about plot. Character-based structure is about using story as a bonding agent between audience and character. This in turn reinforces the narrative because audience is now a character in the film experiencing the story. This leads us to…

The 8-Turn Structure

The beats of the 8-turn structure provide the main points of insertion for the audience. They are moments where plot meets the character. In other words, when we are looking at the 8-turn structure, we are looking at the <u>interface between character and narrative</u>, and that interface comes together in the audience because <u>these structural beats form the insertion points an audience can use to interact with character and with story</u>.

What this means is that we can detail how to insert an audience into a story by looking at the functions served at each of these structural beats. As the story evolves, you may notice the major structural beats become ever more character-related. This is because the purpose of this structure is not to reveal plot – it's to use plot to reveal character, and in so doing, <u>reveal ourselves</u>.

What appears to be story structure on the surface is really a tool for self-discovery designed to do one thing: create a movie where character, story and audience are united as a single entity.

To this end, the insertion points of the 8-turn structure function as steps in the process of uniting character, story and audience -- and this process starts from the very moment the movie begins.

The Beats of the 8-Turn Structure

Hook (1-5 minutes into the movie)
The first beat of the 8-turn structure and one of the most important.

Everyone talks about the need for a hook, but many beginning filmmakers start their stories without it. The hook is essential for inserting an audience into a story because it is designed to create the <u>desire</u> to enter your story. Hooks don't have to be exciting. They must simply serve as an invitation -- a promise that the story is worth the effort of getting to know the characters.

The function of the hook is to provide objective proof, something we can see with our own eyes, that this story is worth entering.

At the same time, hooks also serve to establish the credibility of the filmmaker. The opening of a film is where you prove you can entertain an audience. And remember:

The audience wants to interact with your film.

So what's this mean for you?

It means in the hook you have to provide a moment of interaction. Something small you can set up and pay off within the first few minutes. This can be something you teach us that we can use within the opening. It can be a line of dialogue that plays back into the scene. Whatever it is, you need to establish:

- That this will be an exciting world, and…

- That you are aware of how audiences want to react to a film, and…

- That you have the skills to get us to interact with the film, and…

- You have something interesting to say, and…

- You have to launch the narrative, and…

- You have to pique our curiosity to experience more.

Sheesh – that's a lot, but no one ever said making movies was easy… Bottom line for successful hook: it's a time to prove you can deliver and implant desire in the audience to enter your movie.

Simply put – the hook is an event that just about anyone on earth would react to in similar fashion.

Remember, we are watching the opening of your film with a high degree of objectivity. It's next to impossible to get a strong emotional reaction here. We haven't had enough time for that. You'll need to hook us another way, and develop bonds with the characters and trust with the audience before they'll give you their hearts – and the next step in that process is…

Inciting Incident (10 minute point)

The inciting incident is something small that kickstarts the movie. It forms our second insertion point. This beat is a tentative place for the audience to enter the story. We still haven't earned the full trust of the audience, so we issue a call to join the story.

Some may ask, why have an inciting incident at all? Why not just launch the main story? Why take the time to have this smaller set up? The answer is complicated, but basically this beat serves as further proof that you can get us to enter the story.

If the hook is an initial invitation into the world of the story, then the Inciting Incident is our first invitation to the notion of characters and story together. Looking at it another way -- hooks are aimed at the audience. The inciting incident is aimed at a character.

We haven't had much time to get to know our protagonist, so this beat is a more generalized insertion into the story. It's a bridge of sorts between character, audience and story. Our first attempt to join these things together.

It's also your first chance to show that you can take what we've seen up to this point and weave it into a story beat. Inciting Incidents are often internal to the story. Unlike a hook, which requires practically no knowledge of the story world to engage us, the inciting incident often does – depending on the nature of the force of antagonism causing this beat.

The timing and position of the inciting incident is often dependent on the antagonist:

If the inciting incident is easily understood and can affect anyone, this beat may come sooner.

For example: the opening shark attack in *Jaws*. We have to put you on the beach, create a desire in you to go for a swim, put you in the water, and then the Inciting Incident can occur. Anyone who has ever gone swimming in an ocean, regardless of age, personality, socio-economic status, etc. can understand this beat instantly.

The line between hook and Inciting Incident is blurred in this example because technically, the inciting incident is a beat joining character and story. However, I contend this is blending the story duties of the beat with its audience functions. In other words, a case can be made that Sheriff Brody *discovering* the shark attack is the Inciting Incident.

<u>A force of antagonism that does not affect everyone requires more time to set up.</u> If the antagonist affects a very specific group of people, you'll need to get us to identify with one of those affected, so we can understand how it could affect us (if we were in the story.) By this point we still may not have bonded with a specific character, so the beat is still a more generalized moment of affectation. It affects the commonality we share with others. This is a more voyeuristic type of moment. We're observing it, but not necessarily affected by it – yet.

<u>An Inciting Incident dependent upon a specific character trait requires even more time to set up</u>. Character-dependent inciting incidents require understanding the character, which takes time to establish. Highly-specific personalities and situations require screentime to explain.

<u>As a plot beat</u>, the inciting incident overturns the hero's world and prompts a reaction.

<u>From a functional standpoint</u>, the inciting incident serves as <u>The Great Unifier</u>. It's a point of unification between audience and character and story. It's the event that pushes us together. We may not be bonded with the main character yet, but we are being nudged into this position. Think of this beat as a <u>transitional reactive force</u>. In other words, the main character reacts to it, and given what we know of this world, we would tend to react the same way as the main character. Because our reactions are similar, it's an invitation to insert ourselves into a character affected by this beat.

If the hook is something anyone would react to in similar ways, the inciting incident is an event that you and your close friends might react similarly to. Or, to put it another way, we've narrowed the focus of the story just a bit.

<u>Between now and our next beat, we will be working mightily to solidify the bond between the main character and audience.</u> We'll do this by having the main character decide what to do about the inciting incident. The main character may hesitate, or may decide to act immediately. But, typically the decision-making process at work is designed to mirror our decision making process during this time.

<u>The hero must decide how to react to the inciting incident, and we have to decide the exact same thing</u> – and because we're doing this at the exact same time as the hero, this starts to build the bond.

This is why movies are experiential – the mutual experiences bond audience to character because we are undergoing and reacting to the events of the story simultaneously.

This mirroring of reactions also frames the "Refusal of the Call" beat in myth structure. Audiences are often skeptical about buying in to the story, and this is reflected in the hero's initial refusal to enter as well. <u>Persuading the hero then serves to also persuade the audience to go on the adventure.</u>

The Central Question (17 minute point)

<u>This is a main insertion point into the story itself.</u> It can be character-based (for character-driven stories) or plot-based (for more plot-intensive stories.) It can be a thematic question or simply an event that will play out through the story, but however it is posed -- <u>the Central Question is the main story engine</u>.

Once the Central Question is <u>definitively</u> answered, the movie is over.

The Central Question marks our attempt to address the story. It contextualizes the film for the audience, letting us know what this is about and also letting us know when the story is finished. In other words, the story can't end until the question is answered – one way or another. We may not like the answer. The answer may prompt more questions. But, the answer to this specific question lets us know that we have finished what we came here to do.

It also frames our conditions for victory. The villain may be defeated, but until you answer the question you popped at your 17-minute point, the story is not done.

In terms of function, this beat marks our transition to character. It serves as a specific question to a specific issue. Prior to this the film has been more generalized. Now that the audience has received more information, we can focus the story into a single, clear question that will serve as our final point of unification at the end of the story. When the character(s) this question affects get their answer – we get our answer, and as a result – story, character and audience are now one. The story is over, the events internalized, absorbed into the audience and characters.

The answer to the Central Question is a <u>beat marker</u> – it lets us know that the internalization process is complete and that there's nothing left to do except go our separate ways. Or, to put it another way, the Central Question forces the audience and characters to come together to solve it. Once this question is answered, we can now part company – our need to work together is done.

This beat shapes nearly every beat to follow and forms the context audiences use to evaluate the information, characters and events in the story. We will look at everything following this beat within the context of the Central Question. This may not be a conscious process, but it's always there, darting around under the surface of the story and resurfacing at critical points throughout it – the next of which is:

Reaction to the Central Question (30 minute point)

A major insertion point for audience into the main character (and the story.)

Main characters now insert themselves into the story. This beat is the hero's first attempt to address the Central Question. Now the hero is shaping the story. Prior to this, the hero is often reactive. The story is acting on the character. At this point, heroes actively begin altering story events through their initial attempts to answer the Central Question.

<u>This is a huge insertion point for the audience.</u> The character we should be identifying with by this point is changing the story and as a result – <u>we</u> are changing the story.

This is the start of our two-way conversation in earnest.

If we have a direct bond with the main character, we get the illusion that we can affect the outcome of the story. If our bond is indirect, we can observe changes to the story. Either way, this is a moment of assertion against the external forces of the story and the beginning of a deeply internal relationship between audience and character.

Vital to this beat is the idea that the main character now drives the story. Otherwise, we're still not participating in the movie.

By this point, the audience should be fully invested in the hero and primed to go on the adventure of a lifetime.

Looking back at our beats to this point will help us define the Reaction to the Central Question because this beat represents a major shift in the story.

<u>The hook is typically an external beat</u> -- often driven by the antagonist. It's a pre-story beat – we haven't started the main story just yet, but this beat serves as our introduction to the story to come.

<u>The Inciting Incident is another external story beat</u>. It's often dominated by the force of antagonism. It's the first real beat of our story, and often the first time the external story comes into contact with a main character. Sometimes we may introduce a character into the story here as well, but this beat is typically dominated by the forces of the story.

The Central Question is the last big, stand-alone story-based beat. After this beat, plot will shift off the main structure and the remaining beats will be character-driven. Yes, major story events will occur at the remaining beats, but our relationship to the story will have changed. Prior to the Central Question, the story was being brought to the characters. Now the characters drive the story.

This brings us back to the Reaction to the Central Question.

It's the first major beat that is character-driven, marking the shifting focus of the narrative from story to character. At this point we are getting insertion points that are part character, part story and, believe it or not, part audience – for you too are being taken inside the narrative.

At this beat, we are now alongside the main character actively trying to answer the Central Question with this character. This first attempt may fail. We may bring in secondary characters to express our frustration at the failure. We may seem to succeed, and have secondary characters warn us that this is the wrong path to success, but this beat marks the first attempt to get us to go on an internal ride, deep inside a character – and consequently ourselves.

From this point on the story becomes internal to itself.
All of the big pieces have been placed. Nearly every major element we need to explore this world has been introduced.

This is an important concept because we will now be evaluating story events with the main character. In other words, we'll be figuring out the answers at the same time the hero is based on the same information the hero has. This will strengthen the bond even further between audience and character as the two of us attempt to solve the Central Question.

The hero will try ways to solve the Central Question, evaluate the results, try new ways. And all through this process we bond with the character as we evaluate the same story information that the hero is evaluating. As a result, we are figuring out the story together. Experiencing the story together. Suffering the same setbacks. Enjoying the same victories. Forging our bond.

This is also the first of two transitional beats, marking the audience's journey from story into character. The next beat will explore this newfound relationship.

The Next Big Hurdle (45 minute point)

Our next insertion point. This one adds some new wrinkles as we realize that things aren't quite as they seem.

By this point we should bonded with the hero – now the film can test this bond by <u>creating a new experience</u> that will come as a surprise to both of us (audience and hero). The purpose of this is not to split up audience and hero, but to draw them even closer together.

Up until this point we've been making progress toward answering the Central Question. Now, the plot pushes back. Often the stakes raise – the hero learns of a new complication, a new issue – the problem is bigger than we thought.

Because this information is new to both of us (hero and audience), it's something we learn at the same time. Up until now, the hero may have had information that we, the audience, did not. Here's something new, that neither of us knew about, and we have to face it together. This strengthens the bond between audience and hero by creating another mutual experience – only this time, it's an experience fully intrinsic to the story. In other words, earlier beats may have relied on skills the hero had prior to us knowing them. It also had to rely on what the audience brings to the movie. Now, here's something the two of us have to face, and the primary means we have to tackle it are what we've learned in our time together during the story.

Deception is the key here – in more ways than one. As the deception is exposed, and the problem revealed to be different than first anticipated, what we're also witnessing is a very subtle psychological set up because the underlying meaning, the underlying message, of this beat is this:

Up until this point you thought you were in a story. Now we reveal that all is not as it seems – because in reality, we're being taken inside a character.

This is not an easy transition, so oftentimes <u>a secondary character is brought in at this point</u> to help do three things:

- push us into the character by providing an In-Group, Out-Group Dynamic to respond to

- give us a different narrative point of view in case we refuse to enter the character

- add additional complications and/or stakes

By upping the stakes and providing additional characters we change the dynamic of the story. Sometimes this serves to increase a sense of urgency, which means we better do something quick, not planned, irrational (such as entering the main character). Sometimes, the heightened problems encourage us to rethink our plans and try something new (like entering the character). And sometimes, it just refreshes the story by providing us with new information we have to process, and help assuage our concerns that we may have bonded with the wrong character – after all, who wants to insert themselves into a character who can't seem to solve the Central Question? The new revelations encountered at this beat can serve to explain why our previous attempts to answer the Central Question have failed – we didn't have all the facts.

This raising of stakes and the newly-heightened urgency creates resiliency in the hero, who may have been dejected by earlier failures.

It also forces the hero to go someplace the hero typically has no desire to visit…

Apex (60 minute point)

This beat is also known as The Big Twist. If we thought the Next Big Hurdle threw us a curve, this beat makes that one look easy because the Apex marks a seismic change in the story.

We are now at the midpoint of our narrative timeline – halfway through the movie. A time to rest, pause, and reflect. We are also at a crossroads in the film, in more ways than one.

Several major shifts occur at this point and, one or all of which may be explored:

- Characters go from passive to active in relation to the events of the story, their flaws or inner wounds.

- The narrative may do a complete turn by introducing a major plot twist.

- The main character may rethink his or her previous attempts to answer the Central Question and formulate a whole new approach.

Whatever form this beat takes, it represents THE major insertion point for the audience into the story. To understand why, we'll need to examine the shifts occurring in this beat.

Apex: Passive to Active in Regards to Character and Flaw

Up until this point, the hero's been trying various ways to address the Central Question and has typically met with failure. This is because the hero has not addressed THE REAL PROBLEM – and this real issue is brought to the surface here in this beat.

Remember, this is a character structure, in which the purpose of story is to explore character. This point is driven home in our Apex beat. Here the main character comes to a realization. The events of the story up to this point have shaken the main character, and the character realizes that he or she cannot address the Central Question without coming to terms with something else – that flaw, that inner wound – the real problem the character faces. To do this, heroes must look inside themselves and come face-to-face with something they've simply been living with up until this point. Often, a hero has learned to cope with his or her flaw. They've been getting by, existing. Once the plot brings that flaw to the surface, the hero recognizes this, and realizes they face a choice – do I deal with this thing that's been affecting me, or do I accept the fact that I'll never be able to fix my inner wound?

This is often an intimate moment for a character, a time of introspection, of looking deep within. As a result, this moment is the major insertion point for an audience into a main character. It is a deep look inside a character and <u>an invitation to the audience to fully enter the main character</u>.

Often a hero is alone during this beat – well, not quite alone... for someone is there, watching.

Yes, the hero may be alone in regards to other characters in the story, but the hero is never truly alone because <u>we</u> are there – the audience. And, we alone share this moment with the main character. We alone are privy to this glimpse inside. And, because of the special status we now hold, this moment creates the strongest of our In-Group, Out-Group bonds, for we are in an In-Group of one – the main character and us. The most exclusive club in the movie. Other characters may be close to the hero, but no one else in the movie knows quite what we know, which forges the tightest of bonds with the hero.

The purpose of this beat is simple: we are being let inside a main character.

<u>The key to understanding this beat is realizing that we're addressing very touchy subject for our hero</u>. Dealing with that flaw, that inner wound, is the last place our hero wanted to go. There's an enormous amount of pain and fear there. This was not part of the plan. Up until now, the story was simple – deal with the antagonist,

go back to our lives. Now the hero has got to face something they don't want to face or sometimes even acknowledge.

And, as our hero realizes this – we realize it, too. Our worst fears are confirmed. This person will never be complete until he or she deals with that innermost problem. Of course, because there's so much pain involved with doing that, our hero is going to try just about anything to avoid dealing with it – including a renewed effort to get rid of the antagonist. If the hero can do that, perhaps he or she won't have to deal with that flaw after all.

This leads us to the exterior story aspects of the shift from passive to active in this beat.

Apex: Passive to Active in Regards to Story

Some movies aren't necessarily geared to form such an intimate, personal bond with the main character. That look inward may be a fleeting moment. It may not even exist at all. But the notion of passive to active still applies because something else is going on halfway through this tale….

The first half of the movie is often dominated by the <u>external forces of plot</u> on the world of a character. The plot's pushing those characters around. The antagonist is running rampant.

Notice that our hero's first attempt to get at the film's Central Question is called the Reaction to the Central Question. <u>Often, the first half of a film is all about hero reacting to the external story world.</u> Yes, the hero may be very active, doing all sorts of things, but almost always <u>these early actions are reactions</u>.

Now, the hero takes charge. The hero wants to change things. He or she is sick of reacting, being pushed around, and decides to take action. By our halfway point the hero realizes that the antagonist is not going to go away. It's not going to quit until it has destroyed the hero. This means the only way for the hero to preserve himself/herself is to destroy the antagonist. Now, rather than reacting defensively, the hero turns to the offense.

In terms of audience insertion, this beat invites the audience into the story by saying simply this: "I'm sick of being pushed around. I say we take this thing out! What do you say? Who's with me?!"

This call to action is an invitation to the audience to join with the hero against a common enemy.

And, this call works because in many says, story represents our interaction with the world. Our expression of self, if you will. And when this notion of self is challenged with the threat of being destroyed, we no longer accept the world around us and must attempt to assert ourselves.

Remember, plot is external -- characters are internal.
Plot represents the external forces in our lives, things beyond our control. Characters represent us, dealing with these external forces. These two come together in the audience because…

Movies serve as test cases, practice runs, simulations for how we deal with the world around us.

<u>Want to know why people prefer happy endings?</u>
Because we want our test runs to tell us how we can change the world around us. A happy ending demonstrates that if we learn the lesson of the movie, we too can survive the scenario presented in the story should some form of it occur in our real lives. Well, okay, that and it feels good. :)

<u>Want to know why unhappy endings typically don't work?</u>
Because we don't want that test scenario to confirm that we are powerless against the outside world. Also, the audience doesn't need much help figuring out what NOT to do. That's easy. It's much more difficult to demonstrate how to solve a problem than how not to solve it.

<u>Want to know how to create a successful unhappy ending?</u>
Change how the audience identifies with the main character. Shift narrative point of view away from the hero, so that we're observing the hero rather than directly identifying with him or her. This turns the story into a test run demonstrating what not to do. If you bond us directly with that hero, and the hero loses, we're being told that we lose as a result of watching your movie.

<u>This notion of external story and internal character brings us back to Apex</u>, because this beat marks the point where the narrative flips. It's no longer about the exterior plot -- it's more about the interior character.

Of course, there's plenty more story to come -- we're only to our midpoint. But now that the hero is in charge, the story takes a twist.

The Apex has let us inside the character. Now the external forces of plot are going to attempt to go inside the character as well. This is the true nature of the Big Twist, the other major aspect of the Apex.

The Big Twist of the Apex
In terms of the story, the Big Twist is a new revelation. For the first half of the movie we thought the story was about one thing, now we're being shown it's about something else entirely. For example, in an action movie, the hero is betrayed by someone trusted, a traitor is revealed, we learn who the real enemy is, etc… This serves to refresh the story and keep it interesting. All of our character insertion points from earlier apply as well. As the characters experience the twist, we experience the twist, which continues to refine and reinforce the bonds between character and audience.

At the core of all things Apex is the notion that we are learning what the story is REALLY about…

And, what we discover is that the movie is about a character dealing with a flaw. Naturally the hero doesn't want to deal with his or her flaws and wounds, so the plot now goes after them. It tries to follow us into the character and starts attacking those inner wounds exposed at the Apex.

This means that our big plot twist isn't really a plot twist at all – it's a new event specifically designed to get after the internal wounds of a character. On the surface it will seem like new twists in the plot, but secretly, underneath that surface, these events have the hidden purpose of going inside the main character make the hero deal with his or her flaw or inner wound.

Remember, heroes will not go inside on their own. They will resist. They'll put all their energies into destroying the force of antagonism as a last ditch effort to avoid dealing with their flaws.

However, the exterior forces of the plot will escalate to a point where the hero has no choice…

These are the dark chapters in the story to come. They'll test the bonds between hero and audience. The story will try to break us apart. Destroy the hero from the inside and get at us as a result.

However, before those dark nights of the soul, we have cause to celebrate!

The False Happy Ending (p. 75)
Our next major story insertion point is a moment of levity. The hero's renewed efforts and new plan resulting from the Apex seem to be paying off. It looks like we've answered the Central Question – and best of all, the hero did it without having to face his or her flaw. Unfortunately for the hero, the victory is false. The real enemy, the flaw, has not been addressed.

In the space between our Apex and the False Happy Ending, we're typically spending quite a bit of time with the hero. We might be training for the big battle to come. We might be in a montage as the romantic couple grows more intimate. But whatever the form, the heart of the function is this: we, the audience, have just entered a new relationship with the hero, and we'll need some time to test that out. The capstone of this new union between audience and hero culminates in a party of sorts – our False Happy Ending.

As a character insertion point, this beat is a celebration. It's a reward for going through the process of inserting yourself into the main character. It serves as proof that you did the right thing by bonding with the hero. And, this beat is the result. The False Happy Ending also serves to reinforce the audience's bond with the hero before its most severe test.

As a story insertion point, we get a sense of hope. The hero is on the right track. As a result, the antagonist realizes the hero has grown strong and renews its efforts to destroy the hero, in similar fashion to what the hero underwent as part of the Apex.

This beat also creates contrast with the beat to come – a moment of light before the dark.

The Low Point (p. 90)
The last major insertion point of the 8-Turn structure. Our journey into character is now complete, and this beat actually <u>marks the beginning of our separation from the hero</u>. Here the hero is at his or her lowest point. We appear to be the farthest away from answering the Central Question. The forces of antagonism are ascendant and appear unstoppable. The hero appears defeated. It seems like the end.

Fortunately, we have the whole third act of the film ahead of us to get out of this jam. But, the Low Point forces the hero to ask a very simple question – "how did I get in this spot in the first place?" It's even more perplexing considering things were going so well in the last beat.

This point in the story forces the hero to question everything, and create a new, <u>final plan</u> to deal with the antagonist. If this fails, the hero is out of options. The antagonist wins.

In this desperate moment, heroes come to a singular conclusion – to preserve themselves and defeat the forces of antagonism, they must come face to face with the one thing they didn't want to deal with – their flaws. And, to do that means they have to change -- or affect change in other characters (including the audience.)

This is a painful process for a hero. Change is never easy.

As the hero changes, the audience has the opportunity to change as well. We both learn the <u>lesson of the movie</u>, and we can then take this lesson and apply it to our lives. <u>This is the point where character, story and audience become one</u>.

The rest of the third act is about separating these elements back into their respective categories. The story has ended, but the characters and the audience go on.

The key to understanding the Low Point is understanding that the audience's relationship with the main character begins to change at this point.

As a result of the Low Point, heroes change and begin <u>asserting their own personalities</u>.

In many ways, the journey in a film narrative is that of a character becoming a complete person. It's an assertion of 'self' against an outside world that threatens to destroy our notion of self. The hero becomes the person he or she needs to be in order to lead a complete life.

Once the hero does this, we are no longer directly bonded with that character. We are now watching the hero solve the problem, take down the antagonist, save the day, etc. In the story's climax, the hero often does something that we ourselves haven't thought of or didn't piece together. To be sure this is a moment of bonding, but of a different sort -- we've shifted from being the hero to admiring the hero, and this paves the way for our eventual separation at the end of the film.

<u>Typically this is the part of the story where you'll encounter a very specific beat – a final test for the hero.</u> In terms of story, this beat is designed to see if the hero has learned the <u>lesson of the movie</u> and to see if this lesson stuck. It's a <u>final temptation</u> to revert back to the hero's old ways. In terms of function, this beat serves as proof for us, the audience, that it's okay for us to separate from the hero – we've just seen

that the hero will be fine without us. We can now leave the movie, content and satisfied, richer for having experienced it.

Even if the movie has an unhappy ending, we can still take away this experience to apply to our own lives. The only issue is that we just discovered what not to do, but let's face it – that's easy. There are numerous ways not to do something, but very few 'correct' paths to follow. This is one reason why movies with unhappy endings tend to not work – the lessons gleaned from them aren't really proactive solutions, but one of a myriad of solutions that do not work. Looking at it another way, if I want a solution that doesn't work, I can come up with that on my own – that's a piece of cake, so why should I watch your movie? This is not an argument against unhappy endings per se; but rather, an assertion that unhappy endings contain no more profundity than their happier cousins. They are simply different.

Conclusion

To summarize the beats examined so far...

The <u>Hook</u> is something that could affect almost anyone. It's designed to create desire to see more.
The <u>Inciting Incident</u> is something that affects somebody in a way that virtually anyone would react.
The <u>Central Question</u> blends the story elements presented in the hook and Inciting Incident with character to explore the combination of the first two beats.
The <u>Reaction to the Central Question</u> is a character response to a combination of the first three beats.
The <u>Next Big Hurdle</u> adds a new element to create another layer of complexity and force the character to rethink things.
The <u>Apex</u>, or Big Twist, goes inside the character or exposes 'the real problem'.
The <u>False Happy Ending</u> celebrates the merger of character and audience. It provides levity and hope to create contrast with the Low Point.
The <u>Low Point</u> is failure. It also marks the beginning of separation between hero and audience. A sad moment that marks a strong attempt to implant doubt in a successful ending for the hero.

The beats of the 8-Turn structure are key moments where character and plot intersect, changing each other and creating renewed story possibilities that are then played out in the ensuing scenes between the beats.

Basically, between the major structural beats we see how these two forces (story and character) have altered each other, creating new mixes for exploration, which revitalizes the story after every beat.

However, alongside these major insertion points are a whole host of smaller beats designed to provide access for audiences to enter the film. These we'll call Intrascene Insertion Points.

Intrascene Insertion Points

These are the small beats within scenes designed to invite an audience into interacting with a movie. They are moments of identification, opportunities for an audience to bond with characters and enter the narrative. These moments may be small, but that doesn't lessen their importance. Intrascene Insertion Points form dozens of tiny bonds with the audience, so they will be more receptive to the larger ones to come.

Simply put, these points are opportunities for the audience to complete the picture, to fill in gaps based on what the filmmakers has taught. They are small set ups and payoffs that reassure the audience the storytellers know what they're doing and provide sources of entertainment within the fabric of the larger film.

Some Intrascene Insertion Points

- Teaching us jargon, then using an In-Group, Out-Group Dynamic with outsiders who don't know the terms. These can be other characters or even people who have not seen the film.
- Teaching us the meanings of other elements, then applying the same In-Group, Out-Group dynamics as above.
- Training the audience to recognize certain things, then paying them off.
- Audience Superior moments (we know things the characters don't.) You can use these to build anticipation – we'll watch to see what happens when the characters find out what we know.
- Audience Inferior moments (the characters know things we don't.) You can use these as teases. We don't want to live in this world for very long, but you can build insertion points around characters filling us in on the information we want to know. Think of them as secrets we want to be told, but remember, if you make us wait for it, the secret better be a good one.
- Humor, wit and clever responses. Things we wish we could say or do in real life.
- Predictions and Outcomes. Based on story information, we want to make and test predictions using your story as our playground. Testing outcomes provides huge insertion opportunities!
- Basically any element you teach us the meaning of, then seamlessly insert into your film.

You may notice a pattern.

At the core of audience insertion is the process of teaching and training, set up and payoff.

Your audience wants to put pieces together and test if they've assembled them correctly. It is a process of assembly, of making and testing predictions, and ultimately, of <u>training an audience how to interact with your film</u>.

To do this, you <u>start with small lessons </u>(our Intrascene Insertion Points.) Simple set ups and payoffs to show the audience they are in that two-way conversation. You invite them into the conversation through these small insertion points. Gradually you increase the complexity until you start hitting the major insertion points of structure. It is this process of reeling an audience into your film that enables it to appeal to an audience made up of so many unique and different personalities.

Think about it.

It's hard enough to get three people to agree on anything – much less 30 people, or 300, or 30 million. Now imagine trying to get these same people to agree on something as complex as a film narrative and actually interact with it. Any way you cut it; this is a daunting task, which prompts the question:

How do you create movies that appeal to large numbers of individuals – all with different tastes, different likes, dislikes? How do you get so many unique individuals to respond to your film?

Simple.

<u>You turn individuals into audience</u>.

You train them to become a group, an audience – <u>your</u> audience.

<u>And, you do it one small step at a time.</u>
Not by appealing to the lowest common denominator, but rather, by teaching people how to interact with your film. Once you do that, anyone, no matter what their background, tastes or personality, can enter your film because they've been taught how to do it, and…

Back to our hook -- you've shown them why they should do it, and…

Through Insertion Points – you've given them the opportunities to enter the conversation we call film. This cuts to the very heart of film because…

Insertion points enable an audience to <u>enter</u> the characters and story.

Enter.
That's an interesting word.
Forms the root of another interesting word:

Entertainment.

Congratulations! You've reached the end!
And now, it's on to a new beginning – your next screenplay. But, before you go, there's a final question – perhaps THE burning question of our times...

SET 1: *Final Departure*   ***Theory***   **Total Reps: 1**
Please answer the following:

What is 2 + 2? _____
And, don't say 4. :)

Bonus Question: What color were those fingernails back in Kansas? _____

WORKOUT PROGRESS – CRAFT
Compile your final total!

| EXERCISE | SKILL GROUP || TOTAL REPS ||
	SET #	TYPE	ACTION	AVAILABLE	COMPLETED
Final Departure	1	Theory	Recall ☺	1	
				TOTAL REPS	

THEORY   TOTAL REPS + BONUS   **1**

I sincerely hope these exercises have helped strengthen your command of screenwriting craft. Now go. Write that beautiful screenplay. And live forever.

                                                       FADE OUT.

Made in the USA
Las Vegas, NV
26 July 2022